W9-ABP-909

ALSO BY KITTY GURKIN ROSATI, M.S., R.D., L.D.N.

The Rice Diet Solution:
The World-Famous Low-Sodium,
Good-Carb, Detox Diet for Quick and
Lasting Weight Loss

Heal Your Heart:
The New Rice Diet Program for
Reversing Heart Disease Through Nutrition,
Exercise, and Spiritual Renewal

THE RICE DIET COOKBOOK

150 Easy, Everyday Recipes and Inspirational Success Stories from the Rice Diet Program Community

KITTY GURKIN ROSATI, M.S., R.D., L.D.N.

SIMON & SCHUSTER

NEW YORK   LONDON   TORONTO   SYDNEY

SIMON & SCHUSTER
Rockefeller Center
1230 Avenue of the Americas
New York, NY 10020

For information regarding special discounts for bulk purchases,
please contact Simon & Schuster Special Sales at 1-800-456-6798
or business@simonandschuster.com

Designed by Charles Kreloff

Manufactured in the United States of America

1   3   5   7   9   10   8   6   4   2

Library of Congress Cataloging-in-Publication Data

Rosati, Kitty Gurkin, 1954–
The rice diet cookbook : 150 easy, everyday recipes and inspirational success
stories from the rice diet program community / Kitty Gurkin Rosati.
p.   cm.
1. Reducing diets.   2. Cookery (Rice).   3. High-carbohydrate diet—Recipes.
I. Title.
RM222.2.R646   2007
641.5'635—dc22   2006052218

ISBN-13: 978-1-4165-3922-3
ISBN-10:   1-4165-3922-0

Build houses and live in them; plant gardens and eat what they produce. Seek the Shalom of the community where I have sent you into exile, and pray to the Lord on its behalf, for in its shalom, you will find your shalom.

JEREMIAH 29:5–7

ACKNOWLEDGMENTS

A special thanks and an abundance of gratitude go to Ricers everywhere, a community that is now growing to include phenomenal numbers. For decades I've heard Ricers admit that the Rice Diet Program *dieta* and this "way of life" that promotes such complete healing is the "best-kept secret" in the world. Although I understood their gratefulness for having regained their health and quality of life, I always detected an unspoken concern that the Rice Diet program might grow too popular and they might thereby lose the intimacy so prized within the community. Rest assured, dear Ricers, that a community such as ours will always feel intimate—not because of numbers but because of the enrichment that you all bring to it.

But as *The Rice Diet Solution*'s *New York Times* best-seller success spiraled, hundreds of Ricers came up to me, e-mailed, or called, expressing their heartfelt joy that the truth was finally out to tens of thousands of people! I have been deeply moved by the participants' generous and sincere desire to share this gift with all who want or need it.

There is truly not a scarcity of anything. There is no scarcity of people who can be healed. There is no scarcity of communities where this healing can take place. And there is no scarcity in the *time* it takes to commit to be alone and away from work or other responsibilities or in the potential for others to grow by being without you. If you truly want to be healed, you can choose to let go of the mind-set that holds to the misled belief that scarcity limits your ability to be healed.

So I want to especially acknowledge all those who have leapt out of their scarcity orbit into an eternally expanding abundant life. Jesus once said, "I am come that they might have life, and that they might have it more abundantly." John 10:10; King James Version.

I also want to acknowledge the many people become Ricers through my previous books. Readers of *Heal Your Heart* and *The Rice Diet Solution* have inspired me, and many others now, through their courageous leap into a life of abundance and healing, without even leaving their own homes! It really is a miracle that people can make that huge a shift in consciousness, *away* from following a disease-promoting lifestyle, *toward* embracing a new way of life that promotes health and healing.

My gratitude is absolutely vast for my publishing and editorial assistance. My editor, Amanda Murray, at Simon & Schuster, who called forth *The Rice Diet Solution* and this cookbook, is a pro. And I will forever be grateful to her for leading me to the other key team players, Billie Fitzpatrick, my collaborator, and Debra Goldstein, my agent. Thank you, team, and thank you, God, for bringing them into my life.

And thanks beyond measure to our incredible staff, whose can-do attitude produced a phenomenal collection of tasty and healthy recipes, with juicy testimonials to inspire you on your home-based journey to health. From Ryan Summerford, our new dietitian, who, after a few weeks of orientation, was thrown into the center of creating, analyzing, and testing more recipes than she had ever imagined; to Susan Levy, our Rice Diet Store manager, whose wealth of product info and culinary knowledge was invaluable. Thank you two for your can-do commitment to see this book be all that it has become. Our kitchen staff, led by Chef JR and Nancy Novarro, deserve an eternal acknowledgment not only for their recipe contributions (which continue to delight our taste buds and warm our hearts 365 days per year), but also for their loving commitment and service. And no one has their fingertips on the pulse of our online Forum and "Ricers at home gang" more than Jayne Levey Charles. She is always keeping me abreast of Ricers' stories that break and heal my heart, and yours. Thank you, Jayne, for caring about every single person you encounter in need. Your loving intentions are so obvious to people, whether they be on the phone or Internet—they have no doubt you really care!

In fact it exceeds my imagination how exceptional interns and friends would appear just when we needed them, but it has happened repeatedly now. Jennifer Harris, Joana Krzmarzick, and Elizabeth Bergman were all incredible! And Anna Brown, Kym Stork, Eilene Bisgrove, and Ann Brookhart were also there to test recipes or offer computer analysis and graphics assistance when it was most needed. Not only are they all smart, beautiful, vivacious, and committed women, but also they arrived with their particular gifts at the optimal time. I love it when experiences feel so "win-win." Thank you, thank you, thank you.

And most important, an enormous sense of gratitude goes to my husband, Bob, and our 10-year-old son, Chess, who have given me much time "off" to do another book so soon. Although they have done without me more than usual, they are also committed to us all doing what we are here to do, which includes inspiring others to actualize their potential.

MEDICAL DISCLAIMER

Before starting any new diet or exercise program, you should check with your personal physician. This is particularly important if you are taking medications. While on the diet, you should experience a sense of well-being. Indeed, most participants say they haven't felt as well in years. If you don't feel well—particularly if you experience any nausea or dizziness upon standing—check in with your doctor immediately.

You should be under the supervision of your personal physician if you are taking medications for diabetes, high blood pressure, or congestive heart failure. If you are being treated for diabetes, you will need to have your medications adjusted by your physician as you lose weight and increase your exercise. You should not combine the diet with diuretics or medications containing diuretics, but, again, you should not discontinue any medications without your physician's approval. If you are taking lithium or the blood thinner warfarin (Coumadin), your physician may have to adjust the dose.

The Rice Diet should not be undertaken by patients who have had resection of part or all of their colon, patients who have had ureteral diversion procedures, or patients with impaired kidney function, without our medical assessment and supervision.

CONTENTS

INTRODUCTION

*"Food to a large extent is what holds a society together and eating is closely
linked to deep spiritual experiences."*

—Peter Farb and George Armelagos

I feel truly blessed that our book *The Rice Diet Solution* has achieved such a wonderful reception by so many people. Many Ricers ("Ricer" is our affectionate
name for any participant or reader who lives the Rice Diet), have been asking for
more recipes, menus, and general practical advice about how to make the Rice Diet a
lifelong venture. And recently, while compiling our Web site's Forum recipe re-
sponses, I was further inspired by the plea "Would some ambitious person please
compile all these great recipes in a book? I would sure buy it!"

So this cookbook is my heartfelt response to the thousands of people who called
us, wrote to us, came to us, or e-mailed us at the Rice Diet Program in Durham, North
Carolina, asking for more recipes and meal plans so they could continue living the
Rice Diet. Indeed, this collection of easy recipes, menus, and meal plans was inspired
by many of you! In this way *The Rice Diet Cookbook* is the ultimate group effort—a
mixed and varied collection of delicious, easy-to-make, personal favorites from our
ever-growing Ricer community. Like a true melting pot, the recipes are the creation of
our chefs in the kitchen, our foodie friends on the medical and Rice Diet Store staff,
veteran and seasoned Ricers themselves, as well as readers of *The Rice Diet Solution*
and Web-Forum participants. And, of course, our family and personal friends also
wanted to contribute their favorite quick and simple meals!

As many of you no doubt know, community is a consistently key component of
the success of the Rice Diet and our program. With the support of like-minded
friends, you are bound to succeed; without them, you face unnecessarily difficult
challenges. This cookbook is both a testament to the inestimable power of commu-

nity and an expression of gratitude. We welcome and encourage you to delve into these recipes and become part of our Rice Diet community!

RECIPES AND MEAL PLANS

The Rice Diet Program was founded in 1939 by Dr. Walter Kempner, who was at that time associated with Duke University. He initially treated many kidney and high-blood-pressure patients using a nutrition plan based on rice and fruit, and produced dramatic, never-before-seen reversals of their symptoms. Dr. Kempner's practice and research then went on to prove that the no-salt-added diet reversed every risk factor of heart disease, faster and more safely than any method known. By the 1960s, thousands who were suffering from many different health problems, especially obesity and diseases precipitated by being overweight, were coming for the diet treatment.

So what began as a simple Rice and Fruit Diet now includes thousands of delectable recipes brimming with flavor, rich in texture, and made of nutritious whole foods that will inspire weight loss and healing beyond your imagination! What is the weight loss magic behind these recipes? Besides being delicious, they continue to respect our tried and proven dietary prescription: they are all low in sodium and low in saturated fat. Anyone who has experienced a no-salt-added approach knows that avoiding it, as with sugar, relieves you of a very powerful appetite stimulant. When sodium is not added to your diet, you get in touch with your natural ability to taste and enjoy moderate portions of whole food. You may already be familiar with how incredibly flavorful low-sodium and low-saturated-fat foods can be if you have read *The Rice Diet Solution* and *Heal Your Heart*. Now we have even more—150 more!—recipes to delight your senses and satisfy your stomachs!

You will find over 150 recipes for Breakfast, Snacks and Dips, Sides, Entrées, Dressings and Toppings, and Desserts. How does beginning your day with *French Toast Sticks* grab you? What about a delectable, savory lunch of *Mexican Lettuce Wraps* to whet your appetite? Have you ever tried greens the Asian way, without relying on high-sodium soy sauce? If not, you might just want to sample our *Gingered Greens* recipe. And on those nights when you are looking to indulge in more protein, what about sampling our *Marinated Grilled Chicken with Fresh Corn Salsa?* Top off the day with the extravagant yet healthy *Chocolate–Banana Cream Custard!* These recipes offer a range of taste and spices, and are all easy and quick to prepare. Not only have they been designed to support your weight loss, weight maintenance, and health goals as you live your Rice Diet, but most can be prepared in less than thirty minutes. Indeed, many of them can be prepared in just five to fifteen minutes! Welcome to our world!

One of the many things we learned from the readers of *The Rice Diet Solution* was that those already familiar with the Diet wanted the recipes categorized by Food Group, since many had learned how to eat in a healthier way by thinking of foods as fruit, vegetable, starch, fat, dairy, or protein. So we have presented the recipes in these categories to make creating a meal easy as pie!

You will find a Healthy Grocery List (see page 71) to help you shop, as well as common ways to prepare and conserve certain foods, such as how to cook grains and pasta; tips on how best to use leftovers for flavorful meals; and some interesting shortcuts to preparing meals on the go.

At the back of the book, you will also find many helpful tables and charts, including both an equation and the Body Mass Index (BMI) chart, which will help you determine your weight loss goals.

Another important feature included is the Sample Journal pages. As you will soon see, we feel it is of the utmost importance to record and keep track of your foods, your activities (i.e., exercise), and your thoughts and feelings—on a daily basis. We also encourage you to keep track of your weight by weighing yourself each and every day at the same time. You may think that that much focus on yourself could get monotonous or make you self-absorbed. We actually think it can be freeing. The more you pay attention to your way of living, the more conscious you become of making the right choices and the less effort it takes.

Throughout the book you will also find incredible, and true, inspirational testimonies from successful Ricers; readers reported that this was one of their favorite features of *The Rice Diet Solution.* We are especially pleased and proud to share these stories with you. You can read firsthand of the challenges, successes, and miraculous changes in people's lives as they committed to the Rice Diet. You will hear from a couple who, together lost a total of 110 pounds (he lost 70 and she lost 40 pounds) at home in just six months; a woman who lost 80 pounds in four months while at the program in Durham and later another 70 pounds, saying, "This is a spiritual quest for me. I have seen people come to the Rice House close to death and I have seen them return to health and hope. This program is my life." You will also meet a 93-year-old woman who has been living the Rice Diet for thirty-three years; participants who reversed life-threatening disease and were able to stop their medications; and many other inspiring stories. And even more than their physical successes are their emotional and psychological victories—they are truly living new lives, co-creating their deepest desires and longest-held goals!

Eating and living the Rice Diet produce, more than any other choice I know, optimal weight and the health to actualize the life you want. With our books and free Web site Forum so easy to access, as well as the recipes and meal plans contained in this book, you will find the Rice Diet not only the quickest and safest way to lose the weight you wish but the key to living an entirely new life, one rooted in self-empowerment and healthy choices.

For most of us, optimal health begins with becoming conscious of the foods we consume and our physical activity, understanding how we can produce health or disease, taking responsibility for improving our choices, losing excess pounds, and opening ourselves to a life of unlimited potential. Weight loss and dramatic improvements in chronic diseases are possible when we choose to perceive life differently and open ourselves to the power within. It is my firm and absolute belief that we all have this power to co-create the health and life we desire—in this present moment, and forevermore.

Enjoy these tasty, satisfying, easy-to-make recipes. Whenever you have a question about the diet, you will find the answer in either *The Rice Diet Solution* or *Heal Your Heart*, where the full diet is demonstrated and explained in detail. Also, feel free to contact us at www.ricediet.com. Again, the Rice Diet community is very warm, welcoming, and helpful. On the Forum, you can post questions, find answers, share stories, and exchange helpful tips and advice. Many Ricers have found that the simple back-and-forth communication with others committed to improving their lives is heartening. You will also find suggestions for inspiring and encouraging books, films, and CDs that have made a pivotal difference in someone's recently transformed life.

PART ONE

THE
RICE
DIET
REDUX

CHAPTER ONE

THE RICE DIET SOLUTION

"If we could give every individual the right amount of nourishment and exercise, not too little and not too much, we would have found the safest way to health."

—Hippocrates

Although most participants who come to our program, and readers of our books, do so to lose weight, they quickly learn that the Rice Diet is really much, much more. It is first and foremost a powerful tool that enables you to reach your dreamed-of weight loss goals and maintain that weight for as long as you wish. Second, but no less important, the Rice Diet enables you to create a new way of living that is the closest you can get to a guarantee for long-term optimal health. Since 1939, the Rice Diet has proved for thousands to be the fastest, safest, and most medically documented approach for weight loss; it has also been the most dramatically effective, natural way of preventing and treating all the other modifiable risk factors of heart disease. So with such long-term documented success, what are you waiting for?

The Rice Diet offers you more than a plan to lose unwanted weight. After only a week or two, you will feel lighter, more energetic, and better able to cope with all of life's stresses and complexities. You will feel more confident and in touch with the real you. You will feel empowered to strive for other goals on your dream list. You will finally have the know-how to co-create the life you have always imagined!

THE RICE DIET *DIETA*

The Rice Diet is much more than an eating plan that you "go on and off." Rather, it's a four-step way of life—a *dieta*, a word that comes from ancient Greek, meaning "way of life." It is in these four steps that the Rice Diet enables you, no matter how many diets you may have tried before, to create a new *dieta* that will inspire you to achieve and maintain your weight loss goals—forever!

This may seem like magic, but it's not. As Kate from Idaho said, "I must say, I have never ever been more alive than I am now! I have enough energy to chase after my six kids—yes, I said six—and twins to boot! Thank you . . . I had trouble sleeping, I never ate unless it was on the go, and now I sleep well, I take quiet time for me, and I share the benefits with my family. So, again, thank you!"

And as Mary Ann, a Spiritual Director, shared on the Rice Diet Forum, "This way of eating has been the latest in a series of growth episodes for me. My whole way of being has been changing and growing for the past seven or eight years, and this *dieta* has come into my life at the perfect time. I have internalized it in ways that I cannot [begin to] express in an e-mail."

As you can begin to sense, the Rice Diet gets under your skin and truly begins to reshape your orientation to the world and to yourself. As you begin to change the way you eat, a new clarity develops, allowing you to see yourself and the world around you in a positive, life-enhancing way. We have witnessed this transformation count-less times within the Rice Diet community. Indeed, since the publication of *The Rice Diet Solution*, as well as *Heal Your Heart*, we have even more evidence of how people change, grow, and heal on an emotional and spiritual level that supports their weight loss and maintenance efforts. We have received hundreds of letters and e-mails with very personal and unique testimonials—further proof of how the Rice Diet inspires individuals when they are ready for this inner journey. When a person is ready and willing to look within, he or she can experience life-transforming change. Participants have awakened from decades of self-medicating with food for depression, tapped into unrealized dreams, and made breakthroughs, such as understanding how they have protected themselves with excessive fat after childhood sexual abuse.

Deanne's story captures the essence of this potential to transform one's life:

Over the years my life has centered around two specific areas—the first has been my weight loss journey, including a pattern of yo-yo dieting, medical challenges, and failures. And the second has been childhood traumas, relationship challenges, dealing with religious expectations and eating disorders, which have left me feeling frustrated, desperate, and alone. During one of my "spurt attempts" to change things, I came across a personal story of an individual who had followed the Rice Diet, successfully lost weight, and had kept it off.

I immediately researched the Internet, found a Web page packed with Rice Diet information and dialed the listed number. I spoke to a dietitian, purchased the book, *The Rice Diet Solution,* and the cookbooks, signed up for the teleclasses, and began following the program at home. *The Rice Diet Solution* provided tools that encouraged simple lifestyle changes that restored my mental, emotional, and spiritual health. The more my physical health improved, the more restored I felt mentally, emotionally, and spiritually. Meditation and journalizing directed and focused my thoughts, improving my sense of self-worth, my joy and my freedom. The results were amazing and I began losing weight.

The success of my journey was a process that moved me from "unawareness living" to "awareness living," from mindless, destructive choices to purposeful, intentional choices. I am eternally grateful to God, the Rice Diet program, and the staff at the Rice House for a second chance at life. The quote that inspires me continually on my ensuing journey is written by Geronimo, "I cannot think that we are (I am) useless—or God would not have created us (me)—the sun, the darkness, the winds are all listening to what we have to say."

As we become conscious of what we think and how we feel, and become aware of what we are eating and where it came from, whether we have exercised our bodies today, practiced meditation, yoga, journalizing, and loved someone in need, we will indeed achieve our optimal weight and health, while co-creating a peaceful, healthy world. Does this sound pretty far out? Yes, it is, but it's also within your reach.

HOW THE RICE DIET WORKS

Many of you may already be familiar with these steps, but for those of you who are coming to the Rice Diet for the first time in these pages, what follows is a brief overview of the four essential steps that make up the Rice Diet and enable you to discover your own new *dieta*.

1. Eat a low-sodium, low-fat (especially low-saturated-fat) diet of whole grains, beans, fruits, vegetables, and consciously selected types and amounts of animal proteins (if health indicators suggest appropriate).

2. Become a conscious eater by learning about the foods you are eating; indeed, the more we know about what individual foods do for our bodies and where they come from, the more mindful we are of eating as a health-promoting activity. We recommend that you also eat organic foods whenever possible, for your health and environment. (More about the importance of organics on page 54.)

3. Take time each day to allow yourself to rest and rejuvenate, reinforcing the mindfulness of your evolving *dieta*. We suggest that people use this "self-time" to rest, meditate, practice yoga or tai chi, or journalize. These mindful activities promote inner awareness and reconnect your brains with your bodies in a new, healthy way. We also recommend that you exercise—walking is fine—for at least one hour each day.

BEFORE BEGINNING THE RICE DIET

It is important to check with your physician prior to beginning any diet, especially if you are taking any medications. Due to the rapid weight loss and low-sodium content of the Rice Diet, it is especially important to consult with your physician before starting. You may be on medication that will need to be altered or discontinued before changing your diet, and your doctor is the best person to help you do this. Do not make any changes in your medication regimen without your physician's advice. Since many physicians and health-care professionals are unfamiliar with the impact of a truly low-sodium diet, you should point out the low-sodium content of the Rice Diet to your doctor. Feel free, as well, to refer your physician to the Rice Diet Clinic, and we will be happy to be of assistance. We can be reached at www.ricediet.com. We also recommend that you keep a record of your weight, any heart disease risk factors, and any other health predictors that you are aware of having. Note the space to record these at the top of the Food Journal on pages 323 and 325; both you and your doctor will benefit from knowing these data.

4. Create or become part of a health-conscious community. You can form a community with just one person or many. The key here is to find people in your life who support, encourage, and understand your new way of life, especially during this challenging time of change.

When these four tools are in place, you will not only lose weight, you will create a new *dieta*, or way of living, that inspires the life you desire. You can lose 10 pounds or 200; regardless of your desired weight loss, you will lose weight and enhance your health safely and quickly.

STEP ONE: THE THREE PHASES

The Rice Diet is comprised of a three-phase eating plan: Phase One is the detox phase and lasts a week. Once you have cleansed your body, you are ready to start Phase Two, which is focused on helping you lose the weight you wish. You stay on Phase Two for as long as it takes to lose your unwanted weight and achieve other desired health goals. Once you have reached your goal, you begin Phase Three, which helps you maintain your new weight and adapt the Rice Diet to your lifestyle long term.

In these pages I will summarize the phases in a general way and focus on practical, easy guidelines to assist you in embracing this way of life as effortlessly as possible. Although those who want the nutritional details can refer to the analyses and allowances that follow each recipe and the appendices in the back of the book, the essence and power of the diet can easily by achieved without counting a calorie, gram of fat, or milligram of sodium. All the recipes can be enjoyed on any Phase, *except* those containing meat, poultry, or seafood, which are not eaten on Phase One.

PHASE ONE

Phase One begins with one day of eating just grains and fruits (the details about actually doing the diet, and a guide for how much you will be eating, portion sizes and allowances can be found on page 23, or you can follow the Quick-and-Easy Guide on page 27). For the other six days of the week, you add in vegetables, beans, and some organic, nonfat soymilk or dairy. The focus or goal of Phase One is to detox your body and mind and get it into shape for true weight loss. We recommend doing Phase One of the diet for one week. You may also want to do Phase One at a later date, to cleanse your palate and perspective, as necessary. This jump start, or "reality check," is obviously very helpful if you lose your focus!

You will find that there is a lot of freedom to make your own choices and adapt the diet to your liking once you are familiar with your routine and are comfortable with the amount of weight you are losing.

PHASE TWO

In Phase Two, your focus becomes lasting weight loss. You will begin each week with one day of eating just grains and fruit, followed by five days of fruit, grains, beans, veggies, and one dairy, then on the seventh day (or day of your choice), you will add in one high-protein source, such as fish or nonfat dairy. In Phase Two you will eat slightly more sodium because seafood and dairy products contain more naturally occurring sodium than do foods grown in the earth, and you will consume a few more calories because of the addition of the high-protein meal. You stay on Phase Two until you have reached your weight and health goals.

PHASE THREE

Once you have reached your goals, you move into Phase Three, our maintenance plan, which is the same as Phase Two but adds more choices and more opportunities to enjoy a little flexibility with the protein and sodium if you choose.

These three phases complete step one of the diet. It all boils down to two simple

THE RICE DIET WORKS BECAUSE IT IS

• a detox diet that cleanses your body, ridding it of excess water weight, sodium, and other toxins from processed foods and the environment. Once your body is returned to a clean, natural state, you slowly but surely begin to retrain it to prefer clean, unprocessed foods.

(continued on next page)

• a low-sodium diet that limits salt and all other sodium-rich ingredients to between 500 and 1,000 milligrams daily. Salt, like sugar, stimulates your appetite. When sodium is not added to your diet, you rid yourself of a powerful appetite stimulant, and get in touch with your natural ability to taste and enjoy moderate portions of whole food. And as a result, you control your eating behavior; your eating behavior does not control you.

• a low-fat diet that especially limits saturated fats. While it is true that the lower your fat intake, the lower your weight and the better your odds of maintaining your desired weight; the most important fat to limit is saturated fat, which comes primarily from animal fats. But keep in mind, some fats are health-promoting and therefore good for you to eat, including olive oil, walnuts, sesame seeds, and fish.

• a diet that relies on complex carbohydrates such as grains, beans, veggies, and fruit—all of which are high in fiber, which that cleanses the body and fills you up. This "whole foods" diet is rich and varied in taste, texture, and nutrients. You no longer crave foods, and you never (or rarely) feel hungry. Slowly absorbed, soluble fiber–rich foods allow everyone, including diabetics and hypoglycemics, to eat complex carbohydrates with confidence and gratitude. Consuming soluble fiber–rich foods, such as oats, beans, and barley, frequently lowers cholesterol, stabilizes blood sugar, and thus helps you feel more full per calorie.

• a diet that is individualized to you; the phases lead you through stages where you are aware of what dietary additions (if any) cause a deleterious health response. Otherwise, the diet includes whatever foods produce the results you desire.

things: eat a wholesome diet very low in sodium and low in saturated fat! In lay terms, this can be simplified further: eat whole foods, which include all grains, beans, fruits, and vegetables, with a daily seafood or nonfat dairy choice.

STEP TWO: BECOME A MINDFUL EATER

One of the reasons why the Rice Diet is so incredibly successful is because of Step Two—Becoming a Mindful Eater—when we ask Ricers to become conscious of the foods they are eating. Indeed, we have observed again and again that one of the truly remarkable ways that people are inspired to commit to their new *dieta*, or lifestyle, is when they understand what they are eating, such as carbs, protein, fats, fiber, sodium, and so on. The more you learn about your foods and how they impact your body, the more likely you are to make better choices about food. These better choices will reinforce your Rice Diet eating plan and put you one step further toward your goal of weight loss and a healthy *dieta*.

Again, this cookbook is not meant to replace our original description of the diet and all the details that appear in *The Rice Diet Solution* but is a basic simplification of our approach that will assist you in producing the results you want.

STEP THREE: MAKE TIME FOR YOURSELF

Step Three gives Ricers practical tools to further reinforce the principles of the Rice Diet, ingraining their new *dieta* into their bodies and brains. While many of us blame our stress-filled lives on "being too busy," few have accepted the truth that we all choose what we do with our time. We may not be conscious that we have choices in every moment, and that we are ultimately responsible for these life decisions—so, why not be awake for them? When you set aside even twenty minutes a day to touch base with yourself, you are better able to stick to the diet, stay more centered, and stay connected to your goals of weight loss and better health.

When you spend time mindfully, you will gain insight and clarity of mind. A simple rest period in the middle of the day will do this; regular exercise will do this; and so will yoga, tai chi, journalizing, and meditation. The more Ricers integrate these mindful activities, the more they maximize the benefits of the Diet itself.

STEP FOUR: CREATE A SUPPORTIVE COMMUNITY

Ricers who are able to participate in the Rice Diet Program in Durham are welcomed into a warm, inviting, helpful community the minute they set foot on the property. We have heard, again and again, and observed for ourselves, just how much this support means to people who are in the midst of a life-changing event. And although all are invited to visit us in Durham, you can create this supportive community on your own, at home. One of the biggest challenges in sticking to a healthy diet over time is that most people get tired of feeling different from the culture that surrounds them. That's why we guide participants to establish nurturing relationships and form new groups of companions or friends for exercise. Who are you looking for? Who could best support you and your desired *dieta*? Anyone who has chosen to take better care of themselves may find support at health clubs, in cardiac rehabilitation programs, in special interest groups such as vegetarians, in yoga and meditation classes, on the Internet, in 12-Step Anonymous groups, and in group therapy. (For further information about resources for professional support services and outreach facilities, contact us at www.ricediet.com.)

The four steps of the Rice Diet work synergistically to support and reinforce your weight loss, as well as the more overarching change in your lifestyle, and actualization of your life's dreams. The Program at its best, when done completely, is a total restructuring of your habits, attitudes, and approach to health and well-being. Your participation will mark the beginning of a new commitment to yourself, a promise of taking time each day for exercise, rest, relaxation, and renewal.

DAILY ACTIVITY

Although exercise is part of Step Three, we want to make sure you understand how important it is to be active on a daily basis. We recommend any exercise that interests you. Many Ricers begin by developing a walking plan that consists of walking an hour per day. Others who have orthopedic problems, who have not exercised in years, or who live where the weather is harsh may prefer swimming, water walking, and water aerobics. It is more important to exercise each day, even for only five minutes, than to do no exercise at all. You will often find that even when you don't think you have the time, if you just begin, you will soon have accomplished more than you imagined. Exercise burns calories, improves cardiovascular fitness, reduces stress, usually reduces your appetite, makes you feel better, and gives you time to be with yourself. Taking time to exercise is almost more important than doing the exercise itself. Most of us do not spend ten minutes a day taking care of ourselves, let alone an hour.

KEEPING YOUR PERSONAL JOURNAL

One way that has proved again and again to help Ricers stay focused on their experience and commitment is by keeping a Personal Journal and recording not only their food intake and exercise but also their thoughts and feelings about their experience on the diet.

Why keep a journal? To heal or manage the conditions that brought you to the point of trying the Rice Diet in the first place. This condition (or conditions) may be overweight, diabetes, hypertension, or some other disease. Far too much medicine is prescribed for symptoms we have the power to heal naturally. The condition(s) may also be unresolved, buried emotions that are not serving you or your higher calling. Journalizing your thoughts and feelings can often uncover angers, fears, and resentments that are actually *fueling* obesity and other health problems without your even knowing it. Journalizing can be a powerful tool for healing the root causes of our problems.

Your Journal is also a place to imagine and design your dreams. If you choose to get in touch with what you truly desire from life, if you have a concrete, specific vision of the future you want, then you will be far more motivated to succeed and heal the belief system or circumstances that have become obstacles to this dream, including your overweight or illness. For further assistance in journalizing your life vision and dreams, see page 321.

THE POWER OF TESTIMONIALS

The tens of thousands of Ricers who have participated in the Rice Diet Program in Durham, North Carolina, since 1939 have enjoyed tremendous weight loss and equally dramatic healings from innumerable diseases. But this past year we have been absolutely amazed by the volume and depth of the transformative testimonies we have received from people who have tried the diet but have never physically been to our facility. Inspired by their success, words of wisdom, and stories of healing, we have expanded our community-created nickname of "Ricer" to participants of the Rice Diet whether they be in Durham, readers of our books, or visitors to our Web site Forum at www.ricediet.com.

Throughout this book you will come upon these Inspirational Stories, examples of just a few of the hundreds that Ricers have shared with us. If their success seems a little too good to be true, read on. Their testimonials of weight loss, increased health, and discovery of joy in living should convince you. Names have been changed to respect the individuals' privacy, but take a look at how their new *dieta* changed these lives:

A doctor from Florida, who has spent his life practicing allopathic (traditional Western) medicine, tells his story:

My first exposure to the Rice Diet was in the 1970s when I was an undergraduate at Duke. We used to see some fairly obese folks walking around campus, and they came to be known as "Ricers." I didn't give the Rice Diet much thought until several decades later.

In February 2005, I woke up with a dull pain in my left shoulder, which I attributed to a muscle ache from sleeping in an uncomfortable position. A few hours later, it was still with me, and I became concerned. Not remembering the nostrum about those who treat themselves have a fool for a patient, I did an EKG, which showed a pattern sometimes seen during or just before a full-blown heart attack. I dutifully reported to the ER. After an uneventful overnight stay, tests showed no signs of a heart attack, and the problem was diagnosed as a musculoskeletal strain.

Even though I was relieved that I had escaped "the Big One," it caused me to take a good look at where my health was, and where I was going. After medical school, I had allowed my eating and exercise routines to fall away, and my weight had ballooned from 185 pounds to 230 pounds. My blood pressure and blood lipid profile wasn't too good either, and I had just been started on an injectable medication to reduce my blood sugar. In medical terms, I was hypertensive, hyper-lipidemic, hyperglycemic, pre-cirrhotic, and almost morbidly obese. I was starting to look like those unfortunate patients I remembered seeing during my clinical rotations in cardiology! These folks were caught in a death spiral of poor eating, weight gain, hypertension, diabetes, lethargy, which led to even *more* eating, *more* weight gain, *higher* blood pressure, and *less* activity. *The common wisdom was and, unfortunately still is, that the lifestyle changes that these patients needed were not achievable.*

Although I had to count myself among these unfortunates, I was convinced I could change things, if I made a total commitment to change. After looking at several weight loss programs around the country, I looked at what the Ricers were doing in Durham. Although it was not the most expensive program, it had the highest long-term success of any. I also knew the credentials of the physicians and nutritionists were impeccable, so I called up and made an appointment. I also told my family, staff, and patients that I would be out of town for the next five weeks. Many thought I was crazy to take that sort of time away from my practice, but I knew I needed to break the routine that had made me ill.

At the Rice House, I learned an entirely new way of looking at food, and also a more rational approach to life in general. The community of Ricers consisted of everyone from country farmers to well-known physicians to CEOs. Here were people with very successful lives, who had not been able to achieve similar success with their weight and health. I learned as much from them as I did from the outstanding lectures and demonstrations from the Rice House Staff.

After completing these five weeks, I felt better than I had in the past thirty years. I was totally off all blood pressure and blood sugar medications! Although medicine is an artful science, we still look at cold, hard numbers when we try to measure effects, and here are ones that tell my story:

	PRE-RICE: 10/2005	RICE: 05/2006
Weight	230	169
BMI	34 (35 is morbidly obese)	25
B/P	140/92	110/68
GLUCOSE	112	88
CHOLESTEROL	170	120
TRIGLYCERIDES	148	78
LDL	90	41

This doctor chose to commit to lifestyle changes, rather than treat his (supposed) chronic diseases with drugs. I, for one, am in awe of how much his willingness "to perceive things differently" and choose the Rice Diet *dieta* has benefited him personally, and now the innumerable lives he influences and inspires.

Here is another profound, life-changing story:

My name is Paula and I am from Alabama and this is a story about how my life begin to change on March 11, 2006. First I would like to start this out by saying that I am so thankful for the chance to get my story out there and share a part of my life with anyone who could benefit.

I am thirty-four years old, married to a wonderful husband, and with four beautiful kids. I started my new way of life after reading the story about the Rice Diet and a woman named Susan in *Women's World* magazine. I could relate to this woman as I have been overweight for seventeen years now. I bought the magazine and instantly began reading the story and said to my husband, "Hey, hunny [*sic*], this is the one for me."

I came home and joined the Rice Diet Web site and life blossomed. This is a new beginning for me and my family because I have been changing everything about me. There has not been a time I have come over to the Forum that I haven't received the strength and willpower to go one more day. I have lost 125 pounds in twenty-eight weeks and still have 168 more to go, but I know I will achieve this goal because this is a new beginning for me and for all of us.

I can finally accept the things that are just out of my control. This *dieta* will work for you if you want it to. Set small goals and work toward each and every one of them. Lean on the Forum for support; you will be so surprised at how these people will become the sister, mother, brother, and best friends you have always wanted.

If I can give one word of advice to anyone it would be to stay focused, and if you slip on the program, do not wait days or weeks to make yourself accountable for your actions, you must get up right then and there and move forward. I would like to thank everyone at the Rice Diet clinic for making this possible for people like myself, also big thanks to Susan for sharing her amazing story and inspiring myself and others, another thank you to all the new friends and family I have made on the Rice Diet Forum, and most of all a huge thank-you to my wonderful husband Rick who has stood by me and loved me throughout the failed attempts of dieting. Hunny, you are my rock.

And yet another powerful story. Angela D'Amico, forty-three, speaks with the fervor of the converted. "I've always battled weight but I've taken the addictive personality that made me overeat and have become equally committed to living mostly salt and dairy free with the Rice Diet Program."

Angela freely admits that her big and extended Italian family (her mother had nine brothers and sisters) made sharing food the center of family life. "By 9:00 A.M. on Sunday mornings, a huge pot of sauce was simmering on the stove and the family came together. My father died before I was born, so it is easy to see how food became my comfort and companion."

Experiencing the usual ups and downs of the scale and on-and-off-again dieting, Angela first came to the Rice Diet Program in 1991. She lost 60 pounds in three months; returned to New York to pursue a career; and married. She became pregnant and was ill and bedridden from the second month of her pregnancy. She gained 140 pounds prior to giving birth to her son, Jayme.

When her son turned four, Angela returned to the program and lost 80 pounds in four months. She lost an additional 70 pounds when she returned home, and successfully maintained this weight loss for more than eight years! Then two years ago Angela broke her ankle, which literally tripped up her maintenance success. Angela described how her inactivity after the ankle break became a nemesis, but thankfully her very-low-sodium diet habit was her saving grace. As soon as her ankle had fully recovered, she made a return trip to the Rice Diet program and has resumed her health-promoting *dieta* and inevitable weight loss. Since that time, she has periodically returned to the program to "refuel" and inspire and support others in their quest.

Angela, now divorced, admits that weight was an issue with her husband and is an ongoing concern of her now fourteen-year-old son, who has his own struggle with weight. She is in the art business and travels widely. Exercise is also a key to her continuing success.

But she asserts that the magic of "salt free" is that it eliminates all the foods that are triggers for food addicts. "Pizza is not an option for me. Eating plain foods plainly is as close as one can get to abstinence for the food addict. I always advise Ricers to keep it simple and remember that when they make mistakes, and we all do, to return to eating fruits, vegetables, and grains immediately."

Why is it so important to share her enthusiasm for the Program? "This is a spiritual quest for me. I have seen people come to the Rice House close to death and I have seen them return to health and hope. This program is my life. There is hope. Nothing tastes as good as feeling fit feels."

CHAPTER TWO

LIVING THE RICE DIET

"The great benefit of slowing down is reclaiming the time and tranquility to make meaningful connections with people, with culture, with work, with nature, with our own bodies and minds. Some call that living better. Others would describe it as spiritual."

—Carl Honoré, author of *In Praise of Slowness*

Most people find that getting the added sodium out of their diet results in the single most dramatic change they have ever experienced in their attempts to reduce their appetite, struggle with hunger, and obsessive-compulsive tug-of-war with food. As anyone who has already experienced the Rice Diet knows, once you detox, cleanse your palate, and embrace an attitude that will maximize your health's potential, the dietary effort decreases and your rewards and benefits increase.

When you decide to lose weight on the Rice Diet, you are not being asked to say good-bye to all your favorite foods and say hello to a life full of deprivation and hunger; you are invited to a lifetime of mindful eating and conscious life choices. Those of us who live the Rice Diet *dieta* enjoy the freedom you will immediately feel when you get off added salt and processed foods (sugar in particular). On the Rice Diet, it truly is rare that anyone feels hungry! As Tammy said, "First I have to say, thanks soooooo much for keeping in touch with me. It really means a *lot*. I lost 6 pounds last week and I weighed in this morning and lost another 5¾ pounds. This is just a great diet. I have never been so excited and I feel so good. I have so much energy and I never have the hunger pains!"

THE FOOD GROUPS

Our growing community of Ricers, who shared questions and feedback on our last book, have largely shaped the content of this one. Despite our great efforts to make nutritional science as lay friendly as possible, we found that numerous readers were so focused on specific details that too many "missed the forest for the trees." And while we have included the food group allowances that correspond to each recipe, some of you may take comfort in the fact that although caloric intake is ultimately the most important factor in weight loss, becoming a mindful eater of whole foods (foods that are primarily unprocessed), in general, can be just as effective as counting calories.

Basically, if you eat an average of 4 vegetables, 3 fruits, 6 starches, 1 to 2 servings of nonfat dairy products, and 0 to 4 servings of fat a day (note Healthy Foods Pyramid, page 28), you don't need to agonize over fractions of any of them. Dietitians tend to want to teach accurate nutritional information, but the reality is so simple that it eludes many people—just eat whole foods without added salt and chemicals! People who have been raised eating fast foods and TV dinners don't realize that the majority of people in the world who eat a whole food diet (that grows primarily from the ground) do not have chronic disease.

Most of the recipes included here have a combination of food groups within them, and calculating the details of each was found by some to be more confusing than helpful. So if you don't want to count allowances, don't be concerned with getting an extra fresh fruit or vegetable; that is rarely a problem. Instead stay conscious of excessive starches, protein, and fat-rich foods, especially if they're processed foods.

At the Rice House, it is easy to follow the three phases because all the food is prepared by our chefs in portions that inspire weight loss. Participants don't have to even think about calories, portion sizes, or allowances! However, we realize that at home, many people begin to wonder how they are going to figure out the right foods to eat and the right portion sizes of those foods.

As I indicated earlier, this cookbook is designed so that you can do the diet in two ways: For those of you who are already familiar with the method for determining what to eat and how much, then you might prefer to follow the General Guide (see opposite) stipulating allowances in each of the three phases (i.e., the number of starch, vegetable, fruit, protein, dairy and fat servings eaten per day). These allowances accompany each recipe and are defined in Appendix A, Food Groups Defined (see page 297). Historically, the caloric amounts, and thus definitions of what constitutes a food group serving (often called "exchanges" or "allowances"), are basically the same as that used by Weight Watchers and by diabetics.

However, for those of you who are more comfortable *not* thinking about portion sizes and would rather just know what foods to eat and what foods to limit, and guesstimate how much to eat by rounding servings, then we have prepared the Quick-and-Easy Guide (see page 27).

For the purposes of doing the diet and enjoying the recipes herein, these are the foods and their allowances (the number of servings) you will be eating daily during each Phase:

GENERAL GUIDE TO FOOD GROUPS AND ALLOWANCES BY PHASE

PHASE ONE: DETOX

Remember, you are doing Phase One for only one week:

FOR ONE DAY A WEEK ONLY:

Breakfast:	2 starches & 2 fruits
Lunch:	2 starches & 2 fruits
Dinner:	2 starches & 2 fruits

FOR SIX DAYS A WEEK:

Breakfast:	1 starch, 1 nonfat dairy, & 1 fruit
Lunch:	3 starches, 3 vegetables, & 1 fruit
Dinner:	3 starches, 3 vegetables, & 1 fruit

PHASE TWO: RAPID WEIGHT LOSS

You stay on Phase Two until you have reached your weight loss goal.

FOR ONE DAY A WEEK:

Breakfast:	2 starches & 2 fruits
Lunch:	2 starches & 2 fruits
Dinner:	2 starches & 2 fruits

FOR FIVE DAYS A WEEK:

Breakfast:	1 starch, 1 nonfat dairy, & 1 fruit
Lunch:	3 starches, 3 vegetables, & 1 fruit
Dinner:	3 starches, 3 vegetables, & 1 fruit

FOR ONE DAY A WEEK:

Breakfast:	2 starches & 1 fruit
Lunch:	3 starches, 3 vegetables, & 1 fruit
Dinner:	3 starches, 3 protein (or 2 dairy), 3 vegetables, & 1 fruit

PHASE THREE: MAINTENANCE

Once you have reached your weight loss goal, Phase Three enables you to add more calories (i.e., portions) until you maintain your new weight. You may also add a little more sodium if blood pressure, weight, and other sodium-related problems (like joint pain, swelling, or breathing challenges) don't return.

FOR ONE DAY A WEEK:

Breakfast: 2 starches & 2 fruits
Lunch: 2 starches & 2 fruits
Dinner: 2 starches & 2 fruits

FOR FOUR DAYS A WEEK:

Breakfast: 1 starch, 1 nonfat dairy, & 1 fruit
Lunch: 3 starches, 3 vegetables, & 1 fruit
Dinner: 3 starches, 3 vegetables, & 1 fruit

FOR TWO DAYS A WEEK:

Breakfast: 2 starches & 1 fruit
Lunch: 3 starches, 3 vegetables, & 1 fruit
Dinner: 3 starches, 3 protein (or 2 dairy), 3 vegetables, & 1 fruit

SERVING SIZES AND ALLOWANCES

Food Group	1 serving size in cup/ounces/ tablespoons/teaspoons	Calories/ serving	Sodium
Starch—most grains, pasta, and starchy vegetables (corn, green peas, potatoes, yams)	½ cup cooked	80	2–5 mg
Starch—rice or dried beans and peas (legumes)	⅓ cup cooked	80	2–5 mg
Starch—bread	1 slice	80	2–160 mg
Vegetables	1 cup raw ½ cup cooked	25	5–20 mg
Fruits	1 medium whole fruit ½ banana ¼ cup dried fruit 2 tablespoons raisins ½ cup unsweetened juice or cooked fruit	60	0–10 mg
Dairy	1 cup nonfat soy, grain, or cow's milk or yogurt ½ cup dry curd cottage cheese or skim ricotta	90–126	126–150 mg
Protein	1 ounce cooked fish 1 ounce cooked skinned poultry 1 ounce cooked lean meat ¼ cup cooked dried beans or peas	55	51 mg
Fat	1 teaspoon olive or canola oil 1 tablespoon sesame seeds or walnuts 1½ teaspoons seed or nut butter or tahini ⅛ avocado	45	0 mg

Keep in mind that most meals include at least two servings each of Starch, Fruit, or Vegetables. Consult the chart on page 23 for further guidance.

SODIUM NOTES

Basically, you do not have to concern yourself with counting the milligrams of sodium you are consuming if you eat a variety of whole foods, plus the one serving of soy or dairy product on all days except your Basic Rice Diet Day (i.e., the first day of each Phase). The menu pattern and samples ensure that Ricers at home average between 300 and 500 milligrams of sodium per day while on Phases One and Two; on Phase Three you will average between 500 and 1,000 milligrams of sodium a day. A general rule of thumb is to not add salt to your food or use, on a regular basis, processed foods to which sodium has been added.

THE QUICK-AND-EASY GUIDE

How you do the diet is up to you. But do keep in mind some advice we have heard over and over again from Ricers themselves: if you want to really lose weight and keep it off, then don't skip meals—eat breakfast, lunch, and dinner. In fact, if you'd like to eat smaller, more frequent meals, or snacks in addition to three meals, that's fine too—just keep up with the day's tally.

The Health-Promoting Pyramid (on page 28) is a good general guide. Journalizing your intake of the food group totals daily is a powerful mindfulness exercise. Don't get obsessed with or overly distracted by fractions of food groups eaten. Instead choose suggested servings from the lower end of the range if you are a smaller woman and from the higher end if you are a larger man or someone approaching your goal or maintenance phase. Note that the calcium-rich foods are italicized, since

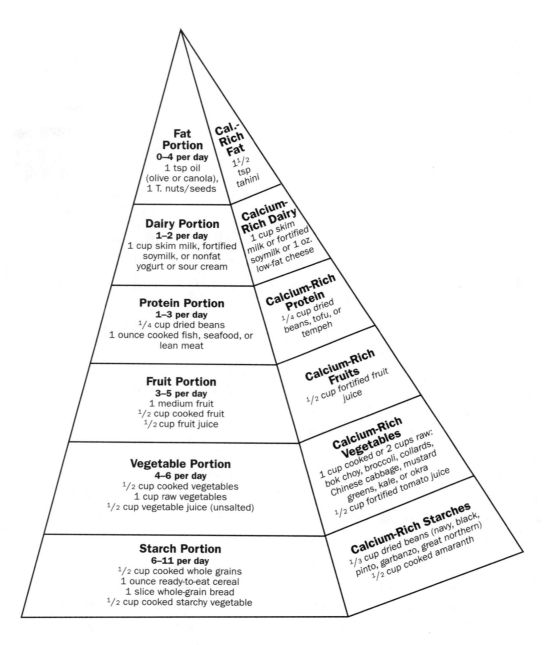

Fat Portion
0–4 per day
1 tsp oil
(olive or canola),
1 T. nuts/seeds

Cal.-Rich Fat
1 1/2 tsp tahini

Dairy Portion
1–2 per day
1 cup skim milk, fortified
soymilk, or nonfat
yogurt or sour cream

Calcium-Rich Dairy
1 cup skim
milk or fortified
soymilk or 1 oz.
low-fat cheese

Protein Portion
1–3 per day
1/4 cup dried beans
1 ounce cooked fish, seafood, or
lean meat

Calcium-Rich Protein
1/4 cup dried
beans, tofu, or
tempeh

Fruit Portion
3–5 per day
1 medium fruit
1/2 cup cooked fruit
1/2 cup fruit juice

Calcium-Rich Fruits
1/2 cup fortified fruit
juice

Vegetable Portion
4–6 per day
1/2 cup cooked vegetables
1 cup raw vegetables
1/2 cup vegetable juice (unsalted)

Calcium-Rich Vegetables
1 cup cooked or 2 cups raw:
bok choy, broccoli, collards,
Chinese cabbage, mustard
greens, kale, or okra
1/2 cup fortified tomato juice

Starch Portion
6–11 per day
1/2 cup cooked whole grains
1 ounce ready-to-eat cereal
1 slice whole-grain bread
1/2 cup cooked starchy vegetable

Calcium-Rich Starches
1/3 cup dried beans (navy, black,
pinto, garbanzo, great northern)
1/2 cup cooked amaranth

HEALTH-PROMOTING PYRAMID

SIX SIMPLE RULES FOR EACH DAY

Here are the six simple rules we tell people about what to eat each day; obviously, eating on the lower end of the range will inspire faster weight loss:

1. 4 to 6 servings of vegetables

2. 3 to 5 fruit servings

3. 6 to 11 starch servings

4. 0 to 4 teaspoons olive oil (or other acceptable fat)

5. 1 to 2 dairy (or calcium-fortified soy products) servings

6. 1 to 3 ounces of animal protein or ¼-cup servings of beans

you're more likely to need supplemental calcium (500 to 800 milligrams per day) if you aren't eating dairy products.

FOR YOUR INFORMATION: USEFUL TIPS TO KEEP IN MIND

Before you delve into the recipes in this book, you might enjoy a quick refresher on a few important FYIs.

SODIUM GUIDELINES

On the Rice Diet, we recommend that your sodium intake be between 500 and 1,000 milligrams, so be sure to check the amount of sodium listed in a product, as sodium inspires overeating. Becoming aware of hidden sodium in processed foods is key, since this is where we typically ingest the greatest amount—without even knowing it! Who would guess that a product can advertise "no salt added," yet still contain other sodium-rich ingredients? Salt is actually sodium chloride, so it is necessary to dramatically limit any products containing salt and anything with sodium in it— monosodium glutamate (a flavor enhancer), sodium benzoate (a preservative), soy sauce, etc. When my weight is ideal, I strive to eat a whole foods, no-salt-added diet with 1 cup of dairy, plus no more than 200 to 300 milligrams of added sodium per day; this allows me space for a regular slice of bread, or cereal, a sorbet, or a glass of wine. There is certainly room for you to personalize this sodium recommendation; just commit to the narrow road until you reach your weight and health goals.

WHEN TO EAT

Most Ricers tend to eat breakfast early, between 7:00 and 8:00 A.M.; they eat lunch between 12:00 and 1:00 P.M. and dinner between 5:30 and 6:30 P.M. Of course, you can eat at whatever times are convenient to you and your lifestyle, but keep in mind that you don't want to wait until you feel desperate or ravenous, because that's a setup to overeat. It's okay to snack or spread out your food intake to create smaller meals throughout the day instead of three major meals—if you do so, we encourage you to become conscious of what you eat and when you eat. This can include any timing you desire; but we highly recommend not eating after your dinner meal, which, preferably, is by 7:00 P.M. Most people who successfully maintain their goal weight do so by creating a routine and sticking to it. Read more on this in "Commonly Asked Questions About the Rice Diet" (page 88).

READ FOOD LABELS

Generally the most important information to note on a food label is: ingredients, serving size, calories, fat grams, saturated fat grams, percent of calories coming from fat, milligrams (mg) of cholesterol and sodium, grams of fiber, and kind and amount of additives, such as refined sugar, artificial sweeteners, preservatives, colorings, etc.

Ingredients are listed in the order in which they are found in a product, by weight. For example, if sugar is the first ingredient listed, that means there is more sugar in the product than any other ingredient. It is important to choose foods that list only whole, unadulterated ingredients that are naturally low in fat, sodium, and refined sugar.

The nutritional information provided on the label is given with respect to the stated serving size. It is crucial to first note the serving size, as many packaged foods state unrealistically small-size servings. For instance, some low-calorie cereals state ¾ to 1 cup as a serving size, whereas some higher-calorie types (such as granolas) might state their serving size as small as ¼ cup! It might surprise a customer that a 15-ounce can of soup is considered to be three servings by some companies. So be aware that many products contain more than one serving per container.

DRINK ENOUGH FLUIDS

Most Ricers will benefit from 40 to 72 ounces of fluid daily, which is approximately 5 to 9 cups per day. Obviously if you are perspiring (in a hot, humid climate or due to significant exercise), your body may need more. We always caution new participants to realize that it is potentially dangerous to push fluids or drink excessive amounts, as some diets that are not low in sodium may recommend this practice. Tune in to your body, and drink when you are thirsty. The best test is to notice the color of your urine and drink more fluid if your urine is darker than pale yellow.

The best fluid to drink is pure water, but you may want to jazz it up. I like to make herb teas in bulk and blend them. For instance, I'm not wild about the flavor of green tea but want its high antioxidant content; so I make a gallon of hot water to pour over

8 tea bags of green tea and 8 fruity flavored tea bags (such as Tazo's Passion). This is very refreshing iced. I also love icing my favorite coffee substitutes, including Orzo, Decopa, and Teeccino Hazelnut Herbal Coffee. As their recipes describe (see pages 120, 119, and 121), they are delicious with soymilk. Once you discover these health-promoting, tasty beverages, it is usually easy to kick your coffee and soda habits. Sodas are simply hard to justify if you are committed to creating a healthy body. Sodas are filled with caffeine, sodium, and sugar or artificial sweeteners, as well as a litany of other questionable chemicals. They are also typically very high in phosphates, which are known to deplete the bones of calcium and are associated with an increased risk of osteoporosis.

ALCOHOL

If you don't already drink alcohol, don't start. Although some people like to cite studies that show that it raises the level of a helpful fat in your body, alcohol typically creates more problems than it solves. In addition to the inherent dangers of intoxication, it offers a lot of calories with few nutrients.

Alcohol is another beverage that is known to affect our bones adversely. From a nutritional perspective, red wine is by far the most nutritionally redeeming alcoholic beverage, offering high amounts of cancer-fighting antioxidants. If you choose to enjoy red wine, do so cautiously. Since alcohol can reduce our inhibitions and thus help us forget our healthy dietary intentions, it is a good practice to limit ourselves to one glass of wine with the meal.

SWEETENERS

At every meal you may have either 1 packet of sugar, Sweet N' Low, Equal, or Splenda, 1 teaspoon of honey, or 1 teaspoon of maple syrup. However, we highly recommend that you eliminate artificial sweeteners. Artificial sweeteners have an intense flavor that gives the taste buds an amazing hit and limits your ability to taste real food. They can also make nonedible foods edible. More than once we've seen people eat reportedly "sour" fruit buried in artificial sweetener rather than the sweetest fresh fruit. Artificial sweetener, like salt, can trigger overeating tendencies. It also definitely continues to train your taste buds to expect foods to taste unnaturally sweet. Why would we consciously want to create that response? When Ricers want to sweeten a steel-cut oat breakfast, a small quantity of raisins and cinnamon is the ultimate!

HERBS AND SPICES

It may seem obvious when you are on a low-sodium diet, but just in case: don't add salt to your food. My favorite substitutes for salt are fresh herbs and spices, which enhance not only the flavor of various foods but also your enjoyment of them. For most people this is a good thing; few people experience food cravings from fresh foods seasoned with herbs and spices. Triggers are much more likely to be from processed, refined foods with added sodium and sugar.

If you are not familiar with using fresh herbs and spices, there is no better time than today—embracing and enjoying a low-sodium diet is the ultimate opportunity to discover them! I used to think that a few foods, like freshly sliced tomatoes and eggs, just had to have added salt, but then I tried fresh basil and ground black pepper on the tomatoes, with a good balsamic vinegar drizzled over the top, and no-salt salsa with cilantro on eggs. I now truly feel sorry for anyone who thinks they need to use a salt shaker rather than enjoy the delicious flavor of fresh herbs and spices!

SAUCES AND DRESSINGS

Ready-made condiments, sauces, and marinades are popular in our fast-paced world, and the low-sodium versions are getting tastier and easier to find. If they taste a bit flat, use your imagination and jazz them up with fresh lemons, limes, horseradish, wasabi, fresh and dried herbs, dried chile peppers, chipotle peppers (smoked jalapeños), no-salt-added vinegars, mustards, and ketchup. The Rice Diet Store sells

INSPIRATIONAL STORIES:

I believe my sister Kathy sent you an e-mail with the news that my high school best friend, Novella, and I were reunited through the RD Forum! We had not seen each other in about nineteen years, and not for lack of trying. We just lost track of each other and since both last names had changed from our last contact, it seemed any hope of reconnecting was pretty slim. Well, due to the RD Forum and a little detective work on my sister's part, Novella and I had a nine-hour reunion this past Saturday at my house! We discovered we had started the diet the same day (June 12); had lost the same amount of weight (10 pounds); had wedding anniversary dates one day apart (October 15, 1994 and October 16, 1993); and *even* wore the same bra brand and style!! (Not the same size though!) And now, we are supporting each other in our weight loss goals and this new *dieta*!

Kathy mentioned you may want to feature the story in your RH newsletter, which would be totally cool with Novella and me! Just as long as we get a copy!

Happy Ricing! Karen M. Hall

And here's another success story, again showing the power of the Rice diet and its *dieta:*

July 20, 2006

As I was leaving the bookstore while Christmas shopping, I remembered the book, *The Rice Diet Solution,* and just about didn't get it. I have a shelf full of diet books—many of which I haven't read. So why buy another? I asked the clerk if they had a copy. One just came in. It was in the back room. And I bought it.

My wife, Joan, started reading the book, and after about a week she said, "We can do this." Little did we know then of the benefits we would receive. After one month, I had lost 20 pounds, and Joan had lost 15. We were so encouraged by the quick results that we continued. I met my goal in six months. I went from 220 pounds in January to 150 pounds in July for a total of 70 pounds. Joan lost a total of 40 pounds with 10 more to reach her goal.

It's not a diet to us anymore. It is a *dieta*. We have embraced many of the tools, such as yoga, teleconference CDs, and journals. We provide support for each other through journalizing discussions. I walk nearly every day with my dog, Molly. We are learning to relax and taking control of our food choices.

Thank you, Kitty and everyone at the Rice Diet.

Sincerely, Arnie and Joan Watson

and ships the best selection of salt-free products we have seen anywhere, from hot sauces, stir-fry sauces, marinades, and dressings to the best balsamic vinegars and extra-virgin olive oils we've tasted.

Karen's and Arnie and Joan's testimonials show not only the power of the Rice Diet to help you lose weight in a safe, quick way, but also how it unites people. The Rice Diet community is growing and thriving because once people try it, they are drawn to like-minded, health-inspired people! Who knows, you might find a long-lost friend, or support beyond what you have imagined!

CHAPTER THREE

THE BASICS:

TIPS FOR BUYING, STORING, AND COOKING WHOLE FOODS

"Make [food] simple and let things taste of what they are."
—Curnonsky (Maurice Edmond Sailland), French writer (1872–1956)

By now, you are probably getting more comfortable thinking in terms of food groups. Veteran Ricers assure me that thinking in terms of simple food groups is the clearest and easiest way to shop and select, plan meals, store, use leftovers, and cook all the wholesome, wonderful foods that are included on the Rice Diet.

What follows is a breakdown of the basics on how to use all the food groups—from soups to nuts—not literally, actually!

STARCHES

Starches supply the majority of calories in the diets of healthy people. You can find short-term research that confirms whatever answer you are seeking to find, but the bottom line is that the longest lived, healthiest people in the world consume primarily a whole-grain and bean–based diet.

Although all whole grains are good for you, rice is especially beneficial because it offers some of the highest-quality protein of any grain. Quinoa, a grain from South America, is also protein packed, in addition to having an exotic, crunchy "mouth feel." Quinoa offers more than twice the protein and iron and five times the magnesium and potassium of white rice. Eating a variety of whole grains helps satisfy anyone who wants to vary the flavor, texture, and appearance of meals. (See the Healthy Grocery List on page 71 for other recommended whole-grain products.)

Most of us know little about grains, especially rice. There are more than 2,000 different rice varieties, but most Americans are familiar with only Uncle Ben's Converted or instant long-grain rice. To add amazing aroma, flavor, and interest to your meals, try fragrant basmati rice from India, jasmine or black rice from Thailand, Chinese sticky rice, Italian short-grain Arborio rice (the main ingredient in risotto), Texmati rice (a Texas-grown cousin of aromatic basmati), and popcorn rice from Louisiana—for starters; they are all equally easy to cook. And considering that what I list above is a fraction of your options, you can only imagine the new discoveries that await you in the world of whole grains—from wheat berries, hull-less barley, polenta, bulgur, hominy grits, millet, and oat groats—this is a diet that will be expanding and enhancing your life options, not restricting them!

COOKING TIPS FOR GRAINS

• Grains are easy to cook; you just need to know the quantity of water to use for the amount of grain you want to prepare and how long to cook it (see Appendix D, page 317, for this summary on a variety of grains). Obviously the most nutritious whole grains take longer to cook than the cracked or slightly processed ones, but don't let this stop you. While your grains are cooking (on average 45 minutes), you can be picking, washing, and making your fresh salad, setting the table, and cooking what will go on top of your grain!

• To cook in a rice cooker: A rice cooker is the ultimate. If you have ever tasted rice cooked by this method, you'll have a hard time not buying one. Besides producing better-tasting rice and being more convenient and efficient, it has the added advantage of keeping the rice warm and ready to eat—all day long! Follow the manufacturer's directions, which usually suggest about ½ cup less water than conventional cooking methods.

• To cook conventionally on the stove top: Brown rice takes a little longer to cook than processed white rice which has had the tougher bran fraction removed, but it is worth the effort given its better flavor, fiber content, and nutrition (especially B vitamins). One cup of regular brown rice cooks in 2¼ to 2½ cups of liquid in about 45 minutes; parboiled or converted rice requires slightly more water. It's a good idea to turn the temperature down for the last 5 minutes of cooking to reduce the odds of scorching it.

• The general rule of thumb for cooking white rice is 2 cups of water to 1 cup of rice to yield moist, soft rice. (Uncle Ben's Converted rice calls for 2½ cups of water to 1 cup of rice.) For firmer, more separate grains, 1¾ cups of water would suffice. Do not stir rice until you think it is done. When rice cooks, little passageways form to allow steam to cook the rice; disturbing the rice results in a gummy, sticky texture.

• You may also choose to dramatically shorten your grain's cooking time by using a pressure cooker. If you have hesitated to venture into the world of pressure cooking because you heard the lids blow off—fear no more! The second-generation pressure cookers are really safe. Rather than risk your family's life by unearthing Grandma's pressure cooker, do yourself a favor and buy a new one, complete with a heavy pot and a stationary pressure regulator (rather than an old-fashioned removable jiggle-top). Although they are more expensive, they are safer, and thus, worth the price.

• Another invaluable, time-saving tip that many Ricers enjoy is a slow cooker. A slow cooker can cook your whole-grain cereal (oat groats, buckwheat groats, or other whole grains that usually take more time than you care to invest in the early morning) overnight, so you literally wake up to a delicious, fully cooked breakfast. Of course, you can also let it cook while you are at work. After an eight-hour day, it's wonderful to walk into your "jasmine-rice-scented" home with your whole-grain main course waiting for you!

• Some people have recommended boiling water and pouring it over the grain (refer to Appendix D on page 317 for the appropriate amount of grain to water) in a wide-mouthed thermos container. Screw on the lid, go to sleep (or work), and awake (or return) for a ready-to-eat, whole-grain-based meal!

PRESERVING FRESHNESS AND IDEAS FOR STORAGE AND LEFTOVERS

• Since whole grains contain the oil-rich germ, they go rancid within a fairly short time if exposed to heat and light. If you have room to store them in the refrigerator uncooked, they will keep for about six months. Obviously you need to replace them if they begin to lose their fresh, nutty taste. White rice and other processed grains have had their germ removed, so they can be safely stored in a cool, dry place for at least a year. You probably already know that keeping them stored in an airtight container is important to protect them from an insect invasion.

• Usually when I cook whole grains, I cook enough to safely store for 4 to 5 days. When whole grains take 45 minutes to cook, why waste the time and fuel (earth's energy) to do this every time you want to eat? To extend the shelf life of your cooked grains, simply refrigerate them in an airtight container. Although I admit that I often prefer freshly cooked grains, I also love them marinated in cold salads (see recipe for *Black-eyed Pea and Barley Salad* on page 171) when I come home ravenous.

• Some Italians I know do not like to purposefully cook more pasta than they plan to eat in that meal. But this busy Mom and hardworking woman finds it downright delightful to come home and discover last night's leftover pasta tossed with the grilled vegetables we enjoyed two days before! I can't think of a better surprise than this, unless it's walking in to find my husband making up patties from last night's risotto (try this by adding a whisked organic egg to make a few patties from *Rachelle's Wild Mushroom Risotto* [see page 227], and frying them up crispy in a teaspoon or two of olive oil! Who said dinner had to be a headache?! Leftover pasta heated up with *Jay's Tomato-Fennel Red Sauce* (see page 268), then topped with some Parmesan cheese, has surely developed my son's palate more than any school lunch program would have. This nutritious, organic lunch (for you or your children) takes from 5 to 10 minutes to prepare and pour into a hot thermos.

• Try keeping no-fat corn or flour tortillas and pita bread on hand to stuff with whatever leftovers you have for lunch. We love having grilled vegetables and roasted peppers around, as well as cooked rice and beans, for quick "stuffers." And packing these items in airtight containers and assembling them just before you eat ensures that they don't get soggy.

QUICK WHOLE-GRAINED SNACKS

• Ezekiel 4:9 bread, toasted and topped with some organic fruit (try *Toasted Ginger Papaya* (see page 292), or a vegetable spread (try *Spinach Dip* or *Sun-Dried Tomato Pesto* (see pages 138 and 271) makes a great quickie meal paired with a fresh green salad.

• Rice, millet, and other grains are popped to create what we know as rice cakes. I had always disliked the Styrofoam-like texture until some Ricer suggested I toast them about half as much as I would regular bread. (Be forewarned; they burn readily, so watch them carefully.) Top with some organic fruit spread and they are divine! When I'm really eating healthfully, this will satisfy my sweet tooth enough to call it dessert!

• Also try Whole Wheat Matzo Crackers, and Ryvita Sesame Rye Crackers ☼ with a teaspoon of tahini and a tablespoon of fruit-only jam or blackstrap molasses.

LEGUMES

Legumes (dried beans and peas) and starchy vegetables make up the rest of the starchy food group. Legumes, like grains, are naturally low in the troublemakers you want to avoid: cholesterol, fat, saturated fat, and sodium. And, together with oats and barley, they are the other highest source of cholesterol-lowering and blood-sugar-stabilizing soluble fiber. They are so high in soluble fiber that they give you a sense of fullness for 4 to 5 hours after you've eaten them.

Dried beans and peas are not only the highest-protein foods in the starch group, they are also the best sources of potassium, calcium, and iron, which are often consumed in inadequate amounts by older Americans. Giving you a generous amount of these nutrients and a lasting sense of fullness, beans are the ultimate substitute for meat and dairy, with significantly less sodium.

Soybeans have almost twice the protein of most other beans and contain complete protein. They are also a good vegetarian source of omega-3 fatty acids and isoflavones, a plant-based estrogen that has been reported to reduce the risk of cancer. If you have never tried soy products, such as tofu (for dishes like *Peach Smoothie* and *Chocolate–Banana Cream Custard*, pages 117 and 284), or tempeh (try *Grilled Tempeh* on page 262)—do yourself a favor! With all the nutritional strengths of legumes, enjoy them daily.

The variety of beans, from lentils or cannellini to black beans or Southern pintos, the amazing variety of their colors, tastes, and textures and the many ways to prepare them are limited only by your imagination. Keep your interest in your diet alive and well by trying beans that you have never seen or tasted. (See Appendix H for sources of beans that may not be available in your local stores.) How about a special dinner with a Black Valentine (bean) dish, filled with elegant ebony-colored beans that retain

NUTRITIONALLY POWER-PACKED BEANS

Beans	Quantity	Calories (kcal)	Fat (g)	Protein (g)	Sodium (mg)	Calcium (mg)	Iron (mg)	Potassium (mg)
Aduki beans, cooked	0.5 cup	147.2	0.11	8.65	9.2	32.2	2.3	611.8
Black beans, cooked	0.5 cup	113.52	0.46	7.62	0.86	23.22	1.81	305.3
Blackeyed, cooked	0.5 cup	99.76	0.46	6.65	3.44	20.64	2.16	239.08
Broad beans, cooked	0.5 cup	93.5	0.34	6.46	4.25	30.6	1.27	227.8
Cannelloni/white kidney beans, w/o salt, canned	0.5 cup	100	1	6	5.75	39	1.62	250
Chickpeas, cooked	0.5 cup	134.48	2.12	7.27	5.74	40.18	2.37	238.62
Cranberry beans, cooked	0.5 cup	120.36	0.41	8.27	0.88	44.25	1.85	342.5
Fava beans, cooked	0.5 cup	93.5	0.34	6.46	4.25	30.6	1.27	227.8
Garbanzo beans, cooked	0.5 cup	134.48	2.12	7.27	5.74	40.18	2.37	238.62
Great northern beans, cooked	0.5 cup	104.43	0.4	7.37	1.77	60.18	1.89	346.04
Kidney beans, all types, cooked	0.5 cup	112.4	0.44	7.67	0.88	30.97	1.96	358.43
Lentil, cooked w/o salt	0.5 cup	114.84	0.38	8.93	1.98	18.81	3.3	365.31
Lima baby beans, cooked	0.5 cup	114.66	0.35	7.32	2.73	26.39	2.18	364.91
Navy beans, cooked	0.5 cup	127.4	0.56	7.49	0	62.79	2.15	353.99
Pinto beans, cooked	0.5 cup	122.26	0.56	7.7	0.85	39.33	1.79	372.78
Soybeans, cooked	0.5 cup	148.78	7.71	14.31	0.86	87.72	4.42	442.9

Data compiled from Food Processor.

their shape beautifully and have a fabulous potatolike flavor and texture? Or how about including in your Christmas tradition a dish of Christmas limas, which are large, flat, lima-shaped beans colored with dramatic splashes of maroon and offering a very creamy texture? Black runners are also unique in that they turn a chocolate brown after cooking, and, most important, have an exquisite chestnutlike flavor. The category of beans is far grander than most of us have ever explored; welcome to this expanding universe!

Starchy vegetables such as yams, sweet and white potatoes, corn, peas, and winter squash get an undeserved bad rap. Although they do convert to blood sugar faster than dried beans and peas, the effects of their high glycemic index status are entirely manageable. For example, when you eat beans and corn together your blood sugar will not rise as high or as fast as it would had you eaten twice the amount of corn and no beans (for the same calories). Plus we all know how good they taste together! There is nothing evil about white potatoes or other starchy, white foods if they grow in the ground. Starchy, unprocessed, white foods are not our problem—eating mega-amounts smothered in butter or gravy is what can lead to serious problems!

QUICK AND BASIC TIPS FOR BUYING, PRESERVING, AND STORING LEGUMES

• Buy a variety of beans that you can store in closed containers in a cool, dark place. Don't be tempted to show off their beauty in glass jars lined up on your windowsill! The best spot to store them is in a cool cupboard as far as possible from the oven or stove. For ease of use, store them in glass bottles and mark the date of purchase.

• If you purchase them from a food cooperative, where you can buy them in bulk for less, you also have the advantage of sorting through them to ensure quality. Beans with dents or dings in them will age faster than whole, intact beans. Many bulk beans seem to have more twigs and grit in them, so while they are a great inexpensive source, they do need your care in selection and later cleaning.

• Beans keep well, but after more than six months of storage, they get increasingly harder to cook, and after two years there is virtually no amount of cooking time that will soften them. Beans can be old without showing outer signs of their age. If you soak beans overnight or for 8 hours, slice one in half, and see that it is not consistent in its appearance, you can be sure that it is too old to justify boiling for hours. After having a pot of old beans take five plus hours to cook, I now buy beans where I expect the turnover is good. For example, consider buying beans from a popular health food store, or a Latin or Asian market, where they would be more likely to have this year's beans than would a store that sells fewer beans.

• Two of the best mail-order sources for unusual and recently harvested beans are The Bean Bag and Phipps Ranch in California. They will send you catalogs upon request (see pages 328–329 for contact info) with varieties and quality that will entice you and inspire your experimentation.

TIPS FOR COOKING LEGUMES

• Dried beans are best if soaked in cold water for about 8 hours before they are cooked. This soaking time ensures that the beans will cook evenly and be easier to digest. Also, rinse them a few times during their soak; this will reduce the gaseousness that eating beans can produce. Don't use hard water. If your tap water is hard, use bottled spring water to boil your beans, and never add acidic foods to beans until they are done; both can cause the bean's skin to stay tough.

• Most people typically soak their beans overnight, but if you have less time, small and medium-size beans usually are sufficiently soaked after 4 hours. To assess if a bean is ready to be cooked, slice a soaked bean in half and see if the inside of the bean is one color. If it has an opaque spot in the center, it needs more soaking; if it is consistently one color—you are ready to cook! FYI: 1 pound of dried beans equals about 2½ cups. Typically, dried beans triple in volume: 1 cup dried = 3 cups cooked. (See Quick and Basic Guidelines for Buying, Preparing, and Storing Dried Beans and Legumes on page 43 for details on specific beans.)

• To cook beans, place soaked beans in a pot with 3 times more water than beans. Add nonacidic herbs and vegetables for seasoning; select two or three of the following, as desired: garlic, onion, leeks, carrot, celery, ginger, thyme, oregano, rosemary sprigs, bay, or sage leaves. Try sautéing the garlic and onions a little, then adding seasonings to them before adding them to the beans. Add an acidic ingredient like tomatoes or lemon only when the cooked beans are tender.

• The Quick and Basic Guidelines for Buying, Preparing, and Storing Legumes (see page 43) guesstimates are just that, educated guesses. Cooking time depends primarily on the beans' size and age—the latter of which we do not know unless we've grown them. Thus, to ensure consistency in tenderness, avoid cooking different batches of beans together. It's a good idea to check the beans 10 minutes or so before the guesstimated cooking time has been reached.

QUICK MEALS AND TIPS FOR LEFTOVERS

Eating whole foods doesn't have to mean spending all day in the kitchen! If you simply get into the habit of keeping healthier staples on hand in your home and office, meals often require only the 5 minutes it takes to toss them together!

• As with whole grains, why not cook enough beans for a few meals since they will be delicious for 3 to 4 days? If you have time and feel ambitious on a weekend, cook them ahead and freeze them in appropriate portions for your family. If you are single and think you will overeat if you cook more than a meal, you may prefer freezing them in ½-cup containers. Larger families may prefer 1-quart, airtight containers. Either way, the beans will freeze beautifully for up to 6 months.

• Some of my favorite quickie bean meals: beans tossed into leftover pasta with marinara sauce; Eden brand canned beans added to a large organic tossed salad; beans jazzed up with a variety of quick sauces, like Mr. Spice Tangy Bangy sauce or *Black Beans with Garlic and Pimentón de la Vera* (see page 148), served in a whole wheat pita (salt free) or with crackers and salad, or spread thickly on a tortilla with grilled veggies, *Roasted Vegetables* (see page 199), or salad, and rice for a burrito wrap.

BEAN ALERT!

When people who have traditionally eaten lower-fiber diets start eating a higher-fiber one, especially one rich in beans, intestinal gas is frequently a problem. Since the enzymes required to digest bean sugars have not been needed, their digestive tract does not have them and the sugars pass undigested into the lower intestine, where bacteria metabolize them and create gas. Rest assured, this annoyance is not dangerous and will pass when your body adjusts to your bean-rich diet. Since your body will start producing the enzymes needed to digest beans without gas production, why not reduce your challenges by introducing them slowly? Most people will not find the problem to be excessive if they increase their bean intake slowly; eating ¼ cup today, ⅓ cup tomorrow, ½ cup the next day, until their body gets accustomed to digesting the sugars. Others claim that adding the seaweed kombu will aid in the digestion of beans. (Eden brand beans contain this ingredient. Even if it doesn't solve your gas problem, you will gain flavor, valuable minerals, and just a little sodium!) Chewing foods slowly and thoroughly could also help the digestive problems. Those who have persistent problems with gas may want to try the product Beano. (See Appendix H, page 327, for ordering information; note that Beano is contraindicated for some people who are allergic to molds.)

• One-half cup of potatoes with ½ cup of cooked beans and a huge tossed salad makes a great meal. The soluble fiber–rich beans dramatically slow the blood sugar rise from the faster-absorbing potatoes—so there is no problem even for a brittle diabetic!

• Starchy vegetables will provide even more fiber if the skin is eaten; just wash with soap and water before cooking, and you won't need to peel them.

• Starchy vegetables are great leftovers for lunches as well. I love a sweet potato the next day—hot or cold. In fact, I'd call that dessert! Be sure to try *Sweetheart Sweet Potato Chips* (see page 129) and *Ryan's Sweet and Spicy Mexi Dip* (see page 133)— they're outrageous!

• A favorite 5-to-10-minute meal is opening up a can of Bearito's Organic Refried Beans (or puréeing some *Pinto Beans* [see page 160] into *Kitty's Refried Beans* [see page 156] ahead of time if you have the time and want to economize), then adding as much no-salt salsa as you like, seasoning with extra chopped tomatoes and minced jalapeños and cilantro as desired, then enjoying with no-fat, no-salt corn chips or in a burrito wrap. What a delicious and fast lunch or appetizer for a UNC basketball game!

• One of the reasons *Dr. Rosati Borlotti Bean Soup* (see page 220) is superb is that he thickens and enriches the soup's stock by puréeing half of the beans. This creates such a flavorful and rich taste and consistency that you'll wonder how you lived this long without this bean technique!

VEGETABLES

Vegetables are not only the lowest-calorie food group, they are nutritional power-houses. Most fresh fruits and vegetables contain significant amounts of vitamin C and A, two of the most important and effective antioxidants. And remember, antioxidants prevent fats from oxidizing in the blood, thus preventing atherosclerosis, the underlying cause of most heart disease, from proceeding. Vitamin C is very high in tomatoes and citrus fruits; vitamin A is very high in all dark orange, red, and green vegetables. Generally speaking, the darker the orange or green fruit or vegetable, the higher the vitamin A content.

BUYING VEGETABLES

• Although vegetables as a group contain more sodium than do fruits, the sodium naturally occurring in whole foods is not our problem (unless you are a kidney or liver patient). By far, our greatest excess of sodium comes from the hidden sodium in processed foods. So, again, read food labels and avoid vegetables with *added* sodium. The best advice is to buy fresh, locally grown, organic vegetables whenever possible. Considering the Rice Diet recommends that your daily sodium consumption should be between 500 and 1,000 milligrams (dependent upon whether one has problems with kidney and liver disease, high blood pressure, congestive heart failure, and edema on this higher range), and this whole foods diet inherently contains approximately 500 milligrams of sodium, you have about 500 milligrams of added sodium to eat where you would most enjoy. For instance, I like occasional bagels, capers, and olives, while others may prefer getting their Phase Three extra sodium splurges via regular cereals and breads. As your food and sodium intake varies, be sure to stay mindful of your daily weight (and blood pressure, if that has been problematic).

• A good-quality, organic, frozen vegetable would be a healthier choice than would a wilted old vegetable that was grown thousands of miles away, then preserved through questionable means (gassed or sprayed with God knows what) and transported.

• The next best choice would be canned, organic vegetables with no salt added. The canning process destroys significant amounts of potassium, and our blood pressure will elevate (or worsen) when we eat excessive sodium *and/or* inadequate potassium.

• Plan to spend most of your grocery shopping time in the produce section. With the exception of the cross-merchandised foods, such as the vegetable dips near the radishes and lettuces, it's the healthiest section in which to shop.

• For those of you who think you will eat more vegetables if they are precut and prewashed, by all means buy them that way. Prewashed, fresh spinach makes *Angela's Spinach with Sun-Dried Tomato* (see page 175) fast, and it is incredible!

CALCIUM-RICH VEGETABLES

The following vegetables are excellent sources of naturally occurring calcium: collards, broccoli, kale, bok choy, mustard greens, Chinese cabbage, and okra.

• Expand your horizons in the vegetable world. You may try a small stretch first, like portabello mushrooms when they are fresh and in season; try them grilled or sautéed and tossed in a marinara sauce for a meaty texture. Then graduate to *Broccoli Rapini* (see page 178) and *Belgian Endive* (see page 177). If you don't think you like greens, open yourself to the conversion experience of the *Gingered Greens* recipe (see page 182). It is hard to have an aahh-haa experience if you don't show up for it. As others have said, "Things didn't change until I did!"

THIS IS NOT A TRICK QUESTION

Guess what part of the United States has the highest incidence of hypertension and strokes? If you guessed the southeastern part, where the people eat not only BBQ and vegetables seasoned with salted fatback and streak of lean, as well as a lot of canned vegetables (which are less expensive and lower in potassium), you are right! We either pay the extra cost for fresh vegetables now, or pay later in unnecessary pharmacy bills and medical complications!

• Focus on buying the majority of your vegetables locally grown—ones that are fresh and in season. Purchasing produce from weekend farmers' markets or work-site local produce sales, has gotten more and more people interested in freshness and quality, knowing where their food is being grown, by whom, and how. Food just tastes better when you can connect with the farmer who tended the vegetables and handpicked them that morning for you to cook and enjoy a few hours later.

QUICK AND BASIC TIPS FOR ENJOYING VEGETABLES

• An effective weight loss and maintenance strategy is to eat at least 3 cups of raw vegetable salad before eating other, higher-calorie foods. Raw vegetables' high fiber fills the stomach and gives your brain time to register that you aren't starving, and you can slow down and enjoy a smaller entrée than you would have had you not eaten the large salad first. Even though Italian waiters may look at you like you have three heads, I always insist upon the salad first so that I won't regret overeating pasta or whatever course may follow! This really works—promise me you will try it!

• Ensure that your vitamin A and C intake is generous by enjoying a dark orange, red, or green vegetable and tomatoes or citrus daily. If you don't care for tomatoes or citrus fruits, many other vegetables contain plenty of vitamin C, including cabbage, broccoli, cauliflower, brussels sprouts, peppers, and any dark green leafy vegetable or sprout. Choose a minimum of 4 servings of vegetables per day, but choosing more will likely assist you better in your weight loss efforts. If you want to eat more of any food group than you have been eating—let it be the vegetable group!

• While a high vegetable intake is typical of populations that have less obesity and cancer, a high cruciferous vegetable intake is an even stronger predictor of low cancer rates. Cruciferous vegetables are a group that includes broccoli, cauliflower, kale, cabbage, brussel sprouts, arugula, watercress, radish, daikon, and various mustard greens. They are very high in sulforophane, which has powerful anticancer properties. Many large, respected studies now show that eating 5 or more servings of cruciferous vegetables per week dramatically reduces your risk of developing numerous different kinds of cancer.

• Sprouts in general offer an abundance of vitamin C and enzymes. Broccoli sprouts, in particular, contain the densest source of sulforophane yet found in any food. What an easy, delicious, and nutrient-dense addition to any salad or wrap! It's a no-brainer way to enjoy and benefit from a highly promising cancer-preventing food. This is certainly inspiring, considering that cancer researchers estimate that dietary modification (like an increase in cruciferous vegetables) reduces cancer risk by 30 to 40 percent! Research has also shown that eating broccoli sprouts daily improves chronic bacterial gastritis (inflamed stomach lining) by fighting H. pylori, the bacteria responsible for many cases of bacterial gastritis and stomach ulcers.

• For those who like to snack or eat more frequently than three times per day, vegetables would be the ultimate choice. Keeping fresh and crunchy, raw, organic vegetables convenient, usually fills the bill when you want something to eat, but you aren't ready for a meal. My mom's friend Barbara used to call that desire for something to be between your teeth "mouth hungry!" Raw vegetables accompanied by a puréed vegetable dip can be just the break you need to tide you over until dinner. I find my afternoon snack is as much a ritual and tradition, as it is a real hunger—so be ready with a low-calorie vegetable snack if you have this munching habit.

• Never forget that your children will assume your food habits far more often than they will follow your free advice or sermons. Setting a good example is the most effective way to teach others you love how to promote their health. Take advantage of their food preferences and offer the healthiest choices just before you expect them to be hungry. For instance, my ten-year old loves vegetables and he's hungriest right after school. Soon after we get home from school, I offer him his favorite snacks: grape tomatoes, and his dad's roasted peppers or artichokes. He (like me) will eat a lot more vegetables when he's hungry than if they are served at the same time as pasta, rice, or seafood at dinner.

STORING AND LEFTOVERS

• Vegetables freeze well. If you have a vegetable garden or can buy in bulk and freeze them when they are freshly picked, then cook and freeze them. You can undercook the vegetables a little so they keep their texture when you reheat them. If you make a big batch of spaghetti sauce or soup and don't finish it within four or five days, simply reheat it and, when it has cooled, pour it into airtight containers and freeze. It's so convenient to have on hand.

• As I said before, leftover grilled vegetables are great the next day over pasta or in a pita pocket. One way to make use of extra veggies is to make a purée, and add it to tomato sauce to add depth, to a soup to enrich the stock, or to create a bisque (soup) that is great during the winter months.

CLEANING AND COOKING TIPS

As more and more people become conscientious about what they eat and have growing concerns about the dangers of pesticide residues in our food supply, the demand for, and thus cost and availability of, organic foods will improve. The following tips may assist you in reducing your pesticide intake and promoting your health:

• Buy organic as often as possible. I don't peel organic fruits and vegetables, simply scrub them lightly with a natural-bristle brush. Use only organic lemon and orange peel for citrus zest.

• Since the recipes in this book constitute a very-high-fiber, nutrient-dense diet, especially if you eat beans daily, do not hesitate to peel all vegetables that are not organically grown. This is especially important for waxed vegetables such as cucumbers and rutabagas. Even with this removal, your fiber and nutritional intake is still far healthier than that of most Americans. Others prefer to scrub their nonorganic produce with a few drops of vegetable-based soap or soak them in water with a drop of Clorox in it.

• When cleaning vegetables that grow in heads or bunches, I remove the outer leaves and soak the inner ones. Salad spinners are the best vegetable cleaning utensil I know for this: in them you can wash, rinse, soak, rinse again, and spin. For produce that cannot easily be peeled or scrubbed, such as cauliflower and broccoli, the salad spinner is invaluable. For peppers that are waxed, I often wash them and then roast them, which helps to remove the outer skin and bring out the flavor!

• Vegetables are versatile and very easy to prepare. You can always eat them raw, which preserves most nutrients and enzymes. The next best way to preserve a vegetable's nutritious value is by steaming; it is so simple a process that many overlook it. There is perhaps no better cooking technique for retaining the purest taste and optimal texture for a perfectly ripe fresh vegetable. Many people simply steam their vegetables in the collapsible metal steamer baskets on legs, but the perforated stainless steel steamers that are the inside liner of a larger pot are the ultimate for people who cook fresh food often. Always have the water boiling before you add the vegetables to the pot. My other favorite type of steamer is the Asian bamboo type that has numerous trays; this type is especially convenient if you like to steam a variety of vegetables that need different cooking times.

• Blanching, which means boiling in a little water for a very short time, is similar in that it quickly seals in the flavor and nutrients of fresh vegetables. Lightly sautéing in a teaspoon of olive oil and stir-frying vegetables are also quick, delicious options that retain most of the valuable nutrients and flavors. The ancient Chinese technique of wok cooking is outstanding because it cooks hot and fast. Although the shape of the wok allows for maximum cooking surface, stir-frying can also be done nicely in a cast-iron skillet, which has the nutritional advantage of imparting iron into the foods cooked in it. For fast and efficient searing with a minimal use of oil, it's best to heat the wok or skillet over a high flame until a bead of water flicked onto the surface evaporates immediately. Then you add a teaspoon or two of oil, tilt and swirl the wok or skillet so that the oil coats the surface and starts to sizzle, and add the previously cut vegetables in the order in which they need to cook. For instance, after flavoring my hot oil with a little garlic and onion, I would add the carrots first since they take

BUYING ORGANIC CAN HELP CHANGE THE WAY THE WORLD THINKS

Both the earth and our bodies can heal if we make the choice to be conscious about what we put into them. If we all took the responsibility to eat primarily organic foods, whether through composting rather than using chemicals on our gardens or getting up on Saturday morning and going down to the farmer's market to meet and support those who are selling their organically grown food and/or signing up with an organic farmer who delivers seasonal produce to your door once a week, we would be taking significant concrete steps toward healthier lives and a transformed world. For more complete information on the hazards of foods treated with chemicals and the benefits of organic foods, see page 83.

the longest, then brussels sprouts (usually halved because they take longer than most veggies to cook), then broccoli, etc.—last would be mushrooms and green leafy vegetables.

• A quick-and-easy way to impart flavor to a stir-fry is to start with frozen cubes of vegetable stock, which is one of the most convenient low-fat and low-sodium ways to season. Also try freezing freshly chopped herbs and olive oil in ice cube trays, which is a great way to capture the fresh herb flavor for later use (when they are not locally available).

• Grilling, roasting, and broiling are cooking methods that add tremendous flavor! Try eating at least half of your produce raw, and then enjoy this range of cooking methods for variety and pleasure.

FRUITS

Fruits were originally selected by the Rice Diet founder, Dr. Kempner, along with grains (specifically rice), to be the mainstay of the diet. Fruit has the lowest content of sodium, fat, and protein of any food group, which is part of the reason why fruit is great for those with many different chronic diseases. The majority of the world that does not suffer from high amounts of chronic disease consumes a lot of fruit. As stated in the vegetable section: the darker the orange and green color of a fruit, the higher the beta-carotene and vitamin A content. You may be surprised to know that dried fruit and watermelon are surprisingly high in iron as well. Fruits are also one of the highest sources of cholesterol-lowering soluble fiber. If you are reducing or elimi-nating dairy products, you may want to enjoy calcium-fortified fruit juices.

TIPS ON BUYING AND STORING FRUITS

• Choose organic fresh, frozen, or dried fruit (in that order) more often than cooked and canned fruit, since they have reduced amounts of vitamin C. Potassium is also significantly reduced in the canning process. Since blood pressure is typically ele-vated by increasing sodium and decreasing potassium and the average American is deficient in potassium, more fresh fruits would be helpful.

• Buy fresh, organic fruit from a farmer as frequently as you can. I'll never forget how incredible it was the first time I bought organic peaches from a farmer who had picked them fresh that morning. I also recall picking blueberries at a Mennonite farm on ladders. It blew my mind that blueberry bushes could grow higher than a house and the berries be twice as big and flavorful as I had ever known. Talk about exquisite!

• If purchasing canned fruit, be sure to buy organic and the type without added sugar or syrup, which gives you extra calories without nutritional value.

ENJOYING FRUITS

• If you drink fruit juice, make sure it is 100 percent fruit juice with no sugar added, and do not drink more than 4 ounces per day. Drinking a lot of your calories in juice is an easy way not to lose weight. Whole fresh, organic fruit is preferable to juice since the whole fruit offers cholesterol-lowering soluble fiber and makes you feel more full per serving.

• If you enjoy fruit juice but want to reduce the calories, try creating fruit juice plus herb tea (and seltzer water if you miss the sparkling soda fizz) blends. They are better than either one "straight up" and have a fraction of the calories of juice alone.

• Eat the skin on fresh organic fruit, whenever possible, for more fiber and vitamins. As with vegetables, when using nonorganic foods, gently scrub fruits carefully with a vegetable-based soap. Since many pesticides are oil-based, washing non-organic produce in water with vinegar or lemon in it is an excellent strategy for removing some of these chemicals. But for delicate fruits like strawberries, raspberries, and blueberries, simply soak and rinse before eating.

• Frozen fresh organic bananas and seedless grapes are two of my favorite all-natural desserts. The bananas taste better and are easier to peel if you get them fairly ripe, peel them, wrap in an airtight wrapper or bag, and freeze. The grapes should be washed, patted, or spun dry, then placed on a cookie sheet in the freezer. After they have frozen individually, scoop them into a plastic ziplock bag for future enjoyment. Red grapes, in particular, are an antioxidant-packed delight. These are a delicious and nutritious alternative to desserts when your sweet tooth is screaming!

• According to the USDA, the most important fruits and vegetables to buy organic include apples, bell peppers, celery, cherries, imported grapes, nectarines, peaches, pears, potatoes, red raspberries, spinach, and strawberries. (See page 83 for complete information on organic fruits and vegetables.)

• To capitalize on the many nutrients and enzymes in fresh, organic fruits, I usually enjoy them raw. But, for variety, and to fulfill my culinary interests and imagination, I also enjoy fruits baked, blended in smoothies, and more recently grilled and broiled. Although when fruit is heated the vitamin C content plummets, it still is more health-promoting than most dessert alternatives. I will admit that eating grilled fruit has been so satisfying for dessert that it has saved me from literally thousands of calories of chocolate! And I do seriously mean thousands! Even the weekly Basic Rice Diet day of grains and fruit is not that challenging when one includes smoothies, *Granny's Baked Apples* (see page 286), *Grilled Pears* (see page 287), and melba toast topped with *Richter Girls Jam* (see page 266)!

PROTEIN

Many people can eat a little meat while maintaining good health, but this is an invitation to do so mindfully and moderately. Detox (Phase One), achieve your optimal weight (Phase Two), and then during maintenance (Phase Three) add what you most desire; do so mindfully and assess your body's response. Most people will detect a slight rise in blood pressure or cholesterol within a month of adding just 3 ounces of skinless chicken breast a couple of times per week! That is why we quit serving chicken on the program, even that infrequently. Seeing that trend repeatedly in our data made us reassess what we were serving. We figured that if our purpose was to educate participants on the power of the detox diet to prevent and reverse chronic diseases and their risk factors, we needed to quit serving chicken, and now the only animal protein we serve here is seafood once per week. Seafood is the only animal protein that does not aggravate heart disease risk factors; in fact, it has been shown to lower triglycerides and blood pressure quite impressively.

Here at the Rice House, dried beans and peas are the protein-rich foods of choice. We include them in both starch and protein categories since nutritionally speaking they are both. I encourage you to experiment with a variety of different and new beans that you have never previously tried. But if you do want to consume protein from animal sources, keep in mind that it is to your advantage to find an organic supplier of your high-protein foods (see page 327 for more information on this topic).

TIPS FOR BUYING, PREPARING, AND CONSERVING PROTEIN-RICH FOODS

• Tempeh, a cultured soy product, is one of the best-kept high-protein, vegetarian secrets. It should be eaten within days of purchasing it as its flavor gets stronger with time. It freezes beautifully if you prefer to keep it on hand for later use. Please transcend your initial judgment that it looks like moldy soybeans, because it is delicious (try *Grilled Tempeh;* see page 262) and certainly no weirder than eating fermented milk as cheese, yogurt, sour cream, or buttermilk. Ignore the black spots, as this sporulation is natural to the product.

• Tofu is a soybean "cheese" that is delicious if you know how to prepare it. It will keep refrigerated for about 10 days if you store it in water and rinse it approximately every other day. It can be frozen; in fact, many people prefer the meatier chew of tofu that has been frozen and thawed before cooking. Tofu is superb at absorbing the flavors of surrounding ingredients. Try *Peach Smoothie* (page 117) and *Apricot-Horseradish Baked Tofu* (page 262) to experience the enjoyable range (from soft to extra-firm types) this food offers.

• Textured vegetable protein, also known as TVP, is a great meat substitute for those missing the "chew" of meat. Simply add one part TVP to 6 parts of vegetarian spaghetti sauce or chili for a texture very similar to that of ground beef. This most popular form of TVP looks very much like a beige version of Grape-Nuts cereal, but larger chunks or strips can be used in stir-fries or stews.

ENJOYING LEAN MEATS—THE BEST CUTS

If you don't have heart disease or significant risk factors and want to enjoy some lean meat, why not choose the cuts lower in saturated fat:

• round cut of beef

• pork tenderloin

• light-meat cuts of poultry, skinned

• When you have the opportunity to purchase some fresh protein-rich foods, you can save some money by buying in bulk and freezing. I do this whenever I go to the Outer Banks, North Carolina (the islands are locally known as the "Outta" Banks). I pack a cooler, loaded with ice, healthy snacks, and drinks for the drive down, and I return with it filled with very fresh fish or soft-shelled crabs. When I arrive home, I rinse the seafood and fill plastic bags with separate portions of fish or crabs, cover with water, and freeze immediately. I challenge anyone to tell the difference between fresh seafood frozen this way and fresh from the sea.

• If you aren't inspired to raise your own chickens, befriending an organic chicken farmer is a brilliant coup. Not only are eggs a great source of protein and iron, they also taste better when really fresh. Organic farmers typically are generous with their chicken manure, which is some of the best compost you can find!

In countries where chronic disease is rare, people typically consume little animal protein. For instance, Ms. Lan, who has done low-sodium cooking schools for Ricers demonstrates how she uses a 4-ounce piece of chicken in a stir-fry for four people. She describes how to use the meat "as a garnish"! What a concept; hold that thought!

SOME FACTS ABOUT FISH

We recommend eating fish from three to five times a week (in 3- to 4-ounce servings) if the Ricer desires. Fish, which is the highest source of omega-3 fatty acids, has been shown to improve overall cardiovascular health. Fish that are a good source of protein, low in saturated fat, and high in omega-3 fatty acids include mackerel, lake trout, herring, sardines, albacore tuna, and salmon. Unfortunately, some of these higher-fat fish are also higher in mercury, PCBs, and other contaminants that can be harmful to your health and have been associated with cancer.

So it is also important to choose your fish wisely. Indeed, the benefits and risks of eating fish vary depending on a person's age and stage of life, so it becomes a question of risk versus benefits:

• Children and pregnant and nursing women usually have less concern about cardiovascular disease (CVD) and more about harmful exposure to mercury in fish; so they should avoid fish with higher mercury levels (see chart in Appendix C, page 315);

• Middle-aged and older men, who are more at risk of CVD, would benefit from eating fish three to five times a week if they avoid or limit those containing the most mercury, or supplement with 1 gram (1,000 milligrams) of EPA + DHA per day if they don't like fish (see chart in Appendix C);

• All people who do not want to be vegetarians would benefit from eating a variety of fish, while minimizing those that may have high mercury and other contaminants.

In 2004, ConsumerReports.org reminded its readers that both the FDA and the EPA warned women of child-bearing age, those pregnant and lactating, and young children to eat no more than 6 ounces of tuna each week because of the high mercury count found in most tuna. It also reminded these populations not to eat king mackerel, shark, swordfish, or tilefish, all of which tend to be high in mercury.

Salmon is one of the more popular and healthy choices; its high omega-3s and low levels of mercury make it worth the high cost. Wild salmon, the preferred choice, has a much stronger flavor and is delicious. In addition, farm-raised fish is more likely than wild to contain high levels of PCBs, dioxins, and other contaminants.

Hot tip: All salmon from Alaska is wild—so enjoy it during salmon season (May to September) and eat canned Alaskan salmon when it's not in season (October to April). Otherwise, Consumer Reports' tests showed that you can pay twice the price for salmon labeled wild, when it actually was farmed!

For a full listing of fish with their omega-3 content and mercury content, see the chart on page 316 in Appendix C.

Another trick is to use fewer egg yolks and more egg whites. While this reduces the cholesterol, it does not have to reduce the flavor. Of course, heart patients may choose to give all the egg yolks to the family dog, who will not get atherosclerosis from the egg yolks' high cholesterol as humans can.

DAIRY

The dairy product category includes all products coming from grain, soy, or animals' milk. On the Rice Diet, we recommend soy and grain milks; skim, ½ percent, or 1 percent cow's milk—in that order. Soy and grain milks have numerous advantages over cow's milk. Soymilk has less saturated fat, more protein, and 20 milligrams of soy isoflavones per cup.

There are many other advantages as well; personally, I can testify to being one of the many soy-consuming women who went through menopause without even knowing it! When I visited my ob-gyn, and she asked whether I was having any menopause symptoms, I told her I had not; her response was "Well, you must eat a lot of soy products!" When I told her that I didn't consider 1 to 2 servings a day "a lot," she laughed and said that is typical of women who do not experience problems with menopause. Although this is anecdotal evidence, when doctors are repeatedly presented with evidence of soy's positive impact, you'd think we'd all be told to do so in advance and save ourselves some sleepless nights and sweats!

Realize that the sooner we teach our children that there are alternatives, the more likely they will be to make health-promoting choices. Children who are weaned on soy formulas, then soymilk, typically prefer it (just be sure to get the calcium-fortified type).

DAIRY TIPS

• Switch to organic dairy and soy or grain milks; this would be one of the best nickels you spend on organic products.

• Replace mayonnaise on sandwiches and in salads, such as potato salad, with nonfat yogurt or *Yogurt Cheese* (see page 143). Adding mustard, horseradish, and other flavorful ingredients will easily disguise any fat flavor you may otherwise miss.

• Try *Yogurt Cheese* mixed with a little fruit-only jelly for an incredible substitute for cream cheese on bagels or crackers.

• If you can find the no-fat (or ½ percent), no-salt-added cottage cheese, try it. First, stir in a few tablespoons of nonfat yogurt into every ½ cup of cottage cheese to provide the familiar consistency. Be aware that full-fat cottage cheese is typically very high in sodium, and the lower-fat types tend to be even higher.

• I personally prefer WestSoy Plus Soymilk, which is fortified with calcium, but any grain or soymilk would be preferable to cow's milk. Grain and soymilks tend to contain more than 110 milligrams of sodium per cup, but occasionally a brand comes out that has as low as 50 milligrams. Brands and companies change frequently, so it's best to continue to read labels and stay alert for lower-sodium milk choices.

• Hard cheeses that claim lower fat content are often higher in sodium, but for instance, one tablespoon of grated Parmesan can offer a lot of flavor without excessive amounts of fat and sodium. The key is stopping at one tablespoon. If cheese is a trigger for you, wait until you have reached your weight loss goal—12-Step travelers often say, "If you don't want to fall down, don't go onto slippery places"!

• Although nonfat dairy products offer a nice texture and taste, be aware of their limitations. While yogurt is terrific in uncooked dressings and sauces, it will curdle when boiled. Remove the sauce from the heat before adding yogurt to it. Nonfat sour cream and milk can be boiled, but if acidic ingredients like lemon juice, tomato, or vinegar are included, they will curdle.

• Sargento's and Calabro's no-fat ricottas have only 65 milligrams and 48 milligrams of sodium, respectively, per ½ cup, and thus are lower in sodium and less grainy than other cottage cheeses currently available.

FAT

Although the populations of the world vary dramatically in fat intake, the National Weight Control Registry has found overwhelmingly impressive evidence that people in the real world who have maintained significant weight losses for long periods of time eat a low-fat diet. Asians and southern Europeans on 10 percent and 40 percent fat diets, respectively, enjoy longer and healthier lives than we do. The probable reason for this wide range of health-promoting fat intakes is that those who eat higher-fat diets tend to eat fat that is high in monounsaturated fat–rich olive oil and omega-3 fatty acid–rich fish.

Since fat has more than twice the calories of protein and carbohydrates, it is just common sense to limit it if your goal is to lose weight. Consuming fat also usually inspires people to want to consume more of it. We just don't eat as much hot air-popped popcorn or baked potato if there is no fat drizzled all over it! The amount of fat our body truly needs is quite minimal, and is found naturally occurring in whole foods— you do not really need to add oils to your diet. (See Appendix A, Food Groups Defined, page 297, for information on essential fats.)

The following tips will assist you in purchasing and storing fats and identifying hidden fats in processed food, as well as give you tricks of the trade to create more flavor in your cooking without the added fat and calories of traditional meals.

TIPS FOR ENJOYING FATS

• Preferred oils and fats (see Food Groups Defined in Appendix A, page 297) to keep stocked, unless you find that they are dangerous triggers for you, are olive oil, canola oil, and oils from walnuts, almonds, flaxseeds, and sesame seeds.

• If fat is solid at room temperature, it will more likely be solid in your arteries than a liquid choice. Simply open your mind to healthier alternatives which are really tastier. I truly feel sorry for anyone who is still using man-made, spreadable fats, when fresh-pressed, extra-virgin olive oils are so exquisite.

• Educate your palate on olive oils; some people prefer the strong, peppery, Tuscan olive oils, especially on vegetables and wild game, whereas others prefer the lighter-flavored Ligurian olive oils, which are much more appropriate on fish. Everyone's palate is different, so experiment to discover what you like best.

• When you buy a liquid oil, you can store it in the refrigerator for ultimate protection. However, olive oil solidifies at cold temperatures, so if you need to get some quickly you will need to immerse the container in warm water until the oil melts. Most people do not have the refrigerator space, so the next safest storage place is in a tightly sealed glass jar placed out of the light, preferably in a cool, dark cabinet. Good olive oils have the pressing date noted on the back label. We use our most recently pressed olive oils for raw use (on salads or bruschetta) and cook with the oils (if we still have them) that were harvested the year before. Olive oil is good for two years, if properly sealed and stored.

• While nuts and seeds contain some protein, the majority of their calories come from fat. The key to protecting your nuts and seeds is to store them in an airtight, cool, dry place. If air is allowed in, the antioxidant-rich vitamin E will be oxidized, and its health benefits lessened.

• Nuts, like nut/seed butters, while delicious, can be quite addictive and easy to overeat. If you find that you can use seeds and nuts as condiments and garnishes rather than megasnacks, they are a delicious way to get your vitamin E. If you're trying to lose weight, pay careful attention to portion sizes. Some may find that flaxseed is the only safe fat to keep in their house!

• Try sautéing with vegetable stock or wine instead of fat, then, after the dish is cooked, drizzling your uncooked, more nutritious and flavorful oil on top.

• I prefer to use most of my oil uncooked and use high-quality oils that have optimal flavor. At 45 calories per teaspoon, I like to enjoy this calorie-packed commodity to the fullest! Try even ½ teaspoon of toasted sesame seed oil on top of your vegetable stir-fries (as a garnish) or ½ teaspoon of walnut oil on a fruit and vegetable salad. It is amazing how much flavor you can get from ½ teaspoon of really good oil!

• As there are a few naturally occurring grams of fat in most starches, 1 to 2 grams of fat in a processed food product are not a problem unless that fat is coming from fat that has been hydrogenated or is animal (and thus highly saturated) in origin.

CONDIMENTS

The number of very-low-sodium and low-saturated-fat products and the variety of herbs and spices that are available now are incredible and sure make eating healthy and quick easier. Try the following flavor-packed options for your health and culinary enjoyment.

While most people are familiar with no-salt versions of mustard, ketchup, horse-radish, and vinegar, fewer have been adventurous enough to try flavor-packed additions like wasabi powder, Pimentón de la Vera, and saffron. Our Rice Diet Store wizard, Susan Levy, and other foodie staff members have gathered the best collection of very-low-sodium and low-saturated-fat foods and condiments I've seen; see the Healthy Grocery List on page 71 for brand names and healthy food additions to catapult you into a new culinary dimension.

INSPIRATIONAL STORY

The following inspirational story is truly remarkable. Kevin Alban, a forty-something-year-old Roman Catholic priest now living in Rome, came to the Rice House last year. As many do, he kept in touch with us, which led to us visiting him when we were in Rome last June. He later wrote us this letter, describing his experience on the Rice Diet and his impressive success back home.

In July 2005 I traveled to Durham, NC, to begin a six-week program at the Rice Diet Program, which had been recommended to me by a colleague in New York. My check-in weight was 304 pounds; blood pressure 180/100; and fasting blood sugar (FBS) was 150 mgs/dl. My check-out

THE BASICS · 67

weight on August 29 was 258 pounds (a drop of 46 pounds); blood pressure 130/76; and FBS 100.

These good results obtained on the program encouraged me to continue with a similar regime when I returned to Italy, where I now live. I eat a low-salt, low-fat diet and make sure that I exercise regularly. Living in a religious community (I am a Roman Catholic priest), it was relatively easy to ask the cook to prepare my meals without salt, sauces, and other additives. Italian cuisine makes much use of fresh vegetables, fruits, and salad; fish is plentiful and there are many varieties available. Rome is a large and beautiful city, so taking a walk each day is no hardship.

The result of my adapted version of the Rice Diet Program has been a further drop of 48 pounds, bringing my current weight to approximately 210 pounds. My goal is to reach 200, which is still a little heavy, but much better than 304 pounds.

Several people have asked me how I have managed to keep losing weight while living in Italy where the cuisine is believed (wrongly) to be rich and high in calories. I believe that there are a number of reasons, which when taken together, have contributed to my weight loss.

1. Low-salt, low-fat, no-meat, no-dairy diet

I would find it hard to overstate the benefits of a cereal/vegetable/fruit diet in continuing weight loss. This has not been without sacrifice and temptation, but I have adopted a number of strategies to cope:

· Generally I turn down invitations to meals in restaurants, but accept them to friends' houses—home entertaining is still important in Italy and cooking is much lighter than in restaurants.

· If I do eat out, then I try to opt for salad with no dressing, and grilled fish. (continued on next page)

• I have decided to not waste calories on inferior quality food—I only eat pasta with sauce or steak if it is excellent.

• I drink plenty of water.

• I snack on fruit or vegetables.

• I use a range of spices and herbs to give flavor, as well as cooking in white wine when preparing meals for myself.

• I do not miss meals and take a regular carbohydrate (oats, pasta, beans, and rice) intake three times a day for energy and a healthy sense of having eaten. I also eat naturally oily fish twice a week.

• If I make an exception, I do not worry about it, but get back on track the next day.

2. Walking an average of six miles a day

• This aspect of my lifestyle has not been hard: Rome has plenty of things to visit and the weather is good year round. Walking requires no training or expensive equipment or membership fees. Committing to a regular exercise time daily, and to the use of a pedometer to ensure my ten kilometers a day has been key for me. The benefits are much more than losing weight: I have noticed much improved concentration and metal alertness, a better frame of mind and attitude, as well as greater physical stamina and endurance.

3. Support from my local community, friends, and from fellow alumni of the Rice House

The initial reaction from everyone upon my return from Durham was so positive that it gave me great heart to continue.

· I briefed my own religious community on what I had done at the Rice Diet Program, and how I hoped to continue. Now, two members of the community eat more or less as I do and have also started to exercise regularly. Both are over 70 years old—so it is never too late.

· I try not to preach or convert others because it seems the quickest way to lose support.

· Most important has been the continuing support from a group of people I met in Durham at the Rice House. There are no secrets and no trying to impress with these friends. They are the most honest and genuinely loving people I have met and their encouragement is vital.

I remember what it was like to weigh over 300 pounds, and I am not going back to that state.

That about says it all!

CHAPTER FOUR

TRANSFORMING YOUR PANTRY THE RICE DIET WAY

"To eat is a necessity, but to eat intelligently is an art."

—La Rochefoucauld

You won't be surprised to learn that I think of food shopping as an activity that also can be mindful. This doesn't mean that shopping has to take a lot of time or energy or money. Like the rest of the Diet, it just may require a little more thought as you become accustomed to the new ingredients and the recipes. And then shopping is simply a part of your routine.

As you may note in the recipes, we have intentionally listed ingredients in a general way, like no-salt-added mustard, and then followed that product with the name of our personal preference, such as Cherchie's Champagne or Cranberry Mustard. The recipes will be tasty if made with generic, no-salt-added products, but after you've tasted some of these ingredients you'll understand why we bothered to specify them.

Stay mindful as you grocery shop; many other brands with the same or a similar product name contain significantly more sodium, fat, or chemical additives, or less than optimal ingredients, like corn syrup.

This ingredient list has evolved after thirty-five years of my commitment to vegetarianism, experimenting with and choosing lower-sodium and lower-saturated-fat foods that taste the best. Our Rice Diet Store manager, Susan Levy, has also devoted much of her life to exploring and acquiring the best products available and using her impressive culinary talents to create interesting combinations for quick, easy, and phenomenally good recipes.

From a taste perspective, the brands that we have specified have all been tried by Rice Diet dietitians, store staff, and numerous Ricers and have been found to be great-tasting products. We appreciate that taste preferences vary from individual to individual and would love any suggestions you have on products that you have found to be your favorites; send them to www.ricedietstore.com and we'll consider carrying them.

The nutritional information at the end of each recipe is based upon all the ingredients specified. If you choose to use other products, be sure to take a moment to examine the ingredients label for sodium and other nasties you want to avoid. For ease in comparison, the nutritional information about specified brands is available on the Rice Diet Store website (www.ricedietstore.com).

As you begin the healthy transformation of your refrigerator and cupboard, use the following Healthy Grocery List as a guide to staples and other products used in the recipes and menus of the Rice Diet.

HEALTHY GROCERY LIST

One way to really make the Rice Diet livable and easy is to fill your refrigerator, cupboard, car, and office with foods that are contained in the Rice Diet recipes and meal plans. Below you will find our Healthy Grocery List. Most of these foods can be found in a big grocery store, health food store, or the Rice Diet Store. Any food that can be purchased from the Rice Diet Store (www.ricedietstore.com) is marked with a ○.

BEANS AND PEAS (LEGUMES)

• Dried beans/peas—any variety (they are less expensive when bought in bulk from food cooperatives). Bean Cuisine ○ makes eight soup kits that start with dried beans; no salt is included in the kit, and each kit makes 14 tasty one-cup servings. These are great for cooking ahead and freezing in one-cup portions for your later convenience.

• Soybean products—As the majority of soybeans are now genetically engineered, buy organic whenever possible.

• Frozen beans/peas—no salt or fat added.

• Canned beans—no salt or fat added (Eden Organic is the best-known high-quality, no-salt-added brand). ○

• Tempeh—Tempeh is a "cultured" soy product, which is made by cooking cracked soybeans, draining the water, and inoculating them with a culture called *Rhizopus oligosporus*. Take care in reading the ingredients; the natural unflavored type, such as Light Life Tempeh, has no sodium.

• Tofu is a soybean cheese found in most chain grocery stores, health stores, and food cooperatives. It is called a cheese because its method of manufacture is similar to that of dairy cheese. Choose the type that is highest in calcium and that suits your texture preferences; it is available in soft and firm.

• TVP is the commonly used abbreviation for textured vegetable protein, which is an excellent meat substitute. TVP and TSP, textured soy protein, are made from low-fat, water-processed soy flour that is cooked, extruded, and dried. They are available in bulk at many natural foods stores and food cooperatives. We prefer Bob's Red Mill TSP, which is organic. ○

BEVERAGES

The average American's beverage is loaded with caffeine, sodium, fat, sugar, and/or artificial sweeteners. All of these can be potentially harmful. Even the decaffeinated beverages have some potentially adverse effects. Decaffeinated coffee and/or tea have been shown to aggravate hernias and inhibit the absorption of iron. If you really want decaffeinated coffee, look for the "naturally decaffeinated" coffee. But, preferably, try some healthier alternatives; such as my personal favorites, Orzo (an Italian coffee substitute made from roasted barley), Teeccino Hazelnut Herbal Coffee, and Decopa, which is roasted dahlia root. ○ See recipes for these drinks on pages 119–121. However, there are many other healthy beverage choices:

• Water: bottled spring or distilled seltzer water—salt-free varieties; good when mixed with 100 percent fruit juices and fruity herb teas.

• Herbal teas, preferably decaffeinated and unsweetened; green tea contains high amounts of health-promoting antioxidants; good-quality brands include Harney & Sons, Tazo, and The Republic of Tea; if you don't care for the taste of green tea straight, mixing it with flavorful fruity blends (like Tazo's Passion) masks the green tea's rather bland flavor, and it is incredibly good iced. ○

• Fruit juices, unsweetened; check ingredients to confirm fruit juice only or fruit juice and seltzer water blends.

• Vegetable juices, unsalted, are great if you add lemon, lime, or other salt- and fat-free condiments. I also like to add full strength no-salt-added prepared horseradish, with a stalk of celery for a virgin Bloody Mary! ○

• Milk: soy and grain milks, skim, ½ percent, and 1 percent are recommended in that order. Soy and grain milks have quite a few advantages over cow's milk. When compared to 2 percent cow's milk, Edensoy Extra Original provides more protein and plant-based estrogens called isoflavones. Isoflavones, especially genistein, are being studied for their reported ability to reduce the risk of cancer. Researchers currently suggest about 50 milligrams of isoflavones each day for the possible prevention of cancer. Soymilk is an excellent replacement for cow's milk, with less saturated fat, more protein, and 41 milligrams of soy isoflavones per cup.

BREADS AND CRACKERS

Most people with overeating problems find that breads and crackers can trigger their desire for excessive consumption and thus weight gain. And traditionally breads or starchy snacks have more than 180 milligrams of sodium per slice or serving, which is too much sodium for someone with hypertension, congestive heart failure, or kidney disease. In addition, almost all of the commercially available products, except for those made at a health-oriented bakery, will contain partially hydrogenated fat. The following choices can be found without any sodium- or saturated fat–rich ingredients.

• Corn tortillas containing only corn, lime, and water

• Bremner Crackers—unsalted ○

• Edward and Sons Sesame Unsalted Rice Snaps ○

• Hol-grain Brown Rice Cracker—no salt added ○

• Old London Sesame and Whole Grain Melba Toasts—no-salt-added varieties ○

• Matzos—no-salt-added variety

• Whole Wheat Pita Bread (see Appendix H for ordering no-salt-added variety)

• Rice Cakes—no-fat and no-salt-added varieties—Koyo Millet ○ has more flavor than regular rice cakes, and all-grain cakes taste much better slightly toasted.

• Ezekiel 4:9 bread is packed with sprouted grains and legumes and is available in the freezer section of natural foods groceries. It has 80 calories per slice and is available in both regular-sodium and low-sodium varieties. It is best toasted and topped with organic fruit-only jam.

COLD CEREALS

Most cereals contain partially hydrogenated fats and 200 to 300 milligrams of sodium. The following have no added fat or sodium and 6 grams or less of added sugar or sucrose, making them superior to the majority of cereals sold in chain grocery stores.

• Puffed Rice and Wheat

• Raisin Squares

• Shredded Wheat

The following cereals are found in a growing number of health food sections in the larger chain grocery stores. Of course, health food cooperatives or stores have the largest selection.

• Grainfield's cereals

• Health Valley cereals

• Most New Morning cereals

• Kashi cereals

• Nature's Path Granola ○

HOT CEREALS

Excellent choices for hot cereals are:

• Buckwheat groats (also known as kasha) ○

• Cream of Rice (or Rice and Shine) ○

• Cream of Wheat (or Cream of Rye) ○

• Grits (be sure to check for a no-salt-added brand like Bob's Red Mill) ○

• Hodgson Mill Multigrain Cereal ○

• Kashi—a brand name for a 7-grain and sesame-mixed cereal

• Oats: Oat groats, steel-cut oats, oat bran, oatmeal ○

• Wheat and Rye Farina (Farina is another name for Cream of Wheat–like products) ○

Most health food stores have numerous other hot and cold cereals. Take care to read the ingredients and choose one without added sodium or fat; the nutritional analysis should read no more than 2 grams of fat, 10 milligrams of sodium, and 6 grams of added sugar and at least 2 grams of fiber.

WHOLE GRAINS

The ultimate cereal is the whole grain itself before it has been puffed, flaked, or processed in any way. Below, the whole grain is listed first, followed by more processed options. Most refined products have half the fiber content and significantly fewer nutrients than the original whole grain. The following can be found at most health food stores and a growing number of chain groceries. These types of grains should be the foundation of starches in your diet. When numerous products are described, they are listed from the least to the most processed.

• Barley: hulled, pearled, flaked, or barley flour ○

• Oat groats or Irish steel-cut oats ○

• Millet ○

• Kasha (roasted buckwheat groats) ○

• Bulgur (cracked wheat) ○

• Couscous and pasta are usually processed wheat products ○

• Polenta (finely to coarsely ground corn) ○

• Popcorn—air popped or microwave from scratch, no oil or salt ○

• Quinoa—South American grain that is relatively new to the United States; it has a great crunch and mouth feel ○

• Rice—brown, wild, basmati, Black Pearl (a blend of rice and other grains), jasmine, or any type that does not contain added fat and sodium ○

• Rye—berries, flakes, or flour

• Wheat berries, wheat germ, and bran—the latter two are fractions of the former whole berry ○

CONDIMENTS

The ultimate condiments to substitute for the traditional salt- and fat-laden ones are herbs, lemon, lime, and the growing varieties of vinegars. But the following condiments are convenient and are usually available at the Rice Diet Store and some grocery stores.

• Vinegars—balsamic vinegar, red and white wine vinegars, and herbed vinegars ○

• Conserves or fruit-only jams/jellies/fruit spreads ○

• Cherchies—no-salt herb seasoning mixes ○

• Frontier no-salt seasoning mixes—many varieties ○

• Diet Zing—low-sodium hot sauce ○

• Enrico's No-Salt Salsa or Desert Pepper Peach Mango Salsa ○

• Heinz or Hunt's—no-salt-added ketchup ○

• Mr. Spice sauces—many to choose from—all no salt/no fat added ○

• Molasses, honey, brown sugar, and anything ending in "ose" should be limited due to their empty calories. Molasses is the only sweetener with any significant nutritional value.

• Paul Prudhomme's Magic seasoning—no-salt-added variety ○

• Angostura low-sodium Worcestershire sauce ○

• The Ginger People make a number of condiments with no salt added: the Sweet Ginger Chili and Sushi Ginger are both excellent, but their sugar content is higher ○

• Kerala Curry Mild Mango Chutney—great flavor and low sodium ○

CONVENIENCE FOODS

As you may have noticed, many products advertise low or no fat, sodium, or sugar, but rarely are they low in all three! The following convenience foods are free of or very low in all of these concerns. Remember to use a little imagination in preparing convenience foods that have no added salt or fat. (See page 313 in Appendix B for specific ideas.)

• No-Salt-Added spaghetti sauce produced by Roselli's ○ or Walnut Acres

• Frozen vegetables for quick stir-fries

• Bearitos Vegetarian Refried Beans—no salt added ○

• Health Valley—no-salt-added products, especially the Vegetarian Chili ○

• Marco Polo Ajvar ○—a mild or hot sauce of peppers, eggplant, and garlic that is an excellent pasta, rice, potato, or veggie topping and can even be used as a pizza sauce on pita pizza

• Muir Glen or Eden Tomato Sauces—no salt added ○

• Tabatchnick—no-salt frozen soups

DAIRY PRODUCTS

All dairy products are fairly high in sodium and protein, averaging 126 milligrams of sodium and 8 grams of protein per cup of skim milk. The following products are your lowest-fat and lowest-sodium choices:

• Friendship low-sodium cottage cheese

• Calabro's Non-Fat Ricotta cheese, and Sargento's Low-fat Ricotta

• Nonfat plain yogurt with active yogurt cultures

• Skim milk

• Soymilk, calcium fortified

NOTES ON SPECIFIC PRODUCTS

Some of the specialty products or brands indicated in the recipes may or may not be familiar to you or your local grocer. As mentioned earlier, although the recipes work just fine with generic products, some of the brands really do warrant at least a try— they are often superior in taste and quality. Take a look at the following notes on some of our favorite brands.

• Ginger People Sushi Ginger: There are many uses for Ginger People Sushi Ginger besides topping your sushi bites. Most pickled sushi gingers have a good portion of sodium as well as dye that turns it pink. Ginger People's Sushi Ginger is easy to mince and add to dressings and salads when you want a sweet flavor with a little ginger bite. Also from the Ginger People brand, we have used Sweet Ginger Chili. It is an excellent zero-sodium, hot-and-sweet sauce for use in stir-fries and salads.

• Safinter Pimentón de la Vera (Hot and Sweet): You may have noticed this seasoning in many of the recipes in this cookbook. Here's why: it seems that every time Susan asks a good cook, "Have you tried this yet? It tastes smoky without the chemicals," a few days or weeks or months later they present us with their favorite recipe using this smoked Spanish paprika. Although you can substitute any paprika, Pimentón de la Vera is superb and very distinctive; it is dried, smoked, and ground in the Vera valley in Spain. Do yourself a favor. Buy the real thing. Look for Pimentón de la Vera on the label. We use the Safinter brand, but there are others.

• Indian Harvest Brand: We use a number of their rice and grain blends in this cookbook as well as in the Rice House kitchen. They are great alone but also make an interesting base for experimenting with salads and pilafs.

• Chef Pascal Orange, Ginger, and Coconut Sauce: This is a ready-made sauce where the chef (a restaurateur in Florida) has done the heavy lifting for you. It has a complex taste that when used in a recipe does not require lots of other seasonings or ingredients.

• Cherchie's: Cherchie's brand has a number of products that contain zero or low sodium. Their three no-salt seasoning blends are excellent without the chemical aftertaste of many no-salt seasonings. They also make two mustards that we think are especially tasty; Champagne and Cranberry.

• L'Olivier Walnut Oil: Because you can't heat walnut oil (when heated it quickly smokes and loses its delightful flavor), it is not as versatile as olive oil. However, it adds a buttery richness to grain salads and a perfect balance to fruit vinegars when making a salad dressing. Since walnut oil is a fragile, polyunsaturate-rich oil, it is important to store airtight in a cool, dark place, preferably in the refrigerator. We like L'Olivier brand for its flavor and intelligent packaging in a ceramic crock for lasting freshness.

• Mr. Spice: Mr. Spice has a full line of sauces. We used Ginger Stir-Fry and Indian Curry Sauce in this cookbook. The Mr. Spice sauces are salt-, fat-, and gluten-free. They don't have the chemical aftertaste of some salt-free sauces and marinades currently on the market. While you can use Mr. Spice sauces in combination with other flavor enhancers like garlic, ginger, and herbs, you can also use them on their own with vegetables or grains for tasty two-ingredient dishes.

• Rapunzel Vegan No-Salt-Added, Vegetable Bouillon: If you have the time and inclination, nothing beats making your own vegetable stock. However, if you need to use a commercial product, we think this is the very best. The folks at Rapunzel don't add salt or chemical flavorings. Each cube makes 2 cups of broth. The cubes are soft, and it is easy to pinch off small quantities to add to grains or vegetables for extra flavor while cooking.

• Honeycup Mustard: This mustard is extra hot and sweet and maybe a little too thick. We always mix it with a "grocery store" balsamic vinegar—a balsamic that isn't aged and has a real vinegar bite. This combination makes an excellent dressing for salads, baked potatoes, and raw veggies.

• Villa Manodori Balsamic Vinegar: While there are a number of very good aged balsamic vinegars, Villa Manodori consistently is chosen as the most popular at our monthly oil and vinegar tastings. When served on a salad or vegetables, it is so smooth that it doesn't need to be combined with oil, which means you can save those calories for something else.

• Kerala Curry Mild Mango Chutney: Compare the sodium content of this chutney (0 milligram) to other well-known mango chutneys (which average 250 milligrams). This is a new product on the market. It is made here locally in North Carolina. It is a smooth chutney and combines easily with other ingredients.

• Sonoma Sun-Dried Tomatoes: Many brands of sun-dried tomatoes are salted and sulfured. This brand is free of added salt, and sulfur is not used in the drying process.

• Téméraire No-Salt-Added Dijon Mustard: Most Dijon mustards contain significant amounts of sodium (usually about 120 milligrams per teaspoon). This Dijon has only 7 milligrams per teaspoon. Mustard is a great ingredient for flavoring many dishes, especially dressings and sauces.

• Bionaturae Apricot Fruit Spread: There are many no-sugar-added fruit spreads on the market. We think this organic import from Italy is the best we've tried.

• Terres Rouges Lemon Ginger Balsamique: This balsamic vinegar has been flavored with figs, cinnamon, coriander, and cloves in addition to the lemon and ginger. Mixed with oil or a no-salt-added sauce (like Chef Pascal Orange, Ginger, and Coconut Sauce), it makes a great marinade or salad dressing.

• Racconto Sun-Dried Tomato Pesto and Traditional Basil Pesto: These two sauces are much lower in sodium than other commercial pestos. They are a convenient addition to your pantry when you don't have homemade pesto on hand.

• Eden Organic Beans: Starting from dried beans continues to be our recommendation, but this is *the* brand of no-salt-added canned beans to keep on your shelves when you haven't been able to plan ahead.

• Marco Polo Ajvar is available in hot. This product is made of eggplant, sweet peppers, and garlic. There are many brands of Ajvar available in specialty food stores, but this brand has the lowest sodium of any we've found.

• Enrico's No-Salt-Added Salsa Hot and Mild: These are chunky salsas that can be used for flavoring almost any dish that needs some extra zip.

SUPPORT AND ENJOY YOUR LOCAL FARMERS' MARKET!

The USDA has created a very-easy-to-use guide that enables you to find great farmers' markets in your area (www.ams.usda.gov/farmersmarkets/). Farmers' markets tend to carry locally grown and/or organic produce, which is not only more healthful for you and your family but also contributes to the growing worldwide effort to support sustainable farms.

• Badia a Coltibuono Red Wine Vinegar: When we first started doing oil and vinegar tastings, everyone tried this vinegar and politely said, yes, it was very nice. Then one day Dr. Rosati brought in a well-known brand of red wine vinegar that most of us had been purchasing from the grocery store for years. Now when we taste them side by side, everyone understands why our recipes read: "use a high-quality red wine vinegar. . . ."

• Villa Manodori Infused Oils: We know there are many brands of infused oils available. We believe that these start with a much higher quality of olive oil than most infused oils and are especially intense.

• Angostura Low-Sodium Worcestershire Sauce: While this product is a great replacement for Worcestershire sauce in any recipe, it also is the best and easiest replacement we've found for soy sauce in a stir-fry.

• Consorzio Mango Dressing: Zero sodium, zero fat; and Ryan has given us two great recipes for this dressing. The vinegar in this product gives a nice bite to offset the sweetness of the mango. We haven't found the same balance in other low-sodium mango dressings.

THE CASE FOR BUYING ORGANIC

Although eating more whole grains, beans, and fruits and vegetables, and eating less meat, saturated fat, and sodium are by far the most important dietary changes we can do for our health, there is a growing body of evidence showing that the more organic foods we eat, the healthier we will be. A recent report published in Britain evaluated more than four hundred scientific studies to summarize a scientific basis for the value of organic food. These studies found that pesticide residues were rarely found in organic crops, and on average, these crops had higher vitamin, mineral, and phytonutrient contents. Unfortunately, the typical American consumer never hears of such studies; the implication is that 98 percent of our conventionally grown food supply is less healthy! Ironically and tragically, political decisions such as food labeling and organic research funding are so heavily influenced by money and big agribusiness, it will take awhile for the true health benefits of organic food and farming methods to be known by the public.

But the dangers of foods treated by chemicals are very real. A May 2003 study published by the Lowell Center for Sustainable Production at the University of Massachusetts showed that "epidemiologic studies have consistently found an increased likelihood of certain types of childhood cancer following parental and childhood exposure to pesticides and solvents." The study also found that children with leukemia were "4 to 7 times as likely" to have been exposed to pesticides used in the yard or garden. Further, another scientific report found that chemicals are up to ten times more toxic in the developing bodies of infants and children than in adults (as reported in 1993 by the National Academy of Sciences [NAS], a nonpartisan, government-funded research body). This increased danger of toxicity is due to the great growth needs of children (between the ages of one and five, children eat three to four times more food per pound of body weight than adults) and the fact that their diet is far more concentrated. Indeed, another study showed that "in the blood samples of children ages 2 to 4, concentrations of pesticide residues are six times higher in children eating conventionally farmed fruits and vegetables compared with those eating organic food" (www.organicconsumers.org).

Another factor to weigh as you become more aware of the sources of the foods you eat is whether that food may be genetically engineered (GE). Biogenetic engineering is the process of splicing or combining one or more genes of a plant or animal into another plant. The majority of American soybeans now contain a gene derived from a microorganism that makes soybeans resistant to herbicides. These plants can later be sprayed with the same herbicide and survive, while the surrounding weeds cannot. However, this does not take into account the harmful effects of foods that are genetically engineered on both our health and environment. GE foods have been linked to increases in toxicity, allergies, resistance to antibiotics, immune-system suppression, and cancer. In addition, their impact on the environment points to uncontrolled biological pollution, thereby threatening numerous microbial, plant, and animal species with extinction (Center for Food Safety, www.centerforfood safety.org).

The USDA estimates that 61 percent of all corn and 89 percent of all soybeans planted in the United States in 2006 were genetically modified, as well as 83 percent of the cotton and maize crops. In addition, it has been estimated that 70–75 percent of processed foods on supermarket shelves—from soda to soup, crackers to condiments—contain GE ingredients (Center for Food Safety and the *Christian Science Monitor*).

Since our food labeling laws do not have to identify GE foods, we are consuming far more than we can imagine. Indeed, Michael Pollan, in his historic account of our history with food and farming in America, *The Omnivore's Dilemma*, points out that we ingest genetically modified corn without ever even knowing because it's disguised in additives such as xanthum gum, high fructose corn syrup, monosodium glutamate, and corn meal. Basically, those who do not eat primarily organic foods are at risk of unwittingly eating foods that have been genetically engineered. (For a thorough list of GE foods on your grocery store shelves, go to www.truefoodnow.org.)

So although organic foods now come with a higher price tag, it seems clear that the long-term health benefits are well worth the extra cost, and more than likely is less costly than the treatment of later disease. These kinds of choices can literally make all the difference in (and to) the world. The grass-roots demand for organic foods, largely accelerated by mothers who intuitively knew that foods with large amounts of concentrated chemicals would be harmful to their children, has catapulted organic foods into a 13.8-billion-dollar business by 2005.

I see this rise in organic purchase power as an invitation and challenge to us all to make the healthiest food and lifestyle choices we can. Growing, buying, and consuming organic food has always been about more than avoiding harm. It is also about benefiting our physical and environmental health, and growing our emotional and spiritual awareness of the interconnectedness and interdependence of all living things.

This invitation to get and give community support for your health has deepened for me since this book was conceived. In fact, as this book goes to press, we at the Rice Diet Program have put our money where our mouths are: we now offer organic, locally grown food choices at every meal.

The recipes in this book, as well as the program and philosophies supporting the Rice Diet lifestyle, also support another grave concern of mine: sustainable agriculture. In her groundbreaking book *Harvest for Hope*, pioneering primatologist Jane Goodall says, "It has become increasingly clear that growing, harvesting, selling, buying, preparing, and eating food plays a central role in the world. And it is equally clear that some things are going wrong." Goodall points to how the takeover of food production by corporations and industrialized farming methods has wreaked havoc on the environment, our food supply, and our health. She points us to a 2005 United Nations report that said "unless we stop pollution and degradation caused by industrial farming and seriously address overfishing and global warming, we will literally run out of enough resources to feed everyone by the year 2050."

The September 2006 *E. coli* outbreak from contaminated spinach is another startling reminder of how industrialized farming methods lead to disease and death—in animals, humans, and plant life. This specific type of *E. coli*, 0157, is a form only found in cows that have been force-fed corn; the spinach more than likely became contaminated from run-off from the infected cattle's excrement. *The New York Times* responded to this alarming outbreak by quoting the *Journal of Dairy Science*, which documented that up to 80 percent of dairy cattle carry 0157, and that when cows were switched from a grain diet to hay for only five days, there was a thousand-fold decline in the 0157! The article then reminded us of the 1993 Jack in the Box fast-food chain *E. coli* outbreak that may well have been prevented by simply switching the cattle to a forage diet seven days before slaughter! In other words, if cattle ate grass as they have done for thousands of years, we would not only eat meat that was healthier (a higher content of omega-3 fatty acids as opposed to higher in omega 6), but we also would not contaminate ground water on and near farms where fruits and vegetables are grown; infect our floodwater and rivers with fatal bacteria; and continue making our cattle so sick from a corn-based diet that most require a lifetime of antibiotics.

We can no longer deny or overlook how we are all connected—people, animals, plants, air, water, earth. As Goodall says, "Remember, every food purchase is a vote. . . . Each meal, each bite of food, has a rich history as to how and where it grew or was raised, how it was harvested. Our purchases, our votes, will determine the way ahead."

So as part of becoming responsible for our health, I implore us all to become responsible for leaving our planet in better shape than we found it, for our children and their children. So as you begin to transform your own pantry and refrigerator, experiment with the recipes in this book, and explore the products and ingredients found in the recipes, I ask you to do so mindfully. I then challenge you to make your commitment to health and healing for yourself, and your community, as wide and as deep as you like!

COMMONLY ASKED QUESTIONS ABOUT THE RICE DIET

Why is limiting sodium such an emphasis on the Rice Diet?

In 1939, when the Rice Diet was initially founded, it was developed as a no-salt-added dietary treatment for those with kidney disease and malignant hypertension (very high blood pressure). Before dialysis and hypertensive medications, the Rice Diet was the only hope for people with these diseases. They either did the Rice Diet or were dead by the age of 40! Dr. Kempner went on to research and publish revolutionary results on the Rice Diet's dramatic beneficial effect not only on kidney disease and hypertension but on cholesterol, cardiovascular disease, congestive heart failure, and diabetes. In addition to weight loss we have also seen significant improvement in such conditions as sleep apnea, psoriasis, pulmonary hypertension, edema, and joint stiffness associated with arthritis.

Within forty-eight hours of eating no-salt-added foods (and usually within twenty-four hours) you will marvel at how little desire you have to overeat! In fact, the more overweight people are, the more they seem to experience this change in appetite or perception of hunger. We believe, after hearing this response from thousands of Ricers, that salt can best be described as a "food trigger," or a food like refined sugar that seems to fuel a desire to overeat. When you hear dozens of people over 500 pounds, who you know were typically eating more than 5,000 calories per day, say after two days on the program that they cannot finish the 1,000 calories they are being served per day and furthermore have no cravings or obsessive thoughts about food for the first time in decades—*you know* something miraculous is going on and needs to be shared.

Most doctors and dietitians, and thus their patients, don't realize that this significant a reduction in sodium intake will make as much difference as it does. I speak as a dietitian who came to the Rice Diet Program after a decade of consulting in cardiac rehabilitation programs, where I had become convinced that vegetarian diets would reverse heart disease, but I was skeptical about whether no-salt diets were really necessary for these results. The power of a no-salt-added, whole food diet so far exceeded the healing potential of anything I had ever seen, it is difficult to distill. Not only did all modifiable heart disease risk factors reverse faster than I could fathom, but there were testimonies of renewed health in every arena imaginable—healing insomnia, daily headaches (that had been suffered for decades despite numerous therapies), psoriasis, arthritis, depression, and general lethargy. Truly, unless you try it, or come here and witness it in dozens of others who are experiencing it, it is hard to believe!

The 2005 Dietary Guidelines for Americans on Sodium and Potassium recognize the direct relationship between increased sodium intake and increased blood pressure. The Guidelines recommend a sodium intake of less than 2,300 milligrams per day, and, for specific populations (persons with hypertension, African Americans and middle-aged and older adults), the recommended daily intake is no more than 1,500 milligrams. In addition, the Guidelines call for increased intake of potassium (found abundantly in fresh fruits, vegetables, and legumes), which blunts the effects of salt on blood pressure and may reduce the risk of kidney stones and osteoporosis. The report also notes that 80 percent or more of Americans' sodium intake is derived from salt added to food by manufacturers or at restaurants, while about 10 percent is the natural content in foods and 10 percent is added at the table.

In the United States, the Center for Science in the Public Interest (CSPI) is encouraging Congress to create a "Division of Sodium Reduction" within the FDA that could advocate for manufacturers to add less salt through regulation. Food products such as Kraft Lunchables manufactured in the United Kingdom have far less salt than the same product in the United States, and CSPI wants the United States to follow Great Britain's enlightened lead.

Given that roughly 90 percent of Americans will eventually develop high blood pressure (which often leads to heart attacks and strokes and is still the leading cause of death in the United States), and how many Americans are African American or over 50 years of age, it seems like we should be giving more than lip service to this 1,500-milligram-sodium recommendation. The CSPI reports that the National Heart, Lung, and Blood Institute (part of the National Institutes of Health) set a target of reducing sodium in the American diet by 50 percent over ten years, but our government has done absolutely nothing to achieve this laudable goal. It would be laughable, if it weren't so downright tragic, that the FDA still considers salt to be "generally recognized as safe" despite the medical evidence that excessive sodium intake is so dangerous.

How much weight can I expect to lose?

While at the Rice Diet Program men lose an average of 30 pounds and women an average of 19 pounds in the first four weeks. The rapidity of your weight loss depends on your age, sex, initial weight, and ability to exercise. Your weight loss is obviously more if you have more to lose, and the same is true of blood pressure, cholesterol, blood sugar, etc. As you lose more weight, the speed at which you lose will slow down, but over a period of months, a weight loss of 2½ to 3½ pounds per week is realistic. Even for those within 10 pounds of their goal weight, although it does get harder, anyone exercising an hour a day and eating as outlined in this book will lose 2 pounds per week.

And more important, as you are losing this weight you will receive the other advantages. You will feel remarkably better: more at peace with yourself, more clear about what you want and why you are here (on planet Earth, that is), and more energetic. Releasing yourself from the grip of processed foods filled with excessive saturated fat, sodium, and sugar is akin to and supportive of releasing ourselves from the ego or the attachments that are not really true for us and who we truly are. Be sure to accompany and undergird your optimal dietary choices with the emotional and spiritual growth that will fuel your commitment to health and healing.

Is the Rice Diet for people who are not overweight?

We all have personal health goals, and one of the most profound qualities of the Rice Diet is that it is easily individualized to everyone's needs regardless of their weight. As stated before, while many initially come to our program to lose weight, usually within days they have realized that the ultimate goal for them is really their *overall* health. Others may come for their blood pressure problems and not think they need to lose any weight, yet find that a month later and 16 pounds lighter their blood pressure becomes optimal. All research done, on about every animal imaginable, shows that being slightly underweight correlates with health and longevity more than any other variable you can examine. So rather than overanalyzing and debating the weight number, we invite people to experience a *dieta*, or lifestyle, that has inspired optimal health predictors for thousands of participants since 1939.

Do you support snacking or spreading your meals out to five to six smaller meals during the day?

We encourage people to get conscious of what, when, and why they eat. This can include any timing you desire, but we highly recommend not eating after your dinner meal, which is preferably by 7:00 P.M. Most people successful with maintaining their goal weight do so by creating a routine and sticking to it. As you learn more about the advantages of soluble fiber–rich foods breaking down into blood sugar more slowly than other whole foods, you may find that you are often satisfied with three meals per day. For example, many years ago I struggled with hypoglycemic problems. If I went more than four hours without eating I would get spaced out, easily irritated, and even disoriented. When a doctor told me that I needed to start eating meat again, I researched healthier alternatives and discovered the natural remedy for my problem. I discovered that the foods highest in soluble fiber (oats, beans, and barley) would satisfy me for five hours or more. Since eating these foods regularly and packing fresh fruit or shredded wheat if I think I might miss a meal, I have not had further problems with hypoglycemia! So keep your health journal and become aware of what, when, and why you eat; in other words, become conscious of your consumption. When people ask if they can skip a meal if they aren't hungry, I caution them not to skip but to delay their food intake until they are hungry and to be prepared with healthy food when that time comes. Always have low-saturated-fat and low-sodium snacks available so that you never abuse the old excuse that you didn't have anything healthy to eat. You can create that reality, or you can create a reality in which you always have healthy food options; the choice is yours. The other key step is to keep track of how many allowances or food group servings you are eating in a day. After all, being at your optimal weight is ultimately determined by the number of calories you consume, and how much exercise you get (e.g., how many calories you expend). The Food Journal and Food Groups Defined in the Appendices (see pages 323 and 297) will be instrumental in assisting you with your conscious consumption of food and the routine that will best support you in achieving your desired weight.

Does my risk of having a heart attack go up if I go off the diet and eat whatever I want for a meal or a vacation period?

A heart attack doesn't just happen one day because of something you ate. It is the result of lifelong eating habits, weight control, and exercise. In fact, what we feed our children when they are young strongly influences the relationship they will have with food for life, and also the decisions they make about habitually creating chronic disease or health.

So I encourage Ricers to view this commitment to creating the health and life of their dreams as a *dieta*—a lifestyle choice—not a diet they would go "off and on." Most of us humans will take detours from our health-promoting choices for celebrations and holidays; the key is to stay conscious of how long these detours take us—or if they are off to never-never land!

What do I do when I hit a plateau and don't lose for days?

We believe that daily weighing is one of the most practical ways to prioritize and remain conscious about our weights. It may be a challenge to know that you are eating and exercising optimally and then not lose weight for days, but this, too, is a lesson in mindfulness and being aware of your body. Plateaus are a normal response to the weight loss process. In fact, weight gain is often part of the weight loss experience. This is not always because we have ingested too many calories or milligrams of sodium, which is one possibility to examine (reread your Food Journal). The other most common reasons people gain weight or plateau is that they are constipated or that they are about to start their period and are retaining fluids. Despite the fact that the Rice Diet is high-fiber, people who start eating a lot of soluble fiber–rich foods (oats, beans, and barley) sometimes have constipation problems. While soluble fiber–rich foods work like magic for lowering cholesterol and stabilizing blood sugar (and making you feel fuller per calorie), the slower transit time may inspire constipation. If this is your problem, adding a few tablespoons of wheat bran per day (mixing it into cereal or moist applesauce) and drinking an extra glass of water or two will solve it; and if this doesn't, a couple of prunes per day will. I would also recommend journalizing your thoughts and feelings when you plateau. On many occasions I have had participants tell me their weight loss was getting stuck despite no caloric increase, then, after journalizing on some issue (they felt was holding them back), they experienced a release in numerous ways. Although this may sound "way out" to some people who have not practiced journalizing, it is one of the easier to believe mind-body epiphanies I have heard shared in my journalizing classes!

Will I be able to keep the weight off this time, for the rest of my life?

If you choose to prioritize achieving your optimal weight and then maintaining it, you will. I do not say this flippantly, as if it were easy, because I know that it requires hard, consistent work to remain that conscious of our choices. Choosing to be aware, day in and day out, and conscious of this present moment and the next present moment is very hard work. Focus, focus, focus. Most everyone wants health, and those who stay focused on their dreams and intentions tend to actualize what they want to manifest. It is easy to get sucked into the mainstream—the drift or current that the majority of people unconsciously choose to join.

During thirty-five years of practicing prayer, yoga, meditation, journalizing, tai chi, and often a combination of these introspective disciplines, I have enjoyed many breakthroughs in consciousness. Although some have led to dramatic healings and epiphanies, more frequently they were simply times when I suddenly awoke to something that I was doing that I previously was not conscious of. My experiences, and those of many Ricers who have shared similar experiences, suggest that these practices we teach at the Rice Diet Program do enhance our likelihood of manifesting our desired weight and dreams. As with everything in life, it takes hard work and discipline to make important long-term changes that last. But when the disciplines so quickly inspire you to feel better than you have in years, you want to maintain the benefits. Focus, and the community to inspire you to keep your focus (visit the forum group at www.ricediet.com), are key to creating and maintaining the health and life you desire.

PART TWO

THREE WEEKS

OF MENUS

AND 150+

RECIPES

A NOTE ABOUT OUR MENUS AND RECIPES

The following menus and recipes were a community birthing if there ever was one! They were inspired, conceived, and delivered by Ricers from around the world, from the loving Rice Diet Program staff to our new Ricers in cyberspace. I especially want to thank Susan Levy, the manager of the Rice Diet Store and a fabulous chef, and Ryan Summerford, our dietitian, who contributed many delicious and inspiring recipes. I thank you all for your generosity and desire to "pay it forward" by sharing what is working for you. Thank you for your willingness for us to tweak the recipes a bit during our testings, to give us the freedom to simplify and to offer an optimal and nutritious product.

To make cooking whole foods way less labor-intensive, the menus reuse many of last night's leftovers for the next day's lunch. You, of course, do not have to follow these menus exactly; they are simply a sample of the many delicious and varied recipes and how realistic and appealing this plan can be.

The sun symbol (☼) beside certain ingredients connotes two things: that you can purchase such an ingredient at the Rice Diet Store (www.ricedietstore.com) and that we prefer this brand, though the brand is not required to try the recipe. After many decades of cooking schools and semivegetarian lifestyle, I have come to appreciate the importance of starting with optimal ingredients. For instance, a bean and vegetable salad is worth eating topped with grocery store olive oil and vinegar, but it can't compare to Susan's *Warm Lentil Salad with Mustard Vinaigrette*, which uses Badia di Coltibuono's Red Wine Vinegar paired with our Ravida's extra-virgin olive oil. It doesn't take a gourmet palate to taste the difference!

Another example that says it all is *Smoky Swiss Chard Sauté*, which could be made with grocery store paprika. But once you've tried it with Pimentón de la Vera (we carry Safinter's, but other companies package it as well), you will make the effort to stock it. It makes a lot of difference when you are committed to eating a healthy, low-sodium, and low-saturated-fat diet, to splurge on your ingredients. The difference you will pay for the best ingredients is still far less than what you'd pay eating more meat, cheese, and restaurant meals!

Salud!

RICE DIET PHASE ONE MENU

MEALS	MONDAY	TUESDAY	WEDNESDAY
Breakfast	Oatmeal, 1 cup Raspberries, 1 cup Fresh pineapple, 1 cup	*Kitty's Favorite Weekday Breakfast*	*Gooey Apple Oatmeal* Soymilk, 1 cup
Lunch	Shredded wheat, 2 cups Raisins, 2 tablespoons Apple	*Susan's Ajvar Hummus with Raw Vegetables* Honeydew melon, 1 cup	*Quick Cauliflower and Garbanzo Curry* (leftover) *De-Anne's Curry Rice,* ½ serving Carrots, 1 cup Pineapple, 1 cup
Dinner	Brown rice, ⅔ cup Peach, 1 medium Strawberries, 1 cup	*De-Anne's Curry Rice* *Quick Cauliflower and Garbanzo Curry* Large spinach salad with dressing of choice Strawberries, 1 cup	*Black Beans with Garlic and Pimentón de la Vera* Brown rice, ⅓ cup *Angela's Spinach with Sun-Dried Tomato* Mango, ½

THURSDAY	FRIDAY	SATURDAY	SUNDAY
Kitty's Gorgeous Granola, ⅓ cup	*Richter Girls Jam*	Cereal, 1 cup	*Peach Smoothie*
Nonfat yogurt, 1 cup	Ezekiel 4:9 bread (reg.),1 slice, toasted	Soymilk, 1 cup	Ezekiel 4:9 bread (reg.), 1 slice, toasted
Berries	Nonfat plain soymilk, 1 cup	Banana, ½ medium	
	Banana, 1 medium		
Whole wheat salt-free tortilla	*Angela's Orzo Salad* (leftover)	*Spicy Potato Skins*	*White Corn Salad*
Black Beans with Garlic and Pimentón de la Vera (leftover)	*Ryan's Grilled Veggie Skewers* (leftover)	*Spinach Dip*	*Pinto Beans,* ½ serving
	Black beans, ⅓ cup	Carrot, 1 raw, sliced	Large spinach and broccoli salad with dressing of choice
Angela's Spinach with Sun-Dried Tomato (leftover)	Cantaloupe, 1 cup	Pear	
Peach, 1 medium			Pear
Angela's Orzo Salad on bed of arugula broccoli sprouts	*Rachelle's Wild Mushroom Risotto*	*Dr. Rosati's Borlotti Bean Soup*	*Mock Macaroni and Cheese*
Ryan's Grilled Veggie Skewers	Large spinach salad with dressing of choice	Tossed salad, 2 cups, with dressing of choice	*Red and Yellow Tomato Salad*
Fresh figs, 2 medium	*Grilled Pears*	Matzo cracker, salt-free, 1	Steamed kale
		Mango, ½	*Granny's Baked Apples*

RICE DIET PHASE TWO MENU

MEALS	MONDAY	TUESDAY	WEDNESDAY
Breakfast	Steel-cut Irish oatmeal, 1 cup Banana, 1 medium	*Ryan's Crunchy Munchy Breakfast*	*Ya Ya's Oatmeal*
Lunch	Puffed wheat, 3 cups Mandarin oranges, ½ cup Honeydew, 1 cup	*Simple Curried Rice* Raw carrots, sliced, 1 cup Broccoli sprouts Cherry tomatoes, 1 cup	*Kitty's Refried Beans,* ½ serving (leftover) Whole wheat flour tortilla 3 tablespoons salsa, no salt added Large tossed salad with dressing of choice Mandarin oranges, ½ cup
Dinner	Brown rice, ⅔ cup Mixed berries, 1 cup Peach, 1 medium	*Kitty's Refried Beans,* ½ serving Salsa, ¼ cup *White Corn Salad* (leftover) *Belgian Endive* Peach, 1 medium	*Jay's Tomato-Fennel Red Sauce* Pasta, cooked 1½ cups *Broccoli Rapini* Mixed berries, 1 cup

THURSDAY	FRIDAY	SATURDAY	SUNDAY
Pineapple Smoothie	*Kitty's Gorgeous Granola*, ⅓ cup	*French Toast Sticks* (using regular whole grain bread)	*Lynnie's Crock-Pot Oatmeal Bars*
Ezekiel 4:9 bread (reg.), 1 slice, toasted	Nonfat yogurt, 1 cup	*My Orzo Eye-Opener*	Soymilk, 1 cup
	Strawberries, 1 cup		Berries, 1 cup
	Banana, ½		
Jay's Tomato-Fennel Red Sauce (leftover)	*Fregole with Roasted Vegetables* (leftover)	*Baba Ganoush*	*Sun-Kissed Quinoa* (leftover)
Baked potato, 1 medium	Large tossed salad with dressing of choice	*Zesty Sweet Potato Chips*	*Chimole*
Broccoli Rapini (leftover)	Figs, 4 medium	Canned black beans (no salt added), ⅓ cup	Large spinach salad with dressing of choice
Honeydew, 1 cup		Strawberries, 1 cup	Mandarin oranges, 1 cup
Fregole with Roasted Vegetables	*Sun-Kissed Quinoa*	*Debbie's Baked or Grilled Tilapia*	*Ryan's Sweet and Spicy Mexi-Dip*
Large tossed salad with dressing of choice	Large spinach salad with dressing of choice	*Grilled Vegetable Medley*	Whole wheat pita, no salt added
Rhubarb–Dried Cherry Crumble	*Toasted Gingered Papaya*	*Grilled Pears*	Salsa, ¼ cup
			Cucumber Salad
			Pear, 1 medium

RICE DIET PHASE THREE MENU

MEALS	MONDAY	TUESDAY	WEDNESDAY
Breakfast	Oatmeal, 1 cup Strawberries, 1 cup Dried cherries, 2 tablespoons	Ezekiel 4:9 bread (reg.), 1 slice, toasted *Richter Girls Jam* Banana, 1 medium	*Elvis Special* (using regular whole grain bread) Nonfat plain soymilk, 1 cup
Lunch	Brown rice, ⅔ cup Banana, 1 small Blueberries, 1 cup	*Black-eyed Pea and Barley Salad* Large spinach salad with dressing of choice Salsa, ¼ cup Cantaloupe, 1 cup	*JR's Grilled Asparagus Salad* (leftover) Salsa, ¼ cup Baked potato, 1 medium Berries, 1 cup
Dinner	Black Pearl medley, ⅔ cup Mango, ½ Pineapple, 1 cup	*Salmon with Summer Salsa* *JR's Grilled Asparagus Salad* Brown basmati rice, ⅔ cup	*Louisiana Cajun Rice,* ½ serving *Baked Okra* Canned kidney beans (no salt added), ⅓ cup Pineapple, 1 cup

THURSDAY	FRIDAY	SATURDAY	SUNDAY
Kitty's Gorgeous Granola	Cream of Wheat, 1 cup	*Ryan's Crunchy Munchy Breakfast*	Ezekiel 4:9 bread, 1 slice, toasted
Nonfat yogurt, 1 cup	Raspberries, 1 cup		Nonfat plain soymilk, 1 cup
Raspberries, 1 cup			Berries, 1 cup
Louisiana Cajun Rice (leftover), ½ serving	*Grilled Tempeh* (leftover)	*Black-eyed Pea and Barley Salad*	*Smoky Swiss Chard Sauté*
Canned kidney beans (no salt added), ⅓ cup	Matzo cracker, 1	*Gingered Greens*, ½ serving	*Angela's Rosemary-Balsamic Mushrooms*
Spinach salad with dressing of choice	Spinach salad with cherry tomatoes and broccoli sprouts	Peach, 1 medium	Brown rice, 1 cup
Mandarin oranges, ½ cup	Peach, 1 medium		Orange, 1 medium
Grilled Tempeh	*Marinated Grilled Chicken with Fresh Corn Salsa*	*Roasted Artichokes alla Rosati*	*Susan's Warm Lentil Salad with Mustard Vinaigrette*
Gingered Greens		*Wild Rice and Mushroom Casserole*	*JR's Spaghetti Squash*
Brown rice, ⅓ cup	*Ilene's Mashed Cauliflower*	Steamed broccoli, 1 cup	Steamed carrots, 1 cup
Pineapple, 1 cup	Couscous, ⅔ cup	Cherries, 1 cup	Mango, ½
	Frozen grapes, 1 cup		

RECIPES

BREAKFAST

STARCHES

ELVIS SPECIAL

Eat like a King for breakfast with Rice Diet's version of Elvis's favorite sandwich.

1 slice whole-grain bread, preferably Ezekiel 4:9 bread, low sodium
1 teaspoon ground cinnamon
1 tablespoon almond butter, no salt added
½ banana, sliced

Toast your favorite whole-grain bread. In a small bowl, mix the cinnamon with the almond butter. Spread on the toasted bread, and top with sliced bananas. This simple sandwich makes a great breakfast that's simple to grab in no time at all.

Yield: 1 serving

Each serving contains approximately: Calories 240, Fat calories 92, Fat 10g, Saturated fat 0.9g, Cholesterol 0mg, Protein 7g, Carbohydrate 34g, Dietary fiber 6g, Sodium 3mg, Omega-3 fatty acids 0.08g

Allowances: 2 fats + 1 starch + 1 fruit

If you can't have almond butter in the house without reaching for it in times of stress, then consider buying it from a store where they have the equipment for you to grind the unsalted almonds yourself, and then keep it in individual serving containers so you're not as tempted to eat more than you truly want.

FRENCH TOAST STICKS

STARCH

Here's a delicious breakfast that is a guaranteed hit! You can, of course, make this with bread in whole slices, but cutting it into strips creates a more delicious, eggier taste—not to mention a more visually appealing plate. And, did I forget to mention—more fun! You can also involve the kids by getting out your favorite cookie cutters, and cutting the bread into shapes (before soaking in the egg) for a memorable breakfast, brunch, or dinner.

2 slices whole-grain bread, preferably Ezekiel 4:9 bread, low sodium

¾ cup egg whites or egg substitute

1 tablespoon ground cinnamon

1 teaspoon pumpkin pie spice

1½ teaspoons canola oil

TOPPING

1½ teaspoons canola oil

1 medium banana

1 teaspoon powdered sugar

1 cup raspberries

Slice the whole-grain bread lengthwise into strips. Mix the egg whites (or egg substitute) and spices in a mixing bowl, and dip the bread slices into the egg mixture; set to the side, turning occasionally to saturate the bread with the egg mixture.

Coat a wide skillet with 1½ teaspoons of canola oil, add the banana and sugar, and cook over low heat. Once the mixture has started to caramelize, add the raspberries, remove from heat, and set aside. Heat another skillet with 1½ teaspoons canola oil over medium-low heat, add the egg-soaked bread, and cook until golden brown. Then flip to the opposite side, and cook until brown.

Blot the French toast sticks between sheets of paper towel, then arrange artfully on an attractive plate and add the fruit topping for a delicious and appealing breakfast treat!

Yield: 2 servings

Each serving contains approximately: Calories 305, Fat calories 84, Fat 9g, Saturated fat 14g, Cholesterol 0mg, Protein 12g, Carbohydrate 47g, Dietary fiber 11g, Sodium 128mg, Omega-3 fatty acids 0.04g

Allowances: 1½ fats + 1 protein + 1 starch + 1½ fruits

Since our 10-year-old tasted French toast made from white Italian bread, he often requests my making it that way. On a recent Saturday morning, after a few months without making either, I asked him if he would like French toast, and he said, "Sure." Since he didn't specify which bread to use, I reverted back to the healthier Ezekiel 4:9 low-sodium bread. After he enjoyed two slices, he asked to be excused and said (without my prompting), "May I be excused? It was a great breakfast, Mom." After picking myself off the floor, I realized the morals to this story are: if you expect a miracle, you usually get it; and if you continue to serve whole grains, you and your family will start to prefer them.

GOOEY APPLE OATMEAL   STARCH

Here is a good old recipe for oatmeal just like Mama used to make. Even if you are on the go, you can still have a "feel-good" meal that is reminiscent of home.

2 cups water

½ cup golden raisins

½ cup applesauce, no salt or sugar added

⅔ cup rolled oats, no salt added

½ teaspoon ground cinnamon

Over high heat, boil 2 cups of water in a small or medium-size saucepan. Before the water reaches a boil, add the raisins and applesauce. When the mixture boils, add the rolled oats, and then the cinnamon. You may add more cinnamon or other spices, if you desire. Reduce the heat to medium and cook for 5 minutes, stirring occasionally. Remove from the heat, cover for 3 to 5 minutes. Serve hot.

Yield: 2 servings

Each serving contains approximately: Calories 256, Fat calories 18, Fat 2g, Saturated fat 0.3g, Cholesterol 0mg, Protein 5g, Carbohydrate 57g, Dietary fiber 6g, Sodium 17mg, Omega-3 fatty acids 0g

Allowances: 1¼ starches + 2½ fruits

KITTY'S FAVORITE WEEKDAY BREAKFAST STARCH

The following is the breakfast I enjoy most weekdays. I find it delicious and am fully satisfied—even if it is a long morning. It is one of the most nutrient-dense meals in the book, so you need not hesitate to enjoy it for lunch or supper! If you don't have all of the ingredients below, feel free to substitute your own favorite organic fresh or dried fruits.

¾ cup nonfat plain yogurt

¼ cup Ezekiel 4:9 Sprouted Grain Cereal or *Kitty's Gorgeous Granola*

2 tablespoons dried cherries

1 tablespoon chopped walnuts or almonds

1 teaspoon flaxseed, freshly ground in a coffee mill or with a mortar and pestle

½ small banana, sliced

Combine the above ingredients except for the fresh fruit, which I like to add to the top for an appetizing finish. My favorite accompaniments are *My Orzo Eye-Opener*, *Dacopa Drink*, or *Teeccino's Hazelnut Finito*. Then all is right with my weekday world!

Yield: 1 serving

Each serving contains approximately: Calories 274, Fat calories 48, Fat 5g, Saturated fat 0.3g, Cholesterol 0mg, Protein 13g, Carbohydrate 48g, Dietary fiber 5g, Sodium 152mg, Omega-3 fatty acids 0.01g

Allowances: 1 fat + ¾ starch + 2 fruits + ¾ dairy

You may notice that I add a little freshly ground flaxseed whenever possible. When freshly ground, flaxseed not only provides a more fatty flavor and thus sense of satiety (or fullness), it is also the highest vegetarian source of omega-3 fatty acid. This type of fat typically lowers blood pressure, triglycerides, and cholesterol, while raising the "good" cholesterol, HDL. So if you don't want fish, which is by far the highest naturally occurring food source of omega-3, 3 to 5 times per week, enjoy a couple tablespoons of freshly ground flaxseed daily.

KITTY'S GORGEOUS GRANOLA STARCH

Cereal from a box is never as good as this gorgeous granola. You can, of course, add whatever you like best in the whole grain, nut and seed, and dried fruit department—and name it after yourself!

1 cup each rolled oats, rye flakes, and barley flakes, or 3 cups oatmeal
¼ cup unhulled sesame seeds

¼ cup pumpkin seeds and/or sunflower seeds, no salt added

½ cup walnuts and/or almonds, coarsely chopped, no salt added

2 tablespoons freshly grated orange zest, preferably organic

½ teaspoon ground cinnamon

¼ cup extra-virgin olive oil

⅓ cup maple syrup or part honey or molasses

2 teaspoons vanilla extract

½ cup raisins, currants, or dried cherries

¼ cup flaxseeds, freshly ground in a coffee mill or by hand with a mortar
     and pestle

Combine the first six ingredients in a 10-inch (or larger) cast-iron skillet. Mix the olive oil, sweetener, and vanilla in a cup and pour over the dry ingredients while stirring. Mix well.

To pan-toast: Toast over medium-high heat, stirring frequently, until the grains, nuts, and seeds become brown and crispy. It will usually take 5 to 7 minutes before the sesame seeds begin to pop and the maple syrup fills the room with its burnt-sugar aroma. Stir in the dried fruit and freshly ground flaxseeds, and mix for another 30 seconds. If you prefer, these last 2 ingredients can be added just before serving. Since flaxseeds contain a very volatile oil, the granola will smell and taste fresher longer if stored separately. You may want to use your granola for the *Five-Minute Granola Piecrust* (where I prefer using granola without fruit in it). Cool to room temperature, stirring occasionally; then transfer to an airtight storage container.

To oven-roast: This method differs only in that you can bake it in the oven at 375 degrees F. You can bake this in anything except cookie sheets, which tend to be challenging to stir in without spilling. Stir every 6 to 7 minutes until the grains are crisp, 25 to 30 minutes. Again, stir in the dried fruit and flaxseed after the granola has browned or just before serving. Cool, stir, then store in an airtight container.

French Toast Sticks (p. 106);
Peach Smoothie (p. 117)

Mexican Lettuce Wrap (p. 230);
Jerk Fingerling Potatoes (p. 155)

Pan-Seared Sea Scallops (p. 240);
Red and Yellow Tomato Salad (p. 206)

Roasted Vegetables (p. 199)
over Israeli couscous

Marinated Grilled Chicken with
Fresh Corn Salsa (p. 256);
Quirky Quinoa Salad (p. 161)

Debbie's Grilled Tilapia (p. 238);
Ryan's Grilled Veggie Skewers (p. 200);
Louisiana Cajun Rice (p. 158)

Rachelle's Wild Mushroom Risotto (p. 227)

Chocolate–Banana Cream Custard (p. 284)

Another variation: Before toasting you could add ⅓ cup of sunflower seeds, dried coconut, and/or wheat or oat bran. Wheat bran would be beneficial if you are prone to constipation; oat bran would be a better addition if you have high cholesterol or blood sugar (diabetes). It is of utmost importance to keep the granola and flaxseed stored in airtight containers. This will keep the fats within them healthier (not oxidized), and it will be much crunchier and more delicious for much longer!

Yield: 20 servings (⅓ cup per serving)

Each serving contains approximately: Calories 156, Fat calories 66, Fat 7g, Saturated fat 0.7g, Cholesterol 0mg, Protein 2g, Carbohydrate 34g, Dietary fiber 3g, Sodium 6mg, Omega-3 fatty acids 0.02g

Allowances: 1½ fats + ¾ starch + ½ fruit

LYNNIE'S CROCK-POT OATMEAL BARS STARCH

Lynnie (Kitty's new friend from the Rice Diet Forum) makes her oatmeal in the Crock-Pot. She says, "This amount lasts me for almost a week's worth of breakfasts. I find this to be very satisfying and filling."

1 cup steel-cut Irish oats
4 cups water
¼ cup dried fruit (raisins, apricots, and cranberries, mixed)
2 tablespoons chopped almonds

Add these ingredients to the Crock-Pot (my Crock-Pot's lowest cooking time is for 4 hours; however, I prefer the texture of the oatmeal in about 2 hours, but have cooked it for the 4 hours, and it is just fine).

When the oatmeal has cooled somewhat (so the fruit stays intact and doesn't become mushy), add the fruits and almonds and blend throughout the oatmeal. After it cools, store it in one large ziplock bag. Serve it in a small container that holds a bit more than a half cup—this size is just big enough to add a bit of milk if you want. Some days I just eat this plain—the fruits and almonds add such a nice flavor to the oatmeal that nothing more is really needed.

You can make this oatmeal blend into bars: After cooking the oatmeal and adding the fruits and almonds, pour the blend into a 10 x 8-inch pan and press it into the corners and smooth out the top. Bake the mixture in an oven at about 350 degrees F and keep an eye on it; it's done when the top is lightly browned. I like the bar when it has shape, but is still very moist. I would imagine that you could bake it longer if you like a crispier texture.

Remove, set on a cutting board, and cut into bars. Wrap each bar with a fresh piece of wax paper, fold it up, and then place it in a ziplock bag. Then they are ready for a "quick grab" when you are on the go.

Yield: 4 servings

Each serving contains approximately: Calories 187, Fat calories 40, Fat 4g, Saturated fat 0.5g, Cholesterol 0mg, Protein 6g, Carbohydrate 33g, Dietary fiber 5g, Sodium 2mg, Omega 3-fatty acids 0g

Allowances: ½ fat + 1½ starches + ½ fruit

RYAN'S CRUNCHY MUNCHY BREAKFAST   STARCH

Ryan discovered this breakfast when she was a student. It's quick, it's delicious, and, for a nutrition student, it replaced the typical "student breakfast staple"—bagels and cream cheese. If you have trouble finding low-sodium cottage cheese, a good substitute is Sargento's Fat Free Ricotta cheese. And if you're out of pineapple, top this with any fruit that you have around.

6 ounces nonfat cottage cheese, no salt added (add 1 tablespoon of nonfat yogurt to moisten if desired)

1 cup crushed pineapple, no sugar added

2 tablespoons chopped walnuts

1 teaspoon ground cinnamon

2 salt-free rice cakes

Stir the cottage cheese, pineapple, walnuts, and cinnamon in a bowl until well mixed. Then spread on two rice cakes for a super-quick-and-easy breakfast that tastes great.

Yield: 1 serving

Each serving contains approximately: Calories 322, Fat calories 95, Fat 11g, Saturated fat 1.1g, Cholesterol 4mg, Protein 12g, Carbohydrate 52g, Dietary fiber 5g, Sodium 105mg, Omega-3 fatty acids 1.4g

Allowances: 2 fats + 1 starch + 1¼ fruits + ¾ dairy

> To keep your rice cakes from tasting like Styrofoam, toast them in the oven or toaster. You will be amazed at how much this dramatically improves the texture. Just keep a careful eye on them while in the toaster; once they are lightly browned, remove them immediately before they burn.

YA YA'S OATMEAL   STARCH

We all have our little favorite combos that become part of our daily rituals. Ryan shares this one of hers. It doesn't take that much longer to combine a few great flavors that turn "ho-hum" oats into a "ya ya" happening!

⅓ cup rolled oats, no salt added

1 teaspoon ground cinnamon

¾ cup fat-free skim milk or soymilk

2 tablespoons raisins

½ cup diced green apple

1 tablespoon chopped walnuts or almonds

Toss the oats with cinnamon. Add the milk and raisins to the oat mixture to soak while dicing the green apple. Add the apple. Microwave for 2 minutes, or boil on the stove top for 10 minutes, or until the oats are tender. Top with chopped nuts and enjoy.

Yield: 1 serving

Each serving contains approximately: Calories 282, Fat calories 38, Fat 4g, Saturated fat 1.3g, Cholesterol 4mg, Protein 11g, Carbohydrate 54g, Dietary fiber 6g, Sodium 101mg, Omega-3 fatty acids 0.24g

Allowances: 1 fat + 1¼ starches + 1½ fruits + ¾ dairy

PROTEIN

POP-ABLE SPINACH QUICHE

Pop these preportioned quiches for a superquick breakfast or brunch. Freeze the leftovers for later, or share them with friends!

1 tablespoon canola oil

2 large eggs

4 egg whites

1 cup spinach leaves

12-ounce can tomatoes, no salt added

2 tablespoons chopped fresh basil

2 tablespoons nutritional yeast, optional

Freshly ground black pepper

Paprika

Preheat the oven to 350 degrees F.

Lightly grease muffin tins with canola oil. Place the eggs and egg whites in the bowl of a mixer and blend on low speed for 2 minutes. Remove from the mixer, add the spinach, tomatoes, and basil, and stir. Pour the mixture into six wells of your muffin tins, and bake for 15 minutes. Top with nutritional yeast, pepper, and paprika to taste!

Yield: 3 servings

Each serving contains approximately: Calories 184, Fat calories 73, Fat 8g, Saturated fat 1.4g, Cholesterol 143mg, Protein 14g, Carbohydrate 16g, Dietary fiber 6g, Sodium 174mg, Omega-3 fatty acids 0.56g

Allowances: 1 fat + 1 protein + 3 vegetables

RACHELLE'S PAN FRITTATA

PROTEIN

Rachelle, our former dietitian, created a stove-top frittata that is perfect for breakfast or brunch. She uses this dish to entertain friends, as well as teach cooking classes down at the Rice House. Thanks, Rachelle!

1 tablespoon extra-virgin olive oil

1 cup chopped red onion

2 cups sliced mushrooms

2 cups cubed baked potato (about ¾ pound)

½ teaspoon dried dill

½ teaspoon dried tarragon

Freshly ground black pepper

2¼ teaspoons nutritional yeast

2 cups frozen mixed vegetables

3 egg whites, lightly beaten

Heat the oil in a skillet that has a lid. Add the onion and sauté for a few minutes over medium heat. Add the mushrooms and cook for 2 minutes more. Add the cubed potatoes. (I usually bake them ahead of time or just microwave for about 6 minutes.) Then add seasonings to suit your taste, plus the nutritional yeast, and mix in well. Add the vegetables and egg whites, and stir around the pan only once or twice. Reduce the heat to low, cover, and simmer. Cook for about 15 minutes, or until the egg whites have firmed up completely and the vegetables are cooked to your liking. Try not to peek—it's the steam that is doing a lot of the cooking!

Yield: 4 servings

Each serving contains approximately: Calories 231, Fat calories 40, Fat 4g, Saturated fat 0.6g, Cholesterol 0mg, Protein 10g, Carbohydrate 42g, Dietary fiber 7g, Sodium 105mg, Omega-3 fatty acids 0.03g

Allowances: ¾ fat + 1 starch + ¼ protein + 4 vegetables

FRUITS

PEACH SMOOTHIE

For a quick breakfast, throw this smoothie in a blender, grab a salt-free rice cake, and you are out the door!

1 very ripe peach
½ cup frozen strawberries
4 ounces soft silken tofu
1 tablespoon fresh lemon juice
1 tablespoon honey
Ice

Mix all the ingredients in a blender until thoroughly smooth. Serve immediately or refrigerate.

This base for a smoothie can be used with all of your favorite fruits. Suggestions for substitutes include pineapple, raspberries, and bananas. For an eye-catching garnish, slide a mint sprig in the side.

Yield: 1 serving

Each serving contains approximately: Calories 170, Fat calories 11, Fat 1g, Saturated fat 0.2g, Cholesterol 0mg, Protein 9g, Carbohydrate 36g, Dietary fiber 3g, Sodium 100mg, Omega-3 fatty acids 0g

Allowances: 2 fruits + ¾ starch

PINEAPPLE SMOOTHIE

FRUIT

Jazz up your side of fruit by whipping it in the blender for a delicious smoothie. It's easy, portable, and ready to go wherever you do!

10.5-ounce package soft silken tofu

1 medium banana

8-ounce can crushed pineapple, no sugar added, chilled

12-ounce can unsweetened pineapple or orange juice

Mix all ingredients in a blender until thoroughly smooth. Serve immediately.

Yield: 2 servings

Each serving contains approximately: Calories 245, Fat calories 43, Fat 4g, Saturated fat 0.7g, Cholesterol 0mg, Protein 10g, Carbohydrate 44g, Dietary fiber 3g, Sodium 11mg, Omega-3 fatty acids 0g

Allowances: 2½ fruits + 1¼ starches

DAIRY

DACOPA DRINK

Dacopa is an instant beverage made from the roasted syrup of the dahlia flower tuber. It is 100 percent caffeine free, while offering a smooth coffeelike flavor. I prefer *My Orzo Eye-Opener* and this *Dacopa Drink* over Pero and Postum a hundred times over!

12 ounces water

1 heaping tablespoon Dacopa ○

½ cup WestSoy Plus Soymilk or other vegan milk of your choice

Boil the water and add the Dacopa; stir until dissolved. Whip the soy, or other grain milk, in a steamer. If you don't own a steamer, you'll be pleased to know that it tastes almost as good without it. Simply stir in the soymilk and enjoy.

Yield: 1 serving

Each serving contains approximately: Calories 34, Fat calories 0, Fat 0g, Saturated fat 0g, Cholesterol 0mg, Protein 3g, Carbohydrate 5g, Dietary Fiber 0.4g, Sodium 9mg, Omega 3-fatty acids 0g

Allowance: ½ dairy

Although I love the taste of a delicious Blue Mountain Jamaican coffee, I began to find that the flavorful rush was not worth what it did to my nervous system. Even decaffeinated coffee unnerves me! I find these coffee-like drinks are just as nurturing, and the ritual with them is equally satisfying. Now I truly look forward to *My Orzo Eye-Opener* in the morning, my *Dacopa Drink* after work, and there's nothing like *Teeccino's Hazelnut Finito* after dinner. Beverages don't need to be a bummer; you can choose for them to be the highlights of your day!

MY ORZO EYE-OPENER

DAIRY

Orzo comes in a dried powder, like instant coffee, or in a pod, which you can put in your espresso or coffee machine. Obviously, like coffee, the latter form is *più forte* (stronger)—and with steamed soymilk, it is literally over the top!

12 ounces water
1 heaping tablespoon Orzo powder, or 1 to 2 pods if you prefer it stronger ○
½ cup WestSoy Plus Soymilk or other vegan milk of your choice

Boil the water, add the Orzo powder, and stir until dissolved; or insert your Orzo pod in an espresso or coffee machine and turn on. I run three rounds of water through each pod in my espresso pod machine (see Appendix H for Capri Flavors store and Web site), stopping each when the color reflects that it is not coming out as strong. In fact, I prefer 2 pods (done with 3 quick flushes each) to this amount of soymilk.

Whip the soy or other grain milk in a steamer, if you have one. Don't let your lacking this piece of equipment stop you; it's good just adding soymilk straight, which I often do when I don't have time to whip it. Stir approximately half of the whipped soymilk into the Orzo, leaving the other half to remain on top. Ahhhh—*delizioso*! This combination is also delicious iced in the summertime.

My Orzo Eye-Opener may not contain caffeine, but it doesn't have to taste like it's lacking that coffee kick!

Orzo is to Italy as Pero or Postum is to the United States. In other words, Orzo is the most popular coffee substitute in Italy. We invested many hours in figuring out how to get it to North Carolina before we did—so you are *fortunato* that you can just order it through www.ricedietstore.com!

Yield: 1 serving

Each serving contains approximately: Calories 45, Fat calories 0g, Fat 0g, Saturated fat 0g, Cholesterol 0mg, Protein 3g, Carbohydrate 5g, Dietary fiber 0.4g, Sodium 9mg, Omega-3 fatty acids 0g

Allowance: ½ dairy

TEECCINO'S HAZELNUT FINITO   DAIRY

Teeccino has produced a deliciously rich, dark, full-bodied drink that is a healthy combination of roasted grains, nuts, and fruits. Containing roasted carob, barley, chicory root, figs, almonds, dates, and natural hazelnut flavor—it's to live for. It is so scrumptious that it can pass for dessert!

16 ounces water
1 rounded tablespoon Teeccino Hazelnut Herbal Coffee ○
½ cup WestSoy Plus Soymilk or other vegan milk of your choice

Boil the water. In the filter of a drip coffeemaker, place the rounded tablespoon of Teeccino Hazelnut. If you prefer using a filter cone, put 1 rounded tablespoon of Teeccino for each cup of water used. Slowly pour the boiling water through the filter.

The Teeccino company offers this suggestion on the box; I paraphrase: "Quit coffee in 2 weeks: Begin blending Teeccino with your coffee. Start with ¾ coffee to ¼ Teeccino and gradually increase the amount of Teeccino until you are drinking 100 percent Teeccino." This sounds like a more humane way of getting off caffeinated coffee than "cold turkey" and headaches for a week!

Steam the milk of your choice, or simply add it directly if you don't own a steamer. I simply couldn't believe how good this was the first time I tried it. As with the other coffee substitutes, if you like iced coffee you will like this cold as well.

Yield: 1 serving

Each serving contains approximately: Calories 64, Fat calories 26, Fat 3g, Saturated fat 0.2g, Cholesterol 0mg, Protein 1g, Carbohydrate 15g, Dietary Fiber 0.8g, Sodium 52mg, Omega-3 fatty acids 0mg

Allowances: ½ dairy + ¼ fat

SNACKS AND DIPS

STARCHES

STARCHY DIPS

PROTEIN DIP

VEGGIE DIPS AND SPREADS

FATS

DAIRY DIPS AND TOPPINGS

STARCHES

EILENE'S PITA OR POCKET BREAD STARCH

Eilene taught the Ricers how to make this bread in a cooking class one day. We all felt like we were back in home economics, keeping our fingers crossed that our creations would turn out just right! These easy pita pockets are great to enjoy plain or with honey, sesame seeds, ground dates, olive oil, hummus, etc.

1 package active dry yeast

½ cup warm water (about 110 degrees F)

2 tablespoons extra-virgin olive oil

2 tablespoons honey or molasses

2 cups warm water

6 cups whole wheat pastry flour

½ teaspoon olive oil

Sprinkle of sesame seeds, optional

Soak the yeast in ½ cup warm water for 10 minutes. In a large bowl, mix the yeast mixture, extra-virgin olive oil, honey, and water. Add 6 cups of whole wheat pastry flour, 1 cup at a time, or until the dough can be rolled into a ball and kneaded. Form into a large ball and knead with floured hands for 5 minutes. Cover with a towel, and let rise in a warm place until double in size, about 1 hour. (If you want a finer texture, you can add 3 cups flour to the liquid mixture and allow it to rise as a "sponge," then add the rest of flour and proceed with kneading.)

Preheat the oven to 400 degrees F. Gently punch down the dough and knead for 1 minute. Form into 12 balls and let rest 10 minutes (for mini rounds make about 18 balls). Roll out into rounds about 5 inches across (mini rounds about 3 to 4 inches across). Place on a baking sheet coated with a little olive oil or covered with a sheet of aluminum foil. Sprinkle the bread rounds with the optional sesame seeds if desired. Bake 8 to 10 minutes. Cool on a board or rack.

Yield: 24 servings

Each serving contains approximately: Calories 134, Fat calories 19, Fat 2g, Saturated fat 0.2g, Cholesterol 0mg, Protein 4g, Carbohydrate 25g, Dietary fiber 3g, Sodium 0mg, Omega-3 fatty acids 0.01g

Allowances: ¼ fat + 1½ starches

EILENE'S "SUPER SEEDY" GRANOLA BARS   STARCH

Warning: The following ingredients are just too delicious for words! Grab a bar and a piece of fruit for a complete breakfast in the morning. Just be careful to limit yourself to one!

2 cups rolled oats

½ cup coarsely chopped almonds

½ cup coarsely chopped peanuts or hazelnuts

½ cup coarsely chopped walnuts

½ cup sunflower seeds

¼ cup flaxseeds

I teaspoon ground cinnamon

2 cups whole wheat flour

¼ cup canola oil

¼ cup honey or maple syrup

½ cup almond butter, no salt added

2 teaspoons vanilla extract

⅔ to I cup water

I cup semisweet chocolate chips, optional

Preheat the oven to 300 degrees F. Mix the oats, nuts, seeds, and cinnamon, spread on a large pan or baking sheet coated with a little olive oil, and toast for 20 minutes. Put the whole wheat flour in a large bowl and stir in the canola oil, honey, almond butter, and vanilla. Add the toasted oats and nuts to the mixture, then gradually add water and mix by hand until a stiff dough forms.

Coat a baking sheet or large cake pan with a little olive oil. Flatten out the dough by hand, or with a roller, until approximately ½ inch thick. Chocolate chips can be pressed into the surface of the dough, if desired. (Note: The bars can be made individually or as a large sheet. Bake at 300 degrees F for 15 to 18 minutes; it may take less time for individual bars.) Allow to cool and carefully cut the sheet of dough into bars. Makes about 2 dozen 1½-x-3½-inch bars.

Yield: 2 dozen bars, 24 servings (1 bar per serving)

Each serving contains approximately: Calories 250, Fat calories 133, Fat 15g, Saturated fat 1g, Cholesterol 0mg, Protein 7g, Carbohydrate 25g, Dietary fiber 5g, Sodium 3mg, Omega-3 fatty acids 0.45g

Allowances: 3 fats + 1½ starches

SLOW SNACK
STARCH

Slow snacks are inspired by our interest in the slow food movement (see Appendix I, under Heal Yourself and Your World Resources, page 330), whose purpose is to spread mindful, conscious consumption. With *slow snacks* you can eat real food while on the go!

2 tablespoons mustard, no-salt-added type, with a touch of honey,
    preferably Honeycup Mustard ⚙
2 tablespoons balsamic vinegar
1 cup baby carrots

Susan has taught our customers this recipe down at the store. It's a great mini meal or snack that you can take with you since it travels so well. Just put your "dip" in a sealable container and the carrots and shredded wheat in bags, and you're out the door.

1 cup shredded wheat

1 apple

Whisk the mustard and balsamic vinegar together. Use the dressing as a dip for the carrots. The shredded wheat and slices of apple taste good dipped in the dressing, too. For dental health the smartest snack ends with an apple, nature's "natural toothbrush"!

Yield: 1 serving

Each serving contains approximately: Calories 165, Fat calories 3, Fat 0g, Saturated fat 0.1g, Cholesterol 0mg, Protein 3g, Carbohydrate 39g, Dietary fiber 5g, Sodium 36mg, Omega-3 fatty acids 0.01g

Allowances: 1 starch + 1 fruit + 1 vegetable

Honeycup brand mustard is good for the dressing because it is sweet and hot. You can substitute your own favorite low-sodium mustard, if you prefer.

SWEETHEART SWEET POTATO CHIPS

STARCH

These chips are just delicious. We typically wouldn't go for a recipe with added sugar, but we couldn't get around the crispness that it adds to the sweet potatoes when they come out of the oven. Just be careful because it doesn't take much. Your whole house will smell like Thanksgiving.

2 large sweet potatoes, very thinly sliced into rounds less than 1/16th of an inch thick
1 tablespoon canola oil
1 tablespoon brown sugar
1 teaspoon ground cinnamon
½ teaspoon freshly grated nutmeg

Preheat oven to 425 degrees F. In a baking dish, combine all the ingredients and toss with the canola oil to coat. Spread the potatoes out evenly on a baking sheet and place on the lowest rack of the oven. Roast, turning occasionally, for 10 to 15 minutes, or until golden brown.

Yield: 4 servings

Each serving contains approximately: Calories 102, Fat calories 33, Fat 4g, Saturated fat 0.4g, Cholesterol 0mg, Protein 1g, Carbohydrate 17g, Dietary fiber 2g, Sodium 36mg, Omega-3 fatty acids 0.33g

Allowances: ¾ fat + 1 starch

TRAIL MIX

STARCH

Here's an easy meal that you can throw in a bag and take on the go!

2 tablespoons raw almonds

¼ cup dried fruit

¾ cup shredded wheat

1 teaspoon ground cinnamon

Put the ingredients in a plastic bag and toss. Another good "slow food" snack that would be perfect if followed with an apple.

Yield: 1 serving

Each serving contains approximately: Calories 337, Fat calories 84, Fat 9g, Saturated fat 0.7g, Cholesterol 0mg, Protein 8g, Carbohydrate 62g, Dietary fiber 8g, Sodium 57mg, Omega-3 fatty acids 0g

Allowances: 2 fats + 1½ starches + 2 fruits

ZESTY SWEET POTATO CHIPS

STARCH

This recipe provides another variation on sweet potatoes that's packed with flavor and nutritional value. It's also nice to have a way to make sweet potatoes without using cinnamon or raisins. When your sweet tooth is bored with fruit, liven up your taste buds with a little zest.

1 large sweet potato, thinly sliced into rounds (as thin as possible)

1 tablespoon extra-virgin olive oil

1 teaspoon ground cumin

1 teaspoon chili powder, no salt added

1 teaspoon paprika

Preheat the oven to 425 degrees F. In a baking dish, combine the ingredients and toss to coat in olive oil. Spread the potatoes evenly on a baking sheet and place on the lowest rack of the oven. Roast, turning occasionally, for 10 to 15 minutes, or until golden brown.

Yield: 2 servings

Each serving contains approximately: Calories 126, Fat calories 66, Fat 7g, Saturated fat 1.0g, Cholesterol 0mg, Protein 1g, Carbohydrate 14g, Dietary fiber 2g, Sodium 38mg, Omega-3 fatty acids 0.06g

Allowances: 1½ fats + ¾ starch

STARCHY DIPS

BARLEY PESTO DIP   STARCH

We found this fresh pesto recipe on the Rice Diet Forum—it's easy to throw in a blender and is a real crowd-pleaser. You can even add leftover barley to save yourself a step.

¾ cup pearled barley
3 cups water
½ cup chopped green onion
1 medium tomato, diced

PESTO
¼ cup chopped flat-leaf parsley
⅛ cup chopped cilantro
2 to 3 mint leaves, chopped
2 garlic cloves, minced
Juice of 1 lemon
3 teaspoons extra-virgin olive oil

Cook the barley in 3 cups of water for about 45 minutes. Add veggies to chilled or room-temperature barley. Place the mixture in a blender and blend until thoroughly combined and you have reached a thickened consistency. Add the pesto dressing, 2 tablespoons at a time, to taste. Garnish with a couple of cilantro or mint leaves, as desired, and serve.

Yield: 4 cups, 4 servings (1 cup per serving)

Each serving contains approximately: Calories 146, Fat calories 29, Fat 3g, Saturated fat 0.5g, Cholesterol 0mg, Protein 3g, Carbohydrate 27g, Dietary fiber 6g, Sodium 10mg, Omega-3 fatty acids 0.04g

Allowances: ¾ fat + 1¼ starches + ½ vegetable

RYAN'S SWEET AND SPICY MEXI DIP STARCH

You can use this supertasty dip for any raw vegetables, no-salt corn chips, or salt-free pita bread. It's a little sweet, a little spicy, and a lotta nutrients!

1 cup baked sweet potatoes
½ cup canned black beans, preferably Eden Organic brand, no salt added ⊙
1 roasted red pepper, cut into 1-inch cubes
2 teaspoons smoked paprika, preferably Sweet Pimentón de la Vera ⊙
1 tablespoon chili powder, no salt added
1 teaspoon ground cumin
Raw vegetables for dipping

Put the sweet potatoes, black beans, and red pepper in the bowl of a mixer and mix on low to medium speed. Add a small amount of water until you reach the desired consistency. Add the spices and stir. Serve with raw vegetables on the side.

Yield: 2 servings

Each serving contains approximately: Calories 83, Fat calories 3, Fat 0g, Saturated fat 0g, Cholesterol 0mg, Protein 3g, Carbohydrate 18g, Dietary fiber 4g, Sodium 26mg, Omega-3 fatty acids 0.02g

Allowance: 1 starch

SUSAN'S AJVAR HUMMUS WITH RAW VEGETABLES

STARCH

Like all of the bean-dip recipes Susan has created, this is not intended as a snack or appetizer. Half of this recipe is a starch serving for a meal. Along with the raw vegetables and a piece of fruit, it makes a great meal that is easy to eat at the office, on a picnic, or on the road.

15-ounce can garbanzo beans (chickpeas), no salt added, preferably
  Eden Organic brand ○
6 tablespoons Marco Polo Hot Ajvar Red Pepper Spread ○
4 cups raw vegetables

Place the beans in a food processor or blender and process until smooth. Add Ajvar and process until well combined. Clean and cut your favorite veggies into pieces and dip into this tasty, quick dip! You can use this for parties or add a piece of fruit and have a meal on the go.

• Traditionally, hummus includes tahini (sesame butter) and lemon juice. This quick-and-easy method sidesteps the calories and fat coming from tahini! The ajvar (red pepper, eggplant, and garlic spread) adds all the zip needed without the lemon juice. Not all brands are low in sodium, so please be sure to check the label, or buy the Marco Polo brand.

• If you are out of fresh ajvar, substitute *Sun-Dried Tomato Pesto* (see page 271).

• Like any hummus, this is especially good with cucumbers.

Yield: 2 servings

Each serving contains approximately: Calories 280, Fat calories 6, Fat 0.7g, Saturated fat 0.02g, Cholesterol 0mg, Protein 5g, Carbohydrate 18g, Dietary fiber 4g, Sodium 35mg, Omega-3 fatty acids 0.02g

Allowances: 2¾ starches + 2 vegetables

SUSAN'S BEAN DIP STARCH

Susan grabs this as one of her quick "throw-together," five-minute meals. When using bean dip for a starch, you can serve it with raw vegetables and a piece of fruit for a complete meal. The desert pepper dip contains red pepper flakes, so be prepared for a little heat. If you need a little more heat, try adding a teaspoon of Diet Zing ○.

15-ounce can navy beans, no salt added, preferably Eden Organic brand ○
2 tablespoons Desert Pepper Trading Co. White Bean Dip ○
2 tablespoons chopped red onions

Purée the ingredients and serve with raw vegetables.

Yield: 2 servings

Each serving contains approximately: Calories 200, Fat calories 10, Fat 1g, Saturated fat 0g, Cholesterol 0mg, Protein 12g, Carbohydrate 36g, Dietary fiber 12g, Sodium 47mg, Omega-3 fatty acids 0g

Allowance: 2½ starches

If you are looking for a substitute for the desert pepper dip in this recipe, try experimenting by replacing it with a dip or pesto (like *Al's Presto Cauliflower Pesto* or *Sun-Dried Tomato Pesto*).

PROTEIN DIP

EILENE'S SIMPLE SALMON SPREAD   PROTEIN

This is just fabulous! Serve on whole-grain crackers, or stuff into *Eilene's Pocket Pita Bread* topped with no-salt salsa and sprouts for a meal that comes together as quickly as it disappears.

7.5-ounce can salmon, or leftover fresh cooked salmon

¼ cup nonfat yogurt

¼ cup freshly squeezed lemon juice

½ teaspoon dried dill or 1 to 2 tablespoon chopped flat-leaf parsley

1 teaspoon minced garlic

1 small or ½ large celery stalk, finely chopped

1 large tomato, chopped, or 1 cup halved grape tomatoes

½ cup chopped onion

⅛ teaspoon freshly ground black pepper

Drain the salmon. Remove the skin and larger bones and break up the fish with a fork. Add the yogurt and lemon juice and stir well. Add the dill (or parsley), garlic, celery, tomato, onion, and pepper and mix well.

Yield: 6 servings

Each serving contains approximately: Calories 69, Fat calories 21, Fat 2g, Saturated fat 0.6g, Cholesterol 20mg, Protein 8g, Carbohydrate 4g, Dietary fiber 0.5g, Sodium 39mg, Omega-3 fatty acids 0.61g

Allowances: 1 protein + 1 vegetable

VEGGIE DIPS AND SPREADS

QUICK AND CRUNCHY VEGGIE SPREAD   VEGETABLE

This is an easy meal that can be thrown together in seconds. To get the right consistency with your cottage cheese, mix in a tablespoon of nonfat plain yogurt for a creamier texture.

¾ cup nonfat cottage cheese, no salt added

½ cup diced green bell pepper

½ cup diced cucumber

Freshly ground black pepper, to taste

2 teaspoons sweet paprika, preferably Sweet Pimentón de la Vera ⦿

2 rice cakes

Mix all of your ingredients (except for the rice cakes) well in a large bowl. Lightly toast the rice cakes. Then spoon the mixture evenly across two rice cakes. Add a piece of fruit, and you have a delicious complete meal that was prepared in seconds!

Yield: 1 serving

Each serving contains approximately: Calories 218, Fat calories 7, Fat 1g, Saturated fat 0.1g, Cholesterol 8mg, Protein 25g, Carbohydrate 26g, Dietary fiber 2g, Sodium 65mg, Omega-3 fatty acids 0.01g

Allowances: ¾ starch + 1 vegetable + 1½ dairy

SPINACH DIP

VEGETABLE

Susan came up with this dish when entertaining a friend at her home one afternoon. This easy dip is great with raw vegetables or to use as a salad dressing.

4 cups baby spinach leaves, washed and dried
½ teaspoon freshly squeezed lemon juice
1 garlic clove
2 tablespoons Kerala Curry Mild Mango Chutney ○

Purée all of the ingredients in a food processor and chill until ready to serve.

Yield: 2 servings

Each serving contains approximately: Calories 52, Fat calories 0, Fat 0g, Saturated fat 0.0g, Cholesterol 0mg, Protein 1g, Carbohydrate 14g, Dietary fiber 2g, Sodium 87mg, Omega-3 fatty acids 0g

Allowances: 2 vegetables + ½ fruit

Obviously this dish is quick, easy, and incredible because this already-prepared chutney is so beautifully flavored. If you don't have this product available to you, try any fruit-flavored chutney, or you can even create your own recipe as a substitute. Since ingredients must be listed in the order in which they are found in the product by weight, you can guesstimate the proportions. For instance, Kerala Curry Mild Mango Chutney's ingredients list includes mango, jalapeño, onions, garlic, and curry, in descending order. Although they may have perfected the exact recipe over the last few years, within minutes you can guesstimate a substitute that will amaze you.

BABA GANOUSH

FAT

Try this tasty dish, straight from the Rice House kitchen!

½ cup water

1 large eggplant, peeled and cubed

1 large Vidalia onion, diced

1 tablespoon tomato purée, no salt added

¼ teaspoon freshly ground black pepper

2 large garlic cloves, minced

1 tablespoon extra-virgin olive oil

1 teaspoon honey

Juice of ½ lemon

1 tablespoon toasted sesame seeds

Put all ingredients (except the lemon and sesame seeds) in a large pot. Cook over medium heat, stirring often, until the eggplant is tender (30 to 35 minutes), adding water if needed. Pour the contents of the pot into a blender and blend until smooth, then transfer to a mixing bowl. Add the lemon juice and sesame seeds and mix well. Chill for 35 to 50 minutes. Divide into equal portions. This could be enjoyed with raw vegetables or toasted pita, quartered, or no-salt crackers for scooping.

Yield: 3 cups, 4 servings

Each serving contains approximately: Calories 102, Fat calories 43, Fat 5g, Saturated fat 0.5g, Cholesterol 0mg, Protein 2g, Carbohydrate 14g, Dietary fiber 5g, Sodium 5mg, Omega-3 fatty acids 0.1g

Allowances: 1 fat + 2 vegetables

RICE HOUSE GUACAMOLE
FAT

Who doesn't love guacamole? But whoever said it had to have over 90 percent of its calories coming from fat? Cutting the traditionally fat-packed guacamole with cauliflower is so good, it is actually hard to believe it! Serve this with salt-free corn chips or pita bread, or use over taco salad. Just be mindful of your portion sizes.

4 cups cauliflower florets

1 avocado, pitted and skinned

4 teaspoons minced garlic

1 Vidalia onion, diced

1 to 2 tomatoes, diced

1 to 2 tablespoons minced jalapeño pepper

2 tablespoons freshly squeezed lemon juice

2 tablespoons chopped fresh cilantro

1 teaspoon freshly ground black pepper

Steam the cauliflower until tender, 20 to 25 minutes. Strain off the water, keeping 1½ cups back, and set aside. Blend the cauliflower until smooth, using leftover cooking water to loosen if needed. Refrigerate for 2 hours, if you have the time.

Mash all the other ingredients together in a large mixing bowl with a potato masher until smooth, then add the chilled cauliflower. Mash together until the consistency is like mashed potatoes, and the color is consistently green.

Yield: 6 cups, 4 servings

Each serving contains approximately: Calories 100, Fat calories 50, Fat 5g, Saturated fat 1g, Cholesterol 0mg, Protein 3g, Carbohydrate 15g, Dietary fiber 7g, Sodium 27mg, Omega-3 fatty acids 0.12g

Allowances: 1¾ fats + 3 vegetables

FATS

WONDERFUL WALNUTS

FAT

Are you in the mood for a sweet, crunchy topping to add to your rice, veggies, or salads? These walnuts add a soul-warming feel to everyday dishes. Again, use this to top your favorite foods, not to enjoy as a main course!

I cup coarsely chopped walnuts
I tablespoon canola oil
I teaspoon ground cinnamon
I teaspoon pumpkin pie spice

Preheat the broiler. Toss the chopped walnuts to coat in the oil and spices. Spread the walnuts out on a nonstick baking sheet and cook for 3 to 5 minutes; be careful not to burn them.

Yield: 8 servings

Each serving contains approximately: Calories 115, Fat calories 104, Fat 11.5g, Saturated fat 1g, Cholesterol 0mg, Protein 2g, Carbohydrate 2g, Dietary fiber 1g, Sodium 0mg, Omega-3 fatty acids 1.5g

Allowance: 2½ fats

RYAN'S ROASTED TOASTED ALMONDS

FAT

Add a little crunch to your salads or veggies with tasty almonds. Again, this is best when used as a condiment, not as a main course.

1 cup coarsely chopped raw almonds

1 tablespoon extra-virgin olive oil

1 tablespoon smoked paprika, preferably Sweet Pimentón de la Vera ○

Preheat the oven to broil. Mix the almonds with the olive oil and paprika. Spread them out on a baking sheet and roast for 3 to 5 minutes. Please be careful not to burn.

Yield: 8 servings (2 tablespoons per serving)

Each serving contains approximately: Calories 94, Fat calories 77, Fat 8g, Saturated fat 1g, Cholesterol 0mg, Protein 3g, Carbohydrate 3g, Dietary fiber 2g, Sodium 1mg, Omega-3 fatty acids 0.01g

Allowance: 2 fats

DAIRY DIPS AND TOPPINGS

YOGURT CHEESE

The uses of yogurt cheese are endless! Try it anywhere you previously might have used mayonnaise, cream cheese, or sour cream, such as on baked potatoes or bean burritos, or in tuna or salmon salads. One of my favorite ways to use it is to add it to a few tablespoons of fruit-only jelly and spread it on bagels instead of cream cheese. If you cook with yogurt cheese, add about 1 tablespoon of cornstarch to 1 cup of yogurt cheese to prevent it from separating when heated.

4 cups plain nonfat yogurt (use a brand that does not contain gelatin or carrageenan)

Line a funnel or colander with a large paper coffee filter or at least three layers of cheesecloth, and place it in a large bowl or pan. Spoon the yogurt into the filter. Cover and refrigerate for 8 to 14 hours; the longer it is allowed to drip, the thicker the product will be. Discard the whey that drips into the bowl; transfer the yogurt cheese from the filter to a covered container and refrigerate until ready to use.

Yield: Approximately 1¼ cups, 10 servings (2 tablespoons per serving)

Each serving contains approximately: Calories 10, Fat calories 0, Fat 0g, Saturated fat 0.8g, Cholesterol 0mg, Protein 4g, Carbohydrate 2g, Dietary fiber 0g, Sodium 25mg, Omega-3 fatty acids 0.02g

Allowance: ¼ dairy

YOGURT SALAD

This staple recipe can be used with any of your favorite vegetables. We've listed some of ours below, but feel free to mix in your own as well!

1 cup nonfat yogurt

½ teaspoon freshly ground black pepper

¼ cup chopped cucumbers

⅓ cup chopped red onion

⅓ cup chopped radishes

1 tablespoon chopped fresh basil, parsley, or mint

Mix the yogurt and black pepper in a small bowl. Then add the cucumbers, onion, and radishes, and herb of choice. Mix together with a fork, chill for 15 minutes, and serve. Delicious with rice and grilled chicken, or rice and beans.

Yield: 2 servings

Each serving contains approximately: Calories 68, Fat calories 0, Fat 0g, Saturated fat 0.0g, Cholesterol 0mg, Protein 6g, Carbohydrate 13g, Dietary fiber 1g, Sodium 76mg, Omega-3 fatty acids 0g

Allowances: ½ dairy + ½ vegetable

SIDES

STARCHY SIDES AND SALADS

VEGETABLE SIDES AND SALADS

FRUITS

STARCHY SIDES AND SALADS

BLACK BEANS WITH GARLIC AND PIMENTÓN DE LA VERA

STARCH

Susan shares a few comments about this fantastic bean recipe: "If you really love garlic, you might want to use the whole head in this recipe; otherwise save the remaining garlic that is mixed with the pimentón and use it to top off a cooked vegetable or as a base for a roasted garlic salad dressing. We used the Sweet Pimentón de la Vera in this recipe, but you could use the hot variety instead. In either case, the smoky flavor is wonderful with the black beans."

1 head unpeeled garlic
15-ounce can black beans, no salt added, preferably Eden Organic brand ⊙
1 tablespoon paprika, preferably Sweet Pimentón de la Vera ⊙

Preheat the oven to 350 degrees F.

Cut off approximately one-fourth of the top of a full head of garlic. Wrap the garlic in foil and bake for about 30 minutes. Remove the garlic from the oven and let sit for a few minutes until cool enough to handle.

Pour the can of black beans into a saucepan. Heat the beans and their liquid over medium heat. If the beans become dry, add a little water. Unwrap the garlic and hold it in your hand over a small bowl. Squeeze the cloves out of the top into the bowl; the cloves will be smooth and buttery. Gently mash the cloves with a fork, add the sweet pimentón, and blend well. Add half of the garlic and pimentón spread to the beans, stir, and taste. Add more garlic spread if desired.

Yield: 4 servings

Each serving contains approximately: Calories 194, Fat calories 0, Fat 0g, Saturated fat 0g, Cholesterol 0mg, Protein 12g, Carbohydrate 34g, Dietary fiber 10g, Sodium 28mg, Omega-3 fatty acids 0g

Allowances: 2 starches + ½ vegetable

BULGUR AND GARBANZO BEAN SALAD STARCH

This recipe is straight from the "Taste of the Rice Diet Store" class here at our program!

1 cup bulgur wheat

¾ cup boiling water

½ cup chopped shallots

1 garlic clove, minced

1 tablespoon walnut oil, preferably L'Olivier Walnut Oil ○

1 tablespoon honey

1 cup canned garbanzo beans (chickpeas), no salt added, preferably Eden Organic
  brand ○

2 tablespoons Marco Polo Hot Ajvar Red Pepper Spread ○ or pureed roasted red
  pepper and roasted garlic

1 cup grape tomatoes, halved

1 Granny Smith apple, chopped

2 tablespoons chopped flat-leaf parsley

Place the bulgur in a bowl. Pour the boiling water over the bulgur and let sit for 10 minutes; the water will be absorbed. Soften the shallots and garlic in a tablespoon of water in a sauté pan over medium heat, about 5 minutes. Whisk the walnut oil and honey together to make the dressing and set aside.

• If you have not invested in walnut oil (yet), you could substitute olive oil in this recipe.

• If you *have* invested in walnut oil, the honey and oil dressing in this recipe is also wonderful on greens or any other grain salad.

Add the drained garbanzo beans and Ajvar to the shallots and stir over medium heat for 2 minutes. Fluff the bulgur with a fork, then add the bean mixture to the bowl. Stir gently to combine. Add the tomatoes, apple, dressing, and parsley and stir to combine. Serve immediately at room temperature.

Yield: 6 servings

Each serving contains approximately: Calories 252, Fat calories 52, Fat 4g, Saturated fat 0.5g, Cholesterol 0mg, Protein 8g, Carbohydrate 49g, Dietary fiber 8g, Sodium 23mg, Omega-3 fatty acids 0.4g

Allowances: ½ fat + 2½ starches + ½ vegetable + ¼ fruit

CANNELLINI BEAN SALAD   STARCHY

Susan created this dish and recommends serving it as a full-starch serving, not as an appetizer salad. Cannellini beans are also called white kidney beans, and they are frequently served cold.

15-ounce can cannellini beans, no salt added, preferably Eden
    Organic brand ○
2 tablespoons minced red onion
2 tablespoons Desert Pepper Trading Co. Tuscan White Bean Dip ○
2 tablespoons red wine vinegar, preferably Badia a Coltibuono brand ○

Drain and rinse the beans, mix with the red onion, and set aside. Now mix the bean dip and vinegar. Toss the beans with the dressing, chill, and serve.

Yield: 2 servings

Each serving contains approximately: Calories 182, Fat calories 17, Fat 2g, Saturated fat 0g, Cholesterol 0mg, Protein 11g, Carbohydrate 31g, Dietary fiber 9g, Sodium 88mg, Omega-3 fatty acids 0g

Allowances: 2¼ starches + ¼ vegetable

While you might enjoy other vinegars more than a red wine vinegar, the strong tart flavor really "stands up" to the beans or grains in a salad. The sweetness of cider vinegar or the sweet mellow taste of an aged balsamic, while good, would create a completely different salad. If you don't have Desert Pepper Trading Co. Tuscan White Bean Dip, you could substitute some mashed cannellini beans and roasted garlic.

CHICKPEA, BULGUR, AND TOMATO PILAF   STARCH

This is a great salad that's an easy staple to enjoy throughout your "menu repertoire" at home: bulgur, beans, veggies, and spices. How simple is that?

1 cup bulgur wheat

15-ounce can garbanzo beans (chickpeas), no salt added, preferably Eden Organic brand ○

5 fresh plum tomatoes, chopped

1 cup finely chopped green onions

½ cup chopped flat-leaf parsley

Juice of 1 lemon

1 tablespoon extra-virgin olive oil

3 garlic cloves, minced

Grated zest from 2 lemons, preferably organic

Freshly ground black pepper, to taste

In a large bowl combine the dry bulgur with 1 cup of boiling water. Cover and let stand for 30 minutes. Fluff the bulgur with a fork, add the remaining ingredients, and stir well. Serve chilled or at room temperature.

Yield: 8 servings

Each serving contains approximately: Calories 145, Fat calories 23, Fat 2.5g, Saturated fat 0.3g, Cholesterol 0mg, Protein 6g, Carbohydrate 26g, Dietary fiber 6.5g, Sodium 22mg, Omega-3 fatty acids 0.02g

Allowances: ¼ fat + 1½ starches + ½ vegetable

DE-ANNE'S CURRY RICE   STARCH

De-Anne, our Canadian ambassador and faith-filled friend, took a family favorite and prepared it without salt, configuring the recipe to fit within the guidelines. De-Anne says, "I made this for my family, and my daughter loved it! And when I made it for the first time without the salt, I must admit I loved it even more."

2 cups Uncle Ben's Converted long-grain white rice, quick cooking time
    (10-15 minutes)

1½ cups water

½ cinnamon stick

½ teaspoon ground turmeric

1 teaspoon curry powder (De-Anne recommends either Indian or Jamaican curry)

2 tablespoons raisins

Place all the ingredients, except the raisins, in a small pot and bring to a boil. When the water begins to boil, spoon the raisins on top of the rice and cover. Turn the heat down to medium-low and cook for 10 to 15 minutes. Remove from heat and let sit, covered, for 5 minutes. Remove the lid and fluff the rice with a fork. Serve the rice with beans or vegetable curry.

Yield: 4 servings

Each serving contains approximately: Calories 159, Fat calories 11, Fat 1.3g, Saturated fat 0.25g, Cholesterol 0mg, Protein 3.5g, Carbohydrate 33g, Dietary fiber 3g, Sodium 9mg, Omega-3 fatty acids 0.02g

Allowances: 1¾ starches + ¼ fruit

DILIP'S VEGETABLE PILAF   STARCH

Dilip is a great chef and friend of our Rice Diet Program nurse, Pat. We found that the flavors in this dish are intense but complement each other just beautifully. It's great on top of a salad, with steamed veggies, or with a good piece of fish—the possibilities are endless!

1 tablespoon canola oil

3 to 4 whole cloves

¼ teaspoon freshly ground black pepper

¼ teaspoon cumin seeds

¼ teaspoon minced garlic

¼ teaspoon minced fresh ginger

¾ cup basmati rice, well washed

¼ cup fresh or frozen peas

½ cup julienned potatoes

1 medium carrot, julienned

2 tablespoons whole raw almonds

¼ cup raisins

¼ cup finely chopped cilantro

In a medium pot, heat the oil. Add the cloves, pepper, cumin seeds, garlic, and ginger, and sauté for a minute or two over medium heat. Add the well-washed rice and sauté for 3 to 4 minutes. Next, add the peas, potatoes, carrot, almonds, raisins, and exactly 2 cups of water. Bring to boil, then reduce the heat to low for 10 to 12 minutes or until a fork inserted comes out easily. Serve on a platter and garnish with chopped cilantro.

Yield: 4 servings

Each serving contains approximately: Calories 248, Fat calories 57, Fat 6g, Saturated fat 0.6g, Cholesterol 0mg, Protein 5g, Carbohydrate 44g, Dietary fiber 3g, Sodium 15mg, Omega-3 fatty acids 0.33g

Allowances: 1¼ fats + 1¾ starches + ½ vegetable + ½ fruit

INDIAN SPICED CEREAL   STARCH

What a unique find from the Rice Diet Forum! The distinctive blend of seasonings in this dish offers a complex taste without having to follow a complex recipe. This is a very good dish to cleanse the digestive system. It's spicy without being overwhelming and is a very nice change of flavors.

3 cups water

1 tablespoon extra-virgin olive oil

1 teaspoon cumin seeds

1 pinch of fenugreek seeds

⅓ cup millet

¼ cup shredded unsweetened coconut

⅓ tomato, chopped

2 jalapeño peppers, chopped

1 slice fresh ginger, chopped

3 dates, chopped

Chopped cilantro for garnish, optional

Place all the ingredients in a large pot and bring to a boil, lower the heat, cover, and simmer for 40 to 50 minutes. Check and stir regularly to keep the grain from sticking to the bottom of the pot, and add water if needed. The cereal should have a soupy consistency.

Yield: 2½ cups, 4 servings

Each serving contains approximately: Calories 146, Fat calories 73, Fat 8g, Saturated fat 3.8g, Cholesterol 0mg, Protein 3g, Carbohydrate 16g, Dietary fiber 3g, Sodium 5mg, Omega-3 fatty acids 0.05g

Allowances: 1¼ fats + ¾ starch + ¼ vegetable + ½ fruit

JERK FINGERLING POTATOES   STARCH

These potatoes are one of our very own Rice House favorites! This popular dish is seen throughout the dining room every time it makes the menu.

4 cups large fingerling potatoes

½ teaspoon paprika

½ teaspoon Frontier No Salt Jamaican Jerk Seasoning ◎

1 teaspoon garlic powder

1 teaspoon extra-virgin olive oil

Preheat the oven to 350 degrees F.

Mix all the ingredients in a large bowl. Place the spice-coated fingerling potatoes on a large nonstick baking sheet. Bake until crisp, 35 to 50 minutes.

Yield: 4 servings

Each serving contains approximately: Calories 132, Fat calories 12, Fat 2g, Saturated fat 0.2g, Cholesterol 0mg, Protein 3g, Carbohydrate 28g, Dietary fiber 2g, Sodium 6mg, Omega-3 fatty acids 0.02g

Allowances: ¼ fat + 1½ starches

Your own version of Jamaican jerk seasoning can be made from scratch if you have allspice, nutmeg, cinnamon, thyme, onion powder, red pepper flakes, and black pepper on hand. Or use another salt-free seasoning flavor and create a new potato recipe!

KITTY'S REFRIED BEANS

STARCH

These refried beans are simply delicious on top of rice, stuffed in a taco, or rolled in a tortilla with *Rice House Guacamole* (see page 140); they are also great as a dip for veggies and corn chips (no-fat, no-salt ones). This is so easy to make and a "must have on hand" for those desiring convenient, yet healthy foods.

3 cups *Pinto Beans* (see page 160)
1 small jalapeño pepper, seeded and minced
½ cup salsa, no salt added, preferably Enrico's Salsa, No Salt Added ⊙
Juice of ½ lime
1 bunch cilantro, chopped

Purée the beans in a blender. Add to a large bowl with the remaining ingredients and mix well. Taste and adjust the heat to your palate!

Yield: 8 servings

Each serving contains approximately: Calories 122, Fat calories 16, Fat 2g, Saturated fat 0.0g, Cholesterol 0mg, Protein 7g, Carbohydrate 19g, Dietary fiber 6g, Sodium 109mg, Omega-3 fatty acids 0g

Allowances: 1¼ starches + 1 vegetable

LENTILS WITH PRUNES   STARCH

Who would have thought that these flavors could complement each other so well? The dietitians were fighting for spoons when this recipe from the Rice Diet Forum debuted for the recipe tasting.

½ pound lentils, cooked
8 ounces pitted prunes
½ cup shredded carrots
Red pepper flakes, to taste
1 teaspoon ground cumin
1 teaspoon dried dill

Mix well and serve chilled.

Yield: 4 servings

Each serving contains approximately: Calories 204, Fat calories 7, Fat 1g, Saturated fat 0g, Cholesterol 0mg, Protein 6g, Carbohydrate 47g, Dietary fiber 9g, Sodium 13mg, Omega-3 fatty acids 0.02g

Allowances: 1 starch + 2¼ fruits

LOUISIANA CAJUN RICE   STARCH

The Rice Diet Forum has turned out to be a fantastic resource for "Rice-Friendly" recipes. One member taught us how to prepare rice "Cajun Style."

2 tablespoons extra-virgin olive oil

1 medium onion, chopped

2 cups water

1 cube vegetable bouillon, no salt added, preferably Rapunzel, Vegan, No Salt Added, Vegetable Bouillon ○

1 large bell pepper, sliced into thin strips

1 teaspoon Safinter's Saffron ○

½ teaspoon dried thyme

¼ teaspoon paprika, preferably Hot Pimentón de la Vera ○

⅛ to ¼ teaspoon cayenne

1½ cups rice

In a medium saucepan heat the olive oil and slowly add in the onion. Cook and stir until the onion is tender but not browned. Place the 2 cups of water in a small pot and bring to a boil; add the bouillon cube and let dissolve. Add the onion, pepper strips, and seasonings to the vegetable bouillon, and bring to a boil. Stir in the rice, cover, and cook for 45 minutes on low heat. Fluff with fork and serve.

Yield: 8 servings

Each serving contains approximately: Calories 125, Fat calories 37, Fat 4g, Saturated fat 0.6g, Cholesterol 0mg, Protein 2.5g, Carbohydrate 20g, Dietary fiber 1g, Sodium 33mg, Omega-3 fatty acids 0.03g

Allowances: ¾ fat + 1 starch + ¼ vegetable

LOW-FAT POTATO SALAD

STARCH

Give your old potato salad a makeover with this new light and fresh recipe. One bite and you'll never look back!

2 cups baby red potatoes

1 cup asparagus tips

¼ cup vegetable stock, no salt added, preferably using Rapunzel's Vegan, No Salt Added Vegetable Bouillon ○

2 tablespoons white wine vinegar

2 tablespoons Dijon mustard, salt free, preferably Téméraire Dijon Mustard ○

1 tablespoon extra-virgin olive oil

1 garlic clove, minced

⅓ cup diced red onion

Freshly ground black pepper, to taste

Place the potatoes in a large pot and cover with water. Bring to a boil, then reduce the heat and simmer for 15 minutes, or until almost tender when tested with a fork. Add the asparagus tips and simmer for 2 to 3 minutes longer, or until the asparagus is bright green and the potatoes are tender. Drain the vegetables and retain this fluid to reconstitute bouillon, if desired. Allow the vegetables to cool a few minutes, then quarter the potatoes. While the potatoes are cooling, whisk vegetable stock, vinegar, mustard, oil, and garlic together in a small bowl. Place the vegetables in a large bowl and top with diced onion. Drizzle the dressing over the salad, add black pepper to taste, and toss gently.

Yield: 4 servings

Each serving contains approximately: Calories 157, Fat calories 71, Fat 8g, Saturated fat 1g, Cholesterol 0mg, Protein 4g, Carbohydrate 18g, Dietary fiber 2g, Sodium 25mg, Omega-3 fatty acids 0.05g

Allowances: 1 fat + 1 starch + 1 vegetable

PINTO BEANS

We've been searching for a good Crock-Pot recipe for beans that is full of flavor, while not full of fat, sodium, and added sugar. Here's a bean recipe with ingredients just as nutritious as they are delicious. Don't worry if you don't have a Crock-Pot; if that's the case, just soak the beans overnight and boil beans in a pot until tender, about 1½ hours. Cook all the other ingredients in a pan while the beans are cooking, then add them to the beans when the beans are tender (refer to Appendix E, page 318, for more details).

1 cup dry pinto beans

1 medium sweet onion, chopped

1 green bell pepper, chopped

2 tablespoons minced garlic

1 bunch cilantro, chopped

2 tablespoons ground cumin

2 teaspoons salt-free chili powder

4 cups water

4 cups vegetable stock, no salt added, preferably Rapunzel's Vegan, No Salt Added, Vegetable Bouillon ⦾

Throw everything in a Crock-Pot and cook on high for 8 hours. (When using a Crock-Pot, there is no need to soak the beans.) This makes a huge batch, so you're ready for days of variations, from *Kitty's Refried Beans* (see page 156) to veggie bean wraps. They also freeze nicely for months.

Yield: 4 servings

Each serving contains approximately: Calories 117, Fat calories 16, Fat 2g, Saturated fat 0g, Cholesterol 0mg, Protein 7g, Carbohydrate 17g, Dietary fiber 7g, Sodium 76mg, Omega-3 fatty acids 0g

Allowances: 1¼ starches + 1 vegetable

QUIRKY QUINOA SALAD

STARCH

Quinoa is such a versatile grain. Since the grain itself is small, very tasty, but not over-powering, it allows the flavors of the ingredients in this dish to really shine through.

1 cup water

½ cup quinoa, rinsed

¼ cup minced shallots

½ cup chopped red bell pepper

1 tablespoon extra-virgin olive oil

¼ cup slivered almonds

Juice of ½ lemon

1 teaspoon smoked paprika, preferably Sweet Pimentón de la Vera ○

1 teaspoon ground cumin

¼ cup chopped dried apricots

In a medium saucepan, bring the water to a boil. Stir in the quinoa, cover, and simmer for 10 minutes. Remove from heat, and let the quinoa remain in the covered pot for another 20 minutes. Transfer the cooked quinoa into a large mixing bowl. Fluff with a fork every few minutes so the heat escapes (this helps prevent sticky quinoa), and let cool for 15 minutes.

Sauté the shallots and the red bell pepper in the oil. When the pepper is tender, add the remaining ingredients. Stir and serve.

Yield: 4 servings

Each serving contains approximately: Calories 180, Fat calories 60, Fat 7g, Saturated fat 0.8g, Cholesterol 0mg, Protein 5g, Carbohydrate 27g, Dietary fiber 3g, Sodium 7mg, Omega-3 fatty acids 0.06g

Allowances: 1¾ fats + ¾ starch + ¼ vegetable + ½ fruit

POLYNESIAN PILAF

STARCH

Here's a pilaf recipe right out of the tropics. Take a South Pacific trip with this at-home meal and never leave the farm, or use this to impress your friends at a luau.

½ cup canned diced pineapple bits or mandarin orange segments

2 cups cooked quinoa

I red bell pepper, diced

2 green onions, halved lengthwise and thinly sliced

½ cup frozen green peas

¼ cup sliced almonds

¼ cup golden raisins

I cup bean sprouts

I teaspoon sesame seeds

DRESSING

¼ cup rice vinegar

¼ cup unsweetened pineapple juice

I tablespoon minced fresh ginger

I large garlic clove, minced

Drain juice from canned fruit; use a few tablespoons in pilaf, as desired. Cook peas as directed on the package.

Prepare the salad ingredients and mix together in large bowl. In a small bowl or glass, mix the dressing ingredients and pour over the salad. Mix thoroughly and chill in refrigerator for 1 hour.

Yield: 6 servings

Each serving contains approximately: Calories 216, Fat calories 43, Fat 5g, Saturated fat 0.4g, Cholesterol 0mg, Protein 7g, Carbohydrate 39g, Dietary fiber 5g, Sodium 13mg, Omega-3 fatty acids 0.06g

Allowances: ¾ fat + 1 starch + 1 vegetable + ¾ fruit

SPICY POTATO SKINS STARCH

Way to go, Rice Diet Forum! One Forum member learned how to take a recipe and convert it to be more "Ricer friendly." They comment: "These tasty potato skins are lower in fat than the original version because they are baked and not fried."

4 medium baking potatoes
2 tablespoons extra-virgin olive oil
1½ teaspoons ground coriander
½ teaspoon freshly ground black pepper
1½ teaspoons salt-free chili powder
1½ teaspoons curry powder
1 teaspoon onion powder
1 teaspoon garlic powder

Preheat the oven to 400 degrees F.

Bake the potatoes for 1 hour. Remove the potatoes from the oven, but keep the oven turned on. Slice the potatoes in half lengthwise, and let them cool for 10 minutes. Scoop out most of the potato flesh, leaving about ¼ inch of flesh against the potato skin (you can reserve the potato flesh for another use, like mashed potatoes). Cut each potato half crosswise into 3 pieces. Place the olive oil in a small cup. Dip each potato skin into the oil and place it on the baking sheet. Combine the spices and sprinkle the mixture over the potatoes. Bake the potato skins for 15 minutes, or until they are crispy and brown.

Yield: 4 servings

Each serving contains approximately: Calories 109, Fat calories 65, Fat 7g, Saturated fat 1g, Cholesterol 0mg, Protein 3g, Carbohydrate 8g, Dietary fiber 4g, Sodium 11mg, Omega-3 fatty acids 0.10g

Allowances: 1½ fats + ½ starch

SUN-KISSED QUINOA   STARCH

This fruity quinoa combo can be served hot or cold. Dress it up by serving over a leaf of crisp romaine lettuce.

1 tablespoon extra-virgin olive oil
½ cup quinoa, rinsed
1 tablespoon grated lemon zest, preferably organic
½ cup orange juice
¼ cup chopped dried apricots

Heat the olive oil over medium heat in a large pot. Add the quinoa and lemon zest, and sauté until lightly browned. Add the orange juice and apricots and bring to a boil. Turn down heat and simmer until the liquid is absorbed.

Yield: 3 servings

Each serving contains approximately: Calories 198, Fat calories 43, Fat 5g, Saturated fat 0.6g, Cholesterol 0mg, Protein 5g, Carbohydrate 35g, Dietary fiber 3g, Sodium 7mg, Omega-3 fatty acids 0.06g

Allowances: 1 fat + 1¼ starches + 1 fruit

SIMPLE CURRIED RICE

STARCH

Susan gives this recipe to patients when they are browsing the Rice Diet Store. She often puts together easy dishes that will be convenient for them when they first return home. She states, "This is an easy starch and fruit dish using leftover rice. Serve with steamed broccoli, tossed with Chef Pascal's Orange, Ginger, and Coconut Sauce."

¾ cup of leftover rice, reheated in microwave

2 teaspoons Mr. Spice Indian Curry Sauce ⊙

2 teaspoons pickled ginger, minced, no salt added, preferably Ginger
   People Sushi Ginger ⊙

2 tablespoons raisins

Mix all the ingredients and serve.

Yield: 1 serving

Each serving contains approximately: Calories 245, Fat calories 13, Fat 1.5g, Saturated fat 0.3g, Cholesterol 0mg, Protein 4g, Carbohydrate 54g, Dietary fiber 4g, Sodium 10mg, Omega-3 fatty acids 0.02g

Allowances: ¼ fat + 2 starches + 1 fruit

We think most of the Mr. Spice sauces are best when heated, but the Indian Curry is great at room temperature. If you don't have any of the Mr. Spice sauces on hand, use a different "no-salt-added" sauce, and maybe a different dried fruit. You can also quickly create your own—see *De-Anne's Curry Rice* (page 152) for spice combos to get this curry flavor.

SUSAN'S WARM LENTIL SALAD WITH
MUSTARD VINAIGRETTE
STARCH

Susan came up with this tasty dish. She writes, "I like to serve this on a bed of lettuce leaves. If you are looking for something a little heartier, try it with oven-roasted vegetables for a warm meal on a cold winter night."

1 cup lentils, preferably Indian Harvest French Green Lentils ○

6 cups water

1 onion, chopped

6 halves sun-dried tomatoes, preferably Sonoma Sun-Dried Tomatoes ○

1 garlic clove, halved

¼ teaspoon dried thyme

2 sprigs flat-leaf parsley

¾ cup diced carrots

2 teaspoons red wine vinegar, preferably Badia a Coltibuono ○

2 tablespoons Dijon mustard, no salt added, preferably Téméraire Dijon Mustard ○

2 tablespoons extra-virgin olive oil

½ cup chopped flat-leaf parsley

Freshly ground black pepper

In a heavy saucepan combine the lentils, water, onion, tomatoes, garlic, thyme, and parsley sprigs and simmer, covered, for 20 minutes. Stir in carrots and simmer the mixture, covered, until the lentils are tender, about 10 minutes more.

Transfer 2 tablespoons of the lentil cooking liquid into a bowl and whisk in the vinegar and mustard. Add the oil, and whisk the dressing until emulsified. Drain the lentils well in a strainer, and discard the parsley sprigs and garlic. Toss the lentils with the chopped parsley and vinaigrette and season with black pepper to taste.

Yield: 4 servings

Each serving contains approximately: Calories 200, Fat calories 60, Fat 7g, Saturated fat 1.0g, Cholesterol 0mg, Protein 10g, Carbohydrate 26g, Dietary fiber 6g, Sodium 30mg, Omega-3 fatty acids 0g

Allowances: 1½ fats + 1¼ starches + 1¼ vegetables

WILD RICE AND MUSHROOM CASSEROLE STARCH

Susan grew up in northern Minnesota, so her family ate lots of wild rice. Wild rice (which is actually grass) is often harvested from a canoe out of shallow lakes. Susan writes: "Where I come from, the sight of this harvest was a harbinger of summer's end."

1 cup wild rice

2 cups vegetable stock, no salt added, preferably Rapunzel's Vegan, No Salt Added, Vegetable Bouillon ○

1 ounce dried porcini mushrooms

2 teaspoons extra-virgin olive oil

Freshly ground black pepper

2 teaspoons chopped fresh tarragon

Preheat oven to 350 degrees F.

Soak the wild rice in cold water for 1 hour. Dissolve the broth cube in 2 cups of boiling water.

Add the drained rice and broth to a casserole dish, cover, and bake for about 30 minutes. Soak the dried mushrooms in hot water for about 30 minutes. Drain and chop mushrooms and sauté in olive oil. Add the mushrooms and black pepper, to taste, to the rice. Cover and bake for an additional 30 minutes. Season with fresh tarragon.

Yield: 4 servings

Each serving contains approximately: Calories 196, Fat calories 32, Fat 4g, Saturated fat 0.4g, Cholesterol 0mg, Protein 9g, Carbohydrate 34g, Dietary fiber 4g, Sodium 38mg, Omega-3 fatty acids 0.14g

Allowances: ½ fat + 1¾ starches + 1½ vegetables

ANGELA'S ORZO SALAD   STARCH

Thank you, Angela, for being a wonderful friend and valuable resource. You (and your recipes) continue to be an inspiration to us all! This would be great with any small or bite-sized pasta or bean; try experimenting with added mustard, citrus juice, and zest.

1 pound orzo pasta

4 cups vegetable stock, no salt added, preferably Rapunzel's Vegan, No Salt Added
    Vegetable Bouillon ○

4 garlic cloves, minced

2 green onions, chopped

1 tablespoon extra-virgin olive oil

1 large red onion, chopped

¾ cup chopped fresh basil

¼ cup balsamic vinegar

15-ounce can garbanzo beans, no salt added, preferably Eden Organic brand ○,
    drained

1 pound grape tomatoes, halved

Freshly ground black pepper

Cook the orzo as directed on the package, using salt-free vegetable bouillon. Sauté the minced garlic and scallions in olive oil until lightly golden. Add the chopped red onion and sauté for 2 to 3 minutes. Next, stir in the basil, vinegar, and cooked orzo pasta along with the garbanzo beans and halved grape tomatoes. Add black pepper to taste.

Yield: 8 servings

Each serving contains approximately: Calories 200, Fat calories 31, Fat 3.5g, Saturated fat 0.4g, Cholesterol 0mg, Protein 8g, Carbohydrate 34g, Dietary fiber 5g, Sodium 55mg, Omega-3 fatty acids 0.04g

Allowances: 2¼ starches + 1 vegetable

You can always substitute homemade vegetable stock for Rapunzel. Did you know that it takes only 10 minutes to cook vegetable stock in a pressure cooker? Just save all your vegetable remnants as you prep them, store in a large plastic bag in the freezer, and boil them for an hour or more, or 10 minutes in a pressure cooker. My recipe for this in *Heal Your Heart* describes how you can then freeze your homemade vegetable stock (after it has cooled) in an ice cube tray. What could be more convenient than popping out a frozen ice cube of vegetable stock to start your next stir-fry? How much oil for stir-frying, and thus fat calories, could this save you?

BASIL-MINT QUINOA SALAD   STARCH

Here's a pilaf with sophistication. Blending the flavors of mint and basil adds a cool, crisp taste that is just delightful.

3 cups canned mandarin orange segments
1 cup thinly sliced baby carrots
2 cups cooked quinoa
6 celery stalks, thinly sliced
Juice of ½ lime
¼ cup chopped fresh mint
¼ cup chopped fresh basil

Drain juice from canned fruit; add a few tablespoons to salad, as desired. Combine all of the ingredients and serve over a bed of lettuce.

Yield: 4 servings

Each serving contains approximately: Calories 214, Fat calories 19, Fat 2g, Saturated fat 0.23g, Cholesterol 0mg, Protein 6g, Carbohydrate 46g, Dietary fiber 5g, Sodium 81mg, Omega-3 fatty acids 0.07g

Allowances: 1½ starches + 1½ fruits + ½ vegetable

BEAN AND VEGETABLE SALAD   STARCH

This is a good staple recipe to follow, while allowing your own personal touches to come into play. Just start with your favorite legume and chopped raw veggies, then experiment with a vinegar that you enjoy. We liked the sweet combo of apple cider vinegar and honey for this one, so we'll loan you ours until you find your own style. Serve it up cold, on top of a green salad. You can also cut your serving in half and fill your remaining starch serving with rice.

15-ounce can garbanzo beans (chickpeas), no salt added, preferably
   Eden Organic brand ○
15-ounce can red kidney or pinto beans, no salt added, preferably
   Eden Organic brand ○
1 cup cherry or grape tomatoes, cut into quarters
1 cup thinly sliced cucumber, cut into quarters
½ cup thinly sliced red onion or green onions
1 cup freshly chopped flat-leaf parsley
⅓ cup apple cider vinegar
1 tablespoon extra-virgin olive oil

½ teaspoon honey

¼ teaspoon freshly ground black pepper

Drain both cans of beans. In a large salad bowl, mix together the beans, tomatoes, cucumber, onion, and parsley. In a separate bowl, whisk together the remaining ingredients. Pour the dressing over the bean salad, and refrigerate before serving.

Yield: 8 servings

Each serving contains approximately: Calories 123, Fat calories 21, Fat 2g, Saturated fat 0.3g, Cholesterol 0mg, Protein 6g, Carbohydrate 20g, Dietary fiber 5g, Sodium 26mg, Omega-3 fatty acids 0.01g

Allowances: ½ fat + 1 starch + ½ vegetable

• You can always substitute 2 cups of cooked dried beans for one 15-ounce can of beans.

• If you are starting with dried beans, be sure to read page 318 about soaking, rinsing, and pressure-cooker alternatives.

BLACK-EYED PEA AND BARLEY SALAD   STARCH

This is a dish that is easy to throw together from ingredients right in your pantry at home. Take your favorite grain, legume, and veggie—a little extra-virgin olive oil and vinegar, and you've got dinner without having to go to the store! But do yourself a favor and try this exact combo once; my 10-year-old liked it so much he asked for three servings!

2 cups cold cooked barley, fluffed with a fork

2 cups cooked black-eyed peas

½ cup diced red and green bell peppers

½ cup chopped red onion

1 cup corn kernels, fresh or frozen

¼ cup chopped flat-leaf parsley

2 tablespoons extra-virgin olive oil

4 tablespoons balsamic vinegar

3 tablespoons lime juice

4 tablespoons sesame seeds, toasted

Mix ingredients together well and chill overnight.

Yield: 6 servings

Each serving contains approximately: Calories 226, Fat calories 66, Fat 7g, Saturated fat 0.8g, Cholesterol 0mg, Protein 7g, Carbohydrate 35g, Dietary fiber 6g, Sodium 14mg, Omega-3 fatty acids 0g

Allowances: 1¼ fats + 1¾ starches + ½ vegetable

WHITE CORN SALAD   STARCH

This dish is simply divine. When testing this recipe, the dietitians were blown away by the flavor, which was packed in just a few simple ingredients. There is nothing overpowering about the vinegar or mustard; it just blends perfectly.

2 cups frozen shoepeg white corn, no salt added, thawed

¾ cup chopped tomato

½ cup chopped cucumber

2 tablespoons chopped green bell peppers

3 tablespoons white wine vinegar

1½ teaspoon Dijon mustard, no salt added, preferably Téméraire Dijon Mustard ○

1 garlic clove, minced
Freshly ground black pepper, optional

Combine the corn, tomato, cucumber, and green bell peppers in a bowl and toss. Combine the vinegar, mustard, garlic, and optional black pepper in a jar. Cover the jar and shake vigorously. Pour the mixture over the corn and toss well.

Yield: 3 servings

Each serving contains approximately: Calories 102, Fat calories 9, Fat 1g, Saturated fat 0g, Cholesterol 0mg, Protein 3g, Carbohydrate 21g, Dietary fiber 3g, Sodium 36mg, Omega-3 fatty acids 0g

Allowances: 1¼ starches + ¼ vegetable

VEGETABLE SIDES AND SALADS

ANGELA'S ROSEMARY-BALSAMIC MUSHROOOMS

VEGETABLE

Another favorite recipe from our dear friend and fellow Ricer Angela, whose heart is as big as the flavor in this dish!

1½ pounds button mushrooms, sliced

1 tablespoon extra-virgin olive oil

3-4 tablespoons balsamic vinegar

1 tablespoon chopped fresh rosemary

1 teaspoon freshly ground black pepper

Preheat the oven to 350 degrees F.

Mix the mushrooms, olive oil, and vinegar on a baking sheet. Then sprinkle with the rosemary and black pepper. Roast in the oven until all the liquid has evaporated.

Yield: 4 servings

Each serving contains approximately: Calories 80, Fat calories 68, Fat 37g, Saturated fat 0.6g, Cholesterol 0mg, Protein 5g, Carbohydrate 8g, Dietary fiber 2g, Sodium 13mg, Omega-3 fatty acids 0g

Allowances: ¾ fat + 1¾ vegetables

ANGELA'S SPINACH WITH SUN-DRIED TOMATO

VEGETABLE

Angela outdid herself on this one! During the recipe-tasting stage of this book, this was a "hands down, don't change a thing" kind of dish. Angela rocks!

2 vegetable bouillon cubes, no salt added, preferably Rapunzel's Vegan,
   No Salt Added Vegetable Bouillon ◯
2 pounds fresh spinach
½ cup sliced white mushrooms
5 garlic cloves, minced
1 large onion, chopped
1 tablespoon extra-virgin olive oil
½ pound (about 2 cups) frozen artichoke hearts, salt free, preferably Birds Eye
   Frozen Deluxe brand
1½ cups sun-dried tomatoes, preferably Sonoma brand ◯
1 cup tomato paste, no salt added

In a large skillet, heat water to dissolve bouillon cube (as instructed on bouillon package).

Boil the spinach in the vegetable bouillon until tender, then drain and chop it. Reserve and set aside most of the bouillon. Next, cook the mushrooms until tender, drain completely, and set aside. Sauté the garlic, mushrooms, and onion over low heat in the olive oil until lightly golden and the onion is translucent. Add the vegetable bouillon to the onion as needed to prevent sticking. Add the artichoke heart halves, sun-dried tomatoes, and tomato paste to the onion. Cook over low heat for 5 to 7 minutes until warm. Add the chopped spinach to the mixture until heated. I can't imagine a starch this would not be good with—crackers, chips, in pitas, or on rice.

Yield: 8 servings

Each serving contains approximately: Calories 124, Fat calories 28, Fat 3g, Saturated fat 0.4g, Cholesterol 0mg, Protein 8g, Carbohydrate 21g, Dietary fiber 9g, Sodium 184mg, Omega-3 fatty acids 0.1g

Allowances: ½ fat + 4 vegetables

BAKED OKRA VEGETABLE

Welcome to Rice House cooking with a little southern flair! You will feel like you've just crossed the Mason-Dixon Line with one bite of this delicious dish. Grits and okra without the "southern" calories, saturated fat, and sodium! When I eat this with some *Pinto Beans*, I've "gone to Carolina in my mind"!

¾ cup grits
1 teaspoon freshly ground black pepper
1 teaspoon paprika
1 teaspoon garlic powder
2 tablespoons hot water
1 teaspoon extra-virgin olive oil
24 ounces cut, frozen okra, salt free

Preheat the oven to 350 degrees F.

Mix all the dry ingredients in a large bowl. Then mix the liquid ingredients and okra together in a separate bowl. When mixed well, add to the dry ingredients and stir to coat the okra thoroughly. Lay the okra evenly across a nonstick baking sheet, and bake for about 1 hour.

Yield: 4 servings

Each serving contains approximately: Calories 178, Fat calories 15, Fat 2g, Saturated fat 0.3g, Cholesterol 0mg, Protein 5g, Carbohydrate 37g, Dietary fiber 5g, Sodium 5mg, Omega-3 fatty acids 0g

Allowances: ¼ fat + 1¼ starches + 2½ vegetables

Although one need not be surprised that this does not taste like deep-fat-fried (and salted) okra, it is surprisingly good—especially after a day of just eating fruits and grains on a Basic Rice Diet day! Ricers love dishes like this—when baked slightly more brown than usual, they offer that chewy, crunchy texture that you can sometimes miss when you avoid fried foods.

BELGIAN ENDIVE
VEGETABLE

This is now my favorite vegetable dish served at the Rice House. Like arugula and other strong vegetables, you either really like it or really don't. In case you are in the former group, don't miss this one!

I teaspoon extra-virgin olive oil

¼ cup balsamic vinegar

8 Belgian endives, halved lengthwise

I teaspoon freshly ground black pepper

½ cup vegetable stock, no salt added, preferably Rapunzel's Vegan, No Salt Added Vegetable Bouillon ○

I tablespoon honey

Preheat the oven to 350 degrees F.

In a wide cooking pot, heat the oil and balsamic vinegar over high heat for 1 to 2 minutes. Carefully place the endive in the pot, cut side down and side by side. Add the black pepper and vegetable stock, cover with lid, and let cook for 5 to 7 minutes until endive is tender. Place the cooked endive side by side on a nonstick pan, cut side up. Drizzle the honey equally over the endive halves. Place in the oven and bake for 10 to 17 minutes, or until the top of the endive is crispy.

Yield: 4 servings (4 halves per serving)

Each serving contains approximately: Calories 72, Fat calories 15, Fat 2g, Saturated fat 0.2g, Cholesterol 0mg, Protein 2g, Carbohydrate 14g, Dietary fiber 5g, Sodium 25mg, Omega-3 fatty acids 0g

Allowances: ¼ fat + ¼ starch + 1½ vegetables

BROCCOLI RAPINI VEGETABLE

This dish is an Italian-inspired way to get your greens! If you're tired of old-style broccoli, try it rapini style.

6 cups broccoli rapini (broccoli rabe)
1 teaspoon extra-virgin olive oil
1 tablespoon minced garlic
1 cup water
1 teaspoon red pepper flakes
Juice of ½ lemon

Rinse the broccoli rapini and trim off ½ inch from bottom of each stem. Heat the oil in a wide skillet over medium heat, add garlic, and sauté until it is lightly browned. Add broccoli rapini stems to the garlic, cover, and cook for 3 to 5 minutes. Add the water, red pepper flakes, and the remainder of the broccoli rapini, stir, cover, and cook for additional 5 to 7 minutes. Stir, sprinkle lemon juice over top, and serve.

Yield: 4 servings

Each serving contains approximately: Calories 54, Fat calories 18, Fat 2g, Saturated fat 0.2g, Cholesterol 0mg, Protein 4g, Carbohydrate 7g, Dietary fiber 3g, Sodium 29mg, Omega-3 fatty acids 0.2g

Allowances: ¼ fat + 1¾ vegetables

CHIMOLE

The Rice Diet family is expanding across the globe. One Forum member sent us this recipe from a close friend in El Salvador. This dish is best when used as a salsa or to top a salad.

3 cucumbers, diced

¼ cup chopped red onions

½ bunch cilantro, chopped

8 plum tomatoes, diced

5 green onions, white and half the green parts, sliced

2 to 3 tablespoons fresh lime juice

(Maybe a drizzle of olive oil)

Mix all ingredients together in a bowl. Chill and serve.

Yield: 4 servings

Each serving contains approximately: Calories 62, Fat calories 15, Fat 1.7, Saturated fat 0.3g, Cholesterol 0mg, Protein 2.5g, Carbohydrate 11g, Dietary fiber 3g, Sodium 13mg, Omega-3 fatty acids 0.02g

Allowances: 2 vegetables

DILIP'S RAITA

Pat, our nurse extraordinaire, brought Dilip into our Ricer family. He has some great recipe ideas. Thanks again, Dilip, for such a creative and tasty dish! This Indian favorite is sometimes enjoyed with dried mustard and cumin; experiment to discover your preferences.

1 medium onion, diced

1 medium cucumber, diced

1 medium tomato, diced

1 medium parboiled potato, diced

6 to 8 green or red seedless grapes

A few sprigs of cilantro, finely chopped

¼ small jalapeño pepper, seeded and minced

8 ounces plain nonfat yogurt

¼ teaspoon fennel seeds

Paprika, to garnish

In a bowl add the onion, cucumber, tomato, and potato. Slice the grapes into ⅓-inch rings. Mix all the veggies and fruit with the yogurt and fennel seeds. Refrigerate for an hour or so before serving, then sprinkle with paprika to garnish.

Yield: 6 servings

Each serving contains approximately: Calories 95, Fat calories 3, Fat 0g, Saturated fat 0g, Cholesterol 1mg, Protein 4g, Carbohydrate 21g, Dietary fiber 2g, Sodium 41mg, Omega-3 fatty acids 0.01g

Allowances: ½ starch + 1 vegetable + ¼ dairy

EASY SUMMER SLAW   VEGETABLE

This supereasy dish is great to whip up ahead of time for a barbecue or picnic. It's a great way to enjoy summer slaw without the added fat and calories from mayonnaise; plus, the mango gives this a refreshingly sweet kick.

16-ounce bag (about 8 cups) shredded cabbage, prewashed

¼ cup Consorzio's Mango Dressing ○ or *Mango Wasabi Dressing*

Mix the cabbage and dressing in a large bowl, cover, and refrigerate. Portion out into ¾-cup servings and enjoy!

Yield: 6 servings (¾ cup per serving)

Each serving contains approximately: Calories 49, Fat calories 0, Fat 0g, Saturated fat 0g, Cholesterol 0mg, Protein 1g, Carbohydrate 8g, Dietary fiber 2g, Sodium 39mg, Omega-3 fatty acids 0g

The Consorzio Mango Dressing was our first choice for this slaw because it has a refreshing mango taste and nice vinegar bite. But you could also use a low-sodium salad dressing of your choice! For future reference, we get a lot of cooking ideas from ingredient lists of products we like. For instance, read the first four or five ingredients on the label of a product you like, then improvise with what you have on hand or can buy locally. Susan did that from a few labels she liked to offer you *Mango Wasabi Dressing*.

If you want to prepare your own mango dressing, try the following:

In a blender, combine

• a fresh mango, plain rice vinegar, fresh ginger, and honey

• a fresh mango, lime juice, honey, and red pepper flakes

• a fresh mango, lime juice, orange juice concentrate, ginger, and fresh jalapeño

GINGERED GREENS

VEGETABLE

Another Rice Diet Forum contributor breaks through her previously held belief that she "didn't like greens"! As she says, "This is a very good way to eat greens, for me at least, since I didn't like them before. The taste has an Asian influence without using soy sauce. You can adjust the amounts of oil, and it makes enough for 6 to 10 servings, depending on how big the bunch of greens. Keeping this recipe on hand really helps me eat greens daily without the hassle of preparation."

1 large onion, thinly sliced

1 teaspoon canola oil

2 cups sliced mushrooms

4 cups chopped Swiss chard, or bok choy, or even turnip greens

2 garlic cloves, minced

1 teaspoon minced fresh ginger

1 tablespoon sesame oil

1 tablespoon sesame seeds

Sauté the onion over medium heat in a pan that has been lightly coated with canola oil. When the onion is soft and translucent, add the mushrooms and stir, and then cover the pan for a few minutes until they begin to soften. Add the greens, garlic, and ginger, and stir it all up. It is not usually necessary to add liquid because the mushrooms tend to release some, but, if needed, add a couple of tablespoons of water. Cover and cook on medium-low heat until the greens are soft. Mix it all thoroughly. At the end of the cooking, add the sesame oil and sesame seeds. Stir and serve.

Yield: 6 servings

Each serving contains approximately: Calories 48, Fat calories 28, Fat 3g, Saturated fat 0.4g, Cholesterol 0mg, Protein 2g, Carbohydrate 4g, Dietary fiber 1g, Sodium 56mg, Omega-3 fatty acids 0g

Allowances: ½ fat + 1 vegetable

GRILLED VEGETABLE MEDLEY VEGETABLE

When compiling the recipes for this cookbook, our staff reached out to friends and family and asked them to share their favorites with the rest of the world. This one comes from Ryan's friend and fellow dietitian Julia. Julia writes that her mother makes this dish as a family favorite. "She is an exquisite chef, and this dish is very tasty as well as nutritious."

1 zucchini

1 yellow bell pepper

1 orange bell pepper

1 red bell pepper

2 leeks, halved and cleaned

2 tablespoons extra-virgin olive oil

1 teaspoon chopped fresh oregano

1 to 4 tablespoons chopped fresh basil, as desired

Freshly ground black pepper

4 garlic cloves, minced

1 cup of crushed tomatoes, no salt added

½ cup vegetable stock, no salt added, preferably Rapunzel's Vegan,
     No Salt Added Vegetable Bouillon ○

Preheat a grill to medium-high (approximately 375 degrees).

Cut the vegetables into ¾-inch-square, approximately equal-size pieces and place in a large bowl. Drizzle with 1 tablespoon of olive oil and toss to coat. Add the oregano, basil, and black pepper to taste, and toss lightly again. Place the vegetables on the grill and grill for approximately 2 minutes per side; the vegetables should be lightly browned but still slightly crisp. Remove the vegetables and allow to cool. Cut the cooled vegetables into smaller bite-size pieces, if desired.

Meanwhile add the remaining tablespoon of oil to a large skillet and place over medium heat. Add the garlic and sauté for 1 minute. Add the cut-up, grilled vegetables. Stir in the tomatoes and vegetable stock and simmer until the mixture thickens and the vegetables are tender, approximately 15 minutes.

Yield: 6 servings

Each serving contains approximately: Calories 94, Fat calories 47, Fat 5g, Saturated fat 0.7g, Cholesterol 0mg, Protein 3g, Carbohydrate 11g, Dietary fiber 3g, Sodium 28mg, Omega-3 fatty acids 0.1g

Allowances: 1 fat + 2 vegetables

ILENE'S MASHED CAULIFLOWER   VEGETABLE

Ilene, our dear friend and fellow Ricer, shares this great replacement for mashed potatoes with half the calories!

1 head roasted garlic, unpeeled
1 head cauliflower
1 teaspoon freshly ground black pepper
⅛ teaspoon paprika

Preheat the oven to 300 degrees F.

Place the entire head of garlic in the oven and roast for 45 minutes. While garlic is roasting, steam the cauliflower until it is fork-tender. Remove the garlic from oven and cool. Remove the skin from the garlic and place the garlic, pepper, and cauliflower in the blender and blend until smooth. Place the purée in a casserole dish and sprinkle with paprika. Then place back in the oven for 20 minutes and serve *hot*!

Yield: 2 servings

Each serving contains approximately: Calories 95, Fat calories 43, Fat 5g, Saturated fat 0.7g, Cholesterol 0mg, Protein 4g, Carbohydrate 11g, Dietary fiber 4g, Sodium 46 mg, Omega-3 fatty acids 0g

Allowances: 3¾ vegetables

JON'S AWESOME ASPARAGUS

VEGETABLE

Ryan's fiancé, Jon, takes all the credit for this veggie dish—asparagus with a kick and full of flavor.

1 bunch asparagus, tough ends removed

1 tablespoon extra-virgin olive oil

3 garlic cloves, minced

2 tablespoons freshly squeezed lemon juice

Freshly ground black pepper

1 tablespoon sesame seeds

Place a large skillet over medium heat. Toss asparagus spears in olive oil to evenly coat, place in skillet, then add the garlic. Use a spatula to turn the asparagus once it has browned on the bottom side. When the asparagus has turned a bright green and is tender, remove from heat and sprinkle with lemon juice, black pepper to taste, and sesame seeds.

Yield: 6 servings

Each serving contains approximately: Calories 121, Fat calories 76, Fat 8g, Saturated fat 0.9g, Cholesterol 0mg, Protein 4g, Carbohydrate 9g, Dietary fiber 3g, Sodium 10mg, Omega-3 fatty acids 0.1g

Allowances: ¾ fat + 3½ vegetables

JR'S CRISPY SWEET PEARL ONIONS

VEGETABLE

This dish is just unbelievably good to be this easy! Leave it to Chef JR!

I cup uncooked Cream of Wheat, preferably Bob's Red Mill no salt added ○
I large pinch of paprika
I large pinch of black pepper
I large pinch of garlic powder
I teaspoon extra-virgin olive oil
I teaspoon honey
I tablespoon water
5 cups peeled, whole pearl onions; frozen are fine

Preheat the oven to 350 degrees F.

Mix all of the dry ingredients together in a small bowl. In a large bowl, mix the liquid ingredients, add the onions, and toss to coat. Stir in the dry ingredients, coating the onions, then spread the mixture evenly over a nonstick baking sheet. Place in the oven and bake for 40 to 60 minutes, or until crispy.

Yield: 6 servings

Each serving contains approximately: Calories 217, Fat calories 7, Fat 1g, Saturated fat 0.1g, Cholesterol 0mg, Protein 4g, Carbohydrate 47g, Dietary fiber 1g, Sodium 30mg, Omega-3 fatty acids 0.01g

Allowances: 1¼ starches + 4 vegetables

JR'S GRILLED ASPARAGUS SALAD
VEGETABLE

Here is another treat that our patients *love* when they come to the Rice House. Our Chef JR has come up with a unique flavor combination that complements the asparagus in a tasty, refreshing way.

36 large asparagus spears, tough ends removed

2 teaspoons extra-virgin olive oil

¼ cup white wine vinegar

I teaspoon freshly ground black pepper

I teaspoon dried oregano

I teaspoon minced garlic

4 large, fresh basil leaves, chopped

2 tablespoons water

½ teaspoon honey

½ Vidalia onion, diced

24 grape tomatoes, halved

Preheat a grill.

Coat the asparagus in 1 teaspoon of the olive oil, then grill for 4 minutes on each side or until crispy. In a small bowl, mix the white wine vinegar, black pepper, oregano, garlic, basil leaves, water, and honey with the remaining olive oil. Whisk well and set aside. Cut each asparagus spear into 3 equal-length pieces. Place the asparagus, dressing, onion, and tomatoes in a large bowl, and mix all ingredients together. Enjoy alone or over your choice of lettuce, spinach, or baby greens.

Yield: 6 servings

Each serving contains approximately: Calories 60, Fat calories 16, Fat 2g, Saturated fat 0.3g, Cholesterol 0mg, Protein 3g, Carbohydrate 10g, Dietary fiber 4g, Sodium 4mg, Omega-3 fatty acids 0.01g

Allowances: ¼ fat + 2 vegetables

JR'S SPAGHETTI SQUASH WITH HONEY MUSTARD SAUCE

VEGETABLE

After trying spaghetti squash thirty years ago, I really wondered what "all the buzz was" about this vegetable. Then I tasted this dish, and it was truly a conversion experience! I get it now: when a vegetable or other food is fairly mild in flavor, you put something incredibly flavorful on it! The squash's texture and the honey mustard flavor are so meant for each other! This is definitely in my top five favorite Rice House recipes!

2 spaghetti squash, halved and seeded

1 cup freshly squeezed lemon juice

½ cup dry mustard

4 tablespoons honey

1 teaspoon freshly ground black pepper

2 tablespoons minced garlic

2 tablespoons chopped flat-leaf parsley

1 tablespoon chopped fresh dill

Preheat the oven to 350 degrees F.

Place the squash cut side down in a 2-inch-deep baking pan with ¼ inch water. Bake for 1 hour. Remove the squash from the oven and scrape out the insides with a fork—it will have a spaghetti-like appearance.

Sauté the remaining ingredients in a saucepan over low heat for 1 to 2 minutes, stirring often. Pour the sauce evenly over the squash and serve.

Yield: 4 servings

Each serving contains approximately: Calories 123, Fat calories 10, Fat 1g, Saturated fat 0g, Cholesterol 0mg, Protein 1g, Carbohydrates 29g, Dietary fiber 2g, Sodium 29mg, Omega-3 fatty acids 0.04g

Allowances: 2½ vegetables + 1 fruit

JR'S SPAGHETTI SQUASH

VEGETABLE

This dish is the second best spaghetti squash recipe I've ever tasted! Go, JR!

2 spaghetti squash, halved and seeded

1 cup cherry tomatoes, halved

1½ cups water

½ cup diced onions

¼ cup tomato purée, no salt added

1 tablespoon honey

1 teaspoon minced garlic

½ teaspoon dried dill

½ teaspoon freshly ground black pepper

1 teaspoon extra-virgin olive oil

Preheat the oven to 350 degrees.

Place the squash cut side down in a 2-inch-deep baking pan with ¼ inch water. Bake for 1 hour. Sauté the remaining ingredients in a saucepan over low heat for 7 to 10 minutes, stirring every 3 to 4 minutes. Remove the squash from oven and scrape out the insides with a fork—it will have a spaghetti-like appearance. Spread the sauce evenly over the squash and serve.

Yield: 4 servings

Each serving contains approximately: Calories 79, Fat calories 16, Fat 2g, Saturated fat 0.3g, Cholesterol 0mg, Protein 3g, Carbohydrate 15g, Dietary fiber 3g, Sodium 10mg, Omega-3 fatty acids 0.1g

Allowances: ¼ fat + 2¾ vegetables

LAURA'S "NO ROOM FOR SECONDS" VEGETABLE SOUP

VEGETABLE

This recipe comes to us from our friend Laura, a Ricer family member. She says this soup is "simply amazing."

½ head cabbage

5 large carrots

5 celery stalks

1 small onion

6 cups vegetable stock, salt free, preferably Rapunzel's Vegan, No Salt Added
    Vegetable Bouillon ○

1 tablespoon minced garlic

1 teaspoon herbes de Provence

½ teaspoon freshly ground black pepper

½ teaspoon ground cumin

1 tablespoon extra-virgin olive oil

1 can chopped stewed tomatoes, salt free

Chop all vegetables, except tomatoes, into bite-sized chunks (no smaller than ¼ inch). Bring the vegetable stock to a boil, and add all the ingredients except for the tomatoes. Simmer over a low heat for 1 hour, or until the vegetables are tender, then add tomatoes. Serve hot!

Yield: 8 servings

Each serving contains approximately: Calories 94, Fat calories 33, Fat 3.5g, Saturated fat 0.3g, Cholesterol 0mg, Protein 3.5g, Carbohydrate 12g, Dietary fiber 3.5g, Sodium 62mg, Omega-3 fatty acids 0.1g

Allowances: 1 fat + 3½ vegetables

OVEN-ROASTED FRENCH BEANS

VEGETABLE

Here is a popular dish straight from the Rice House kitchen. Now you can have the quality, as well as nutritional value, of a meal prepared here at the Rice Diet, right in the comfort of your own home.

1 large red bell pepper, cored, seeded, and thinly sliced lengthwise
1 large yellow pepper, cored, seeded, and thinly sliced lengthwise
1 tablespoon minced garlic
2 tablespoons water
2 tablespoons balsamic vinegar
1 teaspoon freshly ground black pepper
60 green beans, ends removed
1 teaspoon extra-virgin olive oil
1 teaspoon honey
4 basil leaves, chopped

Preheat the oven to 350 degrees F.

Place the sliced peppers, garlic, water, balsamic vinegar, and black pepper onto a nonstick baking sheet and bake in the oven for 45 minutes. Stir the peppers every 15 minutes to prevent burning, and add a small amount of water if necessary.

In a large mixing bowl, toss the beans in the olive oil, then lay them on a nonstick baking sheet, side by side. Bake for 15 to 25 minutes, until the beans are tender, shaking the pan every 5 to 7 minutes to move the beans around.

Remove the peppers from the oven and pour the honey over them. Put 15 green beans on your plate in a bunch, and spoon one-fourth of the peppers over the beans. Sprinkle the chopped fresh basil over the top, and enjoy!

Yield: 4 servings

Each serving contains approximately: Calories 75, Fat calories 16, Fat 2g, Saturated fat 0.2g, Cholesterol 0mg, Protein 2g, Carbohydrate 13g, Dietary fiber 3g, Sodium 6mg, Omega-3 fatty acids 0g

Allowances: ¼ fat + 2½ vegetables

OVEN-ROASTED VEGGIES WITH HONEY MUSTARD
VEGETABLE

Susan is the master when it comes to roasted vegetables. Her root vegetable choices in this recipe shouldn't surprise us for a girl from Minnesota. Their mouthwatering flavors, contrasting colors, and very few calories make this a keeper.

20 baby carrots

3 beets, peeled

3 parsnips, peeled

12 pearl onions, peeled

½ cup honey mustard or honey mustard sauce, low fat, no salt added, preferably
    Mr. Spice Honey Mustard Sauce ○

1 teaspoon seasoned pepper, no salt added, preferably Frontier Veggie Pepper ○

1 teaspoon extra-virgin olive oil

Preheat the oven to 400 degrees F.

Cut the carrots crosswise in half and cut the beets and parsnips into ¾-inch cubes. Place the carrots, beets, parsnips, and pearl onions in a bowl and toss with the Honey Mustard Sauce and Veggie Pepper.

Place the veggies in shallow baking ban. Roast for 1 hour, stirring every 15 minutes. If the veggies begin to dry out and stick to the pan, stir in 1 teaspoon olive oil. Remove from oven. Serve warm, or chill the salad for at least 2 hours before serving.

Yield: 4 servings

Each serving contains approximately: Calories 98, Fat calories 13, Fat 1.5g, Saturated fat 0.1g, Cholesterol 0mg, Protein 2g, Carbohydrate 9g, Dietary fiber 2g, Sodium 24mg, Omega-3 fatty acids 0g

Allowances: ¼ fat + ½ fruit + 2 vegetables

TWO-PEA AND ASPARAGUS STIR-FRY VEGETABLE

One faithful member of our Rice Diet Forum has shown us how to make a stir-fry without the sodium. Throw your favorite veggies into a wok and heat it up!

1 tablespoon sesame seeds
½ teaspoon sesame oil
1 garlic clove, minced
1 tablespoon finely chopped fresh ginger
¼ teaspoon red pepper flakes
6 ounces sugar snap peas, trimmed and cut diagonally
6 ounces snow peas, trimmed and cut diagonally
6 ounces asparagus, trimmed and cut diagonally
1 teaspoon low-sodium Worcestershire sauce

Toast the sesame seeds under the broiler in a glass pie plate. Heat the sesame oil in a nonstick wok until hot but not smoking. Add the garlic, ginger, and red pepper flakes. Stir-fry until the garlic is golden, approximately 1 minute. Add the sugar snap peas, snow peas, and asparagus. Stir-fry until crisp tender, approximately 5 minutes. Stir in the Worcestershire and stir-fry for 1 minute. Sprinkle with the toasted sesame seeds.

Yield: 4 servings

Each serving contains approximately: Calories 75, Fat calories 18, Fat 2g, Saturated fat 0.2g, Cholesterol 0mg, Protein 4g, Carbohydrate 10g, Dietary fiber 3g, Sodium 52mg, Omega-3 fatty acids 0g

Allowances: ¼ fat + 2½ vegetables

RED CABBAGE

VEGETABLE

Who needs dessert when you have a nutrient-packed, sweet, and delicious dish like this? After enjoying this sweet cabbage dish, your sweet tooth will be satiated!

4 cups shredded red cabbage

1 tablespoon extra-virgin olive oil

Freshly ground black pepper, to taste

½ teaspoon nutmeg, preferably freshly grated

1 tablespoon maple syrup

1 medium onion, chopped

2 cups hot water

1 apple, sliced

4 whole cloves

1 tablespoon vinegar, preferably apple cider vinegar

Slice the cabbage and soak in cold water. In a saucepan, add the cabbage, oil, pepper, nutmeg, maple syrup, and onion. Simmer for about 20 minutes. Then add the hot water, apple, cloves, and vinegar. Cover and cook slowly until tender.

Yield: 4 servings

Each serving contains approximately: Calories 95, Fat calories 34, Fat 4g, Saturated fat 0.7g, Cholesterol 0mg, Protein 2g, Carbohydrate 16g, Dietary fiber 3g, Sodium 16mg, Omega-3 fatty acids 0.1g

Allowances: ¾ fat + 1¼ vegetables + ½ fruit

RICE HOUSE ROASTED EGGPLANT SALAD VEGETABLE

JR came up with yet another great way to enjoy eggplant—those Italians know how to prepare it. Most Americans we meet here rarely, if ever, cook it; so if you are in their club—this one is for you! The recipe tastes better when the eggplant is sliced really thin, so make sure that you have a good, sharp knife handy.

2 large eggplants, unpeeled and thinly sliced crosswise

2½ teaspoons extra-virgin olive oil

I tablespoon minced garlic

½ teaspoon dried oregano

½ teaspoon freshly ground black pepper

2 tablespoons red wine vinegar

2 tablespoons water

½ teaspoon dried marjoram

I large red onion, thinly sliced

I large bell pepper, thinly sliced, preferably orange or yellow

I teaspoon chopped flat-leaf parsley

I tablespoon fresh lemon juice

6 cups romaine lettuce, shredded

24 cherry tomatoes, halved

Preheat oven to 350 degrees F.

Lay the eggplant slices on a nonstick baking sheet. Drizzle the tops with ½ teaspoon olive oil. Roast in oven for 20 to 25 minutes, then set aside to cool. Place the remaining ingredients into a large mixing bowl, except for eggplant. Mix well and set aside. Cut the eggplant rounds into long strips. Place the salad mixture on a serving plate. Top with the eggplant, and enjoy.

Yield: 6 servings

Each serving contains approximately: Calories 102, Fat calories 28, Fat 3g, Saturated fat 0.4g, Cholesterol 0mg, Protein 3g, Carbohydrate 17g, Dietary fiber 7g, Sodium 13mg, Omega-3 fatty acids 0g

Allowances: ½ fat + 3 vegetables

ROASTED ARTICHOKES ALLA ROSATI   VEGETABLE

It's almost hard to believe how good and easy this recipe is—a "basic" and "must-have-on-hand-at-all-times" item. If you like artichokes, they make virtually everything taste better with their addition to everything from salads to bruschetta to risotto.

Two 9-ounce packages frozen artichoke hearts, preferably Birds Eye Frozen Deluxe, no salt added
1 tablespoon extra-virgin olive oil
Freshly ground black pepper, to taste

Defrost the artichoke hearts and toss with the olive oil. Place under the broiler and cook for about 15 minutes, turning once. They are ready when they look slightly browned or roasted on both sides. Remove from the oven and top with freshly ground black pepper, to taste. You can marinate them in the fridge and enjoy as a topping for days.

Unless you are adding them to a dish that is already flavorful, you may want to add balsamic vinegar or freshly squeezed lemon or lime juice for a nice punch.

Yield: 6 servings

Each serving contains approximately: Calories 54, Fat calories 24, Fat 3g, Saturated fat 0.4g, Cholesterol 0mg, Protein 2g, Carbohydrate 6g, Dietary fiber 5g, Sodium 40mg, Omega-3 fatty acids 0g

Allowances: ½ fat + 1¼ vegetables

ROASTED BEET PURÉE

VEGETABLE

Here's another recipe created by Susan, who says that the spices make the whole kitchen smell good! Obviously, when you are heating the oven for this long, remember to utilize your space and energy by cooking sweet potatoes, baking potatoes, winter squash, or baked beans at the same time. You'll be set for the week!

4 beets
2 unpeeled garlic cloves
2 bay leaves
4 whole cloves
4 allspice berries
1 teaspoon walnut oil, preferably L'Olivier brand ○

Preheat the oven to 400 degrees F.

On a sheet of heavy aluminum foil (or a double sheet) place the beets, garlic, bay leaves, cloves, and allspice. Seal the package and roast for about 2 hours, or until the beets are tender. Open the foil and peel the beets, then discard the other package ingredients. Purée the beets in a food processor with the walnut oil and serve!

Yield: 4 servings

Each serving contains approximately: Calories 62, Fat calories 22, Fat 2g, Saturated fat 0.2g, Cholesterol 0mg, Protein 1.5g, Carbohydrate 9g, Dietary fiber 3g, Sodium 64mg, Omega-3 fatty acids 0.2g

Allowances: ¼ fat + 2 vegetables

ROASTED GARLIC

VEGETABLE

Roasted garlic is so flavorful, yet so much richer and mellower than it is raw. If you've never tried garlic prepared this way, please do yourself a favor. After you enjoy the "garlic-y" paste from one of these cloves on bread, you will forever feel sorry for those who still use butter!

1 head garlic
1 tablespoon extra-virgin olive oil
1 sprig fresh thyme, flat-leaf parsley, rosemary, or other herb of your choice
Freshly ground black pepper, to taste

Preheat the oven to 375 degrees F.

Place the garlic head bottom side down onto the shiny side of a piece of aluminum foil. Brush with olive oil and season with the herb of your choice. Wrap the sides of the foil to enclose the garlic. Bake for 30 minutes until tender, or until the garlic has taken on a slightly brown color. Prick the small-tipped end with a sharp paring knife, and squeeze the garlic out of its skin by pinching with your fingers; or you can put the entire clove (peeled) into dishes that are prepared with a blender or processor.

Yield: 4 servings

Each serving contains approximately: Calories 41, Fat calories 22, Fat 3g, Saturated fat 0.4g, Cholesterol 0mg, Protein 1g, Carbohydrate 4g, Dietary fiber 0g, Sodium 2mg, Omega-3 fatty acids 0g

Allowances: ¼ fat + 1¼ vegetables

ROASTED VEGETABLES

VEGETABLE

One member of the Rice Diet Forum shows us how she likes to prepare her vegetables. This dish is incredibly easy to prepare, and requires very little attention—just put this into the oven and let it go.

6 large whole mushrooms, wild or domestic

I cup yellow bell pepper, cored, then sliced lengthwise in ¼-inch-wide strips

I cup red bell pepper, cored, then sliced lengthwise in ¼-inch-wide strips

I red onion, or Vidalia onion if available, peeled and quartered

6 new potatoes, halved

2 small fennel bulbs, sliced ¼ inch thick

I medium zucchini or yellow crookneck squash, sliced lengthwise into ¼-inch-thick rounds

4 tomatoes, quartered

2 sweet potatoes, sliced into ⅛-inch-thick rounds

2 tablespoons extra-virgin olive oil

½ cup fresh herbs, minced (thyme, oregano, basil, and/or parsley)

Freshly ground black pepper, to taste

Preheat the oven to 375 degrees F.

Arrange the vegetables in a large baking dish. Sprinkle on the oil, herbs, and black pepper to taste, and toss to coat evenly. Bake, uncovered, for 30 minutes. Stir, then raise the oven temperature to 425 degrees F and roast for 15 minutes more.

Yield: 10 servings

Each serving contains approximately: Calories 105, Fat calories 35, Fat 4g, Saturated fat 0.5g, Cholesterol 0mg, Protein 2g, Carbohydrate 17g, Dietary fiber 4g, Sodium 43mg, Omega-3 fatty acids 0g

Allowances: ½ fat + ¾ starch + 1 vegetable

RYAN'S GRILLED VEGGIE SKEWERS   VEGETABLE

This is Ryan's favorite way to prepare vegetables. It's superquick and easy, as well as a real crowd-pleaser. You can impress your friends at a barbecue or serve it up at home. If you have a George Foreman Grill, this takes seconds to heat up and you're ready to go!

2 small red onions

2 medium zucchini

1 red bell pepper

1 green bell pepper

½ pound medium-size mushrooms

1 cup cherry tomatoes

¼ cup balsamic vinegar

Juice of one freshly squeezed lemon

Freshly ground black pepper, to taste

18 metal skewers or bamboo skewers, soaked in water

Chop the vegetables into uniform-size pieces, about 1-inch cubes. Place the veggies into a sealable container. Mix together the balsamic vinegar, lemon juice, and black pepper to taste, and pour over the vegetables. Cover and refrigerate for 30 minutes. Preheat your grill. Thread skewers with the marinated vegetables, place on the grill, and cook until they become tender, which takes only 6 to 8 minutes.

Yield: 6 servings, 3 skewers per serving

Each serving contains approximately: Calories 44, Fat calories 3, Fat 0g, Saturated fat 0g, Cholesterol 0mg, Protein 2g, Carbohydrate 10g, Dietary fiber 2g, Sodium 15mg, Omega-3 fatty acids 0.04g

Allowances: 1¾ vegetables

RYAN'S SWEET AND SPICY GREEN BEANS VEGETABLE

Ryan was trying to get tips for cooking class one night and was inspired to create this dish while watching Rachel Ray. The crisp of the green beans, crunch of the almonds, and sweet of the raisins just make a mouthful of this so satisfying.

I pound fresh green beans (approximately 4 cups), cut into thirds

¼ cup golden raisins

I tablespoon paprika, preferably a good smoked paprika such as
    Sweet Pimentón de la Vera ○

1½ teaspoons extra-virgin olive oil

2 tablespoons *Ryan's Roasted Toasted Almonds* (page 141)

Remove the ends from the green beans and snap into thirds. Place in a large pot with the golden raisins and boil for 10 to 12 minutes. Drain in a colander and place in a large bowl. Stir the paprika into the olive oil, then mix it into the green beans and raisins. Top with 2 tablespoons of the roasted toasted almonds for a mouthwatering crunch. Enjoy!

Yield: 4 servings

Each serving contains approximately: Calories 101, Fat calories 35, Fat 4g, Saturated fat 0.2g, Cholesterol 0mg, Protein 2g, Carbohydrate 16g, Dietary fiber 5g, Sodium 2mg, Omega-3 fatty acids 0g

Allowances: 1 fat + 1 vegetable + ½ fruit

SKILLET SENSATION

VEGETABLE

One of our Forum members gave us this recipe, and it's a great meal to put together quickly on the stove top. With very little preparation time, it comes together with ease. The flavors are an amazing combination. Just don't get carried away with the Romano cheese—a little can go a long way.

1 teaspoon extra-virgin olive oil

¼ cup chopped asparagus

¼ cup chopped baby carrots

7 grape tomatoes, halved

2 fresh basil leaves, chopped

1 large garlic clove, minced

1 tablespoon grated Romano cheese

Sauté all veggies until cooked, then add the basil, garlic, and cheese. This is great served over pasta!

Yield: 1 serving

Each serving contains approximately: Calories 122, Fat calories 50, Fat 6g, Saturated fat 1.1g, Cholesterol 1mg, Protein 5g, Carbohydrate 15g, Dietary fiber 5g, Sodium 59mg, Omega-3 fatty acids 0.04g

Allowances: 1 fat + 3 vegetables + ¼ dairy

SMOKY SWISS CHARD SAUTÉ

VEGETABLE

This recipe from Susan works well for any sturdy greens (collard, turnip, kale, or mustard). The Sweet Pimentón de la Vera adds the smoky flavor without the use of chemicals or smoked animal products. You can also use Hot Pimentón de la Vera (smoked paprika) made from hot peppers if you like *hot* foods.

¾ pound Swiss chard, stems removed

2 teaspoons extra-virgin olive oil

3 garlic cloves, minced

⅓ cup diced tomatoes, no salt added, preferably Eden Organic brand ○

½ teaspoon paprika, preferably Sweet Pimentón de la Vera ○

½ teaspoon fennel seeds

1 teaspoon red wine vinegar, preferably Badia a Coltibuono ○

Coarsely chop the chard. Bring 2 cups of water to a boil, put the chard leaves into a vegetable steamer, and cook over high heat until tender, about 8 minutes. Drain well.

Add the olive oil to a skillet and heat until simmering. Add the garlic cloves and cook over moderately high heat, stirring, until lightly browned. Drain the juice from the tomatoes and add the tomatoes to the garlic with the pimentón and cook for 2 minutes. Add the cooked chard, fennel seeds, and 2 tablespoon of water and cook over moderate heat for 2 to 3 minutes. Stir in the red wine vinegar, and serve.

Yield: 2 servings

Each serving contains approximately: Calories 85, Fat calories 45, Fat 5g, Saturated fat 0g, Cholesterol 0mg, Protein 1g, Carbohydrate 5g, Dietary fiber 1g, Sodium 132mg, Omega-3 fatty acids 0g

Allowances: 1 fat + 1½ vegetables

CUCUMBER SALAD   VEGETABLE

This refreshing salad is best when served cold and crisp. The flavors blend beautifully, and will give your taste buds something to talk about.

3 cucumbers, peeled and chopped

5 tomatoes, quartered

1 bunch green onions, chopped

9-ounce package frozen artichoke hearts, no salt added, preferably Birds Eye
    Frozen Deluxe ○

¼ cup white wine vinegar

1 tablespoon extra-virgin olive oil

1 teaspoon minced garlic

1 teaspoon Italian blend seasoning, preferably Cherchie's brand ○

Mix all ingredients together and serve. If you want to take the time to roast the artichokes first, they will, of course, be even better.

Yield: 4 servings

Each serving contains approximately: Calories 78, Fat calories 27, Fat 3g, Saturated fat 0.4g, Cholesterol 0mg, Protein 3g, Carbohydrate 12g, Dietary fiber 5g, Sodium 30mg, Omega-3 fatty acids 0.02g

Allowances: ¾ fat + 1¾ vegetables

JULIA'S HOLIDAY SALAD   VEGETABLE

Ryan's friend Julia contributed this dish, which she serves during the holidays. "This is a family favorite, spinach salad recipe. I make it on Christmas as a tradition now. It's well tested and always gets devoured!"

¼ cup minced onion

3 tablespoons apple cider vinegar

3 teaspoons white wine vinegar

1 tablespoon sesame seeds

¼ teaspoon paprika

2 tablespoons sugar

1 tablespoon extra-virgin olive oil

Freshly ground black pepper, to taste

2 tablespoons slivered almonds

10-ounce bag prewashed spinach

2 medium Granny Smith apples, quartered, cored, and thinly sliced

Combine the onion, cider vinegar, white wine vinegar, sesame seeds, and paprika in a small bowl. Mix in 1 tablespoon sugar. Gradually whisk in ½ tablespoon of olive oil.

Season the dressing to taste with black pepper. Heat the remaining olive oil in a skillet and add the almonds. Stir until the almonds begin to color, about 2 minutes. (Really watch them, they will burn quickly!) Sprinkle the remaining tablespoon sugar over the nuts. Stir until the sugar melts and begins to turn golden, about 2 minutes more. Transfer the almonds to a bowl and cool. The dressing and almonds can be prepared 4 hours ahead. Cover separately and let stand at room temperature.

Combine the spinach and apples in large bowl. Toss with enough dressing to coat, mix in the almonds, and serve. Any remaining dressing can be served separately.

Yield: 4 servings

Each serving contains approximately: Calories 136, Fat calories 68, Fat 7g, Saturated fat 0.7g, Cholesterol 0mg, Protein 4g, Carbohydrate 17g, Dietary fiber 3g, Sodium 62mg, Omega-3 fatty acids 0g

Allowances: 1¼ fats + 2 vegetables + ½ fruit

RED AND YELLOW TOMATO SALAD

VEGETABLE

This wonderful and colorful salad is simply delicious. It's quick to make and will please any palate—perfect for summer, when tomatoes are in season!

20 red grape tomatoes, halved

20 yellow grape tomatoes, halved

4 fresh basil leaves, chopped

1 teaspoon oregano, dried

⅛ teaspoon freshly ground black pepper

1 teaspoon minced garlic

¼ cup white wine vinegar

Juice of ½ lemon

1 teaspoon honey

Place all the ingredients in a large bowl, except for the honey. Mix well and chill for 30 to 40 minutes. Pour the honey over the tomato salad and mix well. Serve over a bed of greens.

Yield: 4 servings

Each serving contains approximately: Calories 42, Fat calories 5, Fat 1g, Saturated fat 0g, Cholesterol 0mg, Protein 2g, Carbohydrate 9g, Dietary fiber 2g, Sodium 24mg, Omega-3 fatty acids 0g

Allowances: 1¾ vegetables

SUMMER SALAD

VEGETABLE

I just love salad recipes. They are so tasty and quick to throw together! They also keep well, and the flavors intensify when they have been stored in an airtight container overnight.

½ cup no-salt-added canned garbanzo beans. drained, preferably
  Eden Organic brand ○
2 celery stalks, chopped
¼ cup shredded carrots
¼ cup raisins or halved red seedless grapes
¼ cup mandarin orange segments
2 tablespoons walnuts
2 tablespoons Consorzio's Mango Dressing ○
4 cups torn romaine lettuce

Put the ingredients into large bowl and toss to coat in the dressing.

Yield: 4 servings

Each serving contains approximately: Calories 104, Fat calories 28, Fat 3g, Saturated fat 0.3g, Cholesterol 0mg, Protein 4g, Carbohydrate 18g, Dietary fiber 4g, Sodium 39mg, Omega-3 fatty acids 0.4g

Allowances: ½ fat + ¼ starch + 1¼ vegetables + ½ fruit

SWEET BABY GREEN SALAD

VEGETABLE

Any variation of raw vegetables is the healthiest thing you can eat. The most important addition to this salad is the broccoli sprouts, which contain more anticancer compounds than any other food! Since discovering them and their great, refreshing crunch, I add them to almost every salad I make. *Salud!*

4 cups mixed baby greens, washed and dried

1 tablespoon extra-virgin olive oil

4 tablespoons balsamic vinegar

¼ cup shredded carrots

½ cup torn arugula

½ cup torn radicchio

10 strawberries, sliced

28 canned mandarin orange segments or 28 grape tomatoes

¼ cup coarsely chopped walnuts

½ cup broccoli florets

1 cup broccoli sprouts or clover sprouts

Mix all ingredients in a large bowl. Any of the ingredients can be adjusted up or down to taste except those that are higher in fat: the olive oil and walnuts.

Yield: 6 servings

Each serving contains approximately: Calories 80, Fat calories 38, Fat 4g, Saturated fat 0.5g, Cholesterol 0mg, Protein 2g, Carbohydrate 10g, Dietary fiber 2g, Sodium 21mg, Omega-3 fatty acids 0.2g

Allowances: ½ fat + 1 vegetable + ½ fruit

VANILLA VINAIGRETTE DRESSING WITH BOK CHOY SALAD

VEGETABLE

Our Rice Diet Forum respondents renew us daily. This recipe was posted by one of our participants after being inspired by following the *Rice Diet Solution* book at home. The flavor combination is unique and a wonderful complement to any meal.

1 teaspoon maple syrup

1 teaspoon vanilla extract

1 tablespoon white wine vinegar

1 tablespoon extra-virgin olive oil

1 head bok choy or cabbage, cut crosswise into thin ribbons

¼ cup golden raisins or currants

Mix the first 4 ingredients to make the vinaigrette dressing, and pour over the bok choy and raisins for a salad.

Yield: 2 servings

Each serving contains approximately: Calories 120, Fat calories 54, Fat 6g, Saturated fat 0.6g, Cholesterol 0mg, Protein 3g, Carbohydrate 14g, Dietary fiber 3g, Sodium 140mg, Omega-3 fatty acids 0.1g

Allowances: 1 fat + 1½ vegetables + ½ fruit

FRUITS

APPLE AND CELERY SALAD   FRUIT

Susan shares an age-old combo that tastes refreshingly new with gourmet mustard and walnut oil flavors. Once again, regular grocery store mustard and oil will work just fine, but after you've tasted this pairing with the real thing, your pantry won't be without these new ingredients.

2 teaspoons freshly squeezed lemon juice

2 teaspoons mustard, no salt added, preferably Téméraire Dijon Mustard ○

1½ teaspoons honey

1 teaspoon walnut oil, preferably L'Olivier Walnut Oil ○

2 celery stalks, leaves included

1 Granny Smith apple

Whisk together the lemon juice, mustard, honey, and oil. Thinly slice the celery stalks, and peel, core, and thinly slice the apple. Add the celery and apples to the bowl with the dressing and toss to coat.

Yield: 1 serving

Each serving contains approximately: Calories 143, Fat calories 50, Fat 6g, Saturated fat 0.4g, Cholesterol 0mg, Protein 1g, Carbohydrate 25g, Dietary fiber 3g, Sodium 45mg, Omega-3 fatty acids 0.5g

Allowances: 1 fat + 1½ fruits

CABERNET MEDLEY STRAWBERRY WALDORF SALAD

FRUIT

The chef from Indian Harvest inspired us with this recipe that we "tweaked" ever so slightly to make it Ricer friendly—now we can all enjoy it! This salad is best served chilled, and sealing it in a airtight container overnight brings out even more flavor. The apple cider vinegar and plain yogurt combination is a good "staple" for any salad that you might make. You could make this with carrots and raisins, if you prefer.

1 cup uncooked rice, preferably Indian Harvest Cabernet Medley ○

1 Granny Smith apple, cored and diced

Juice of ½ lemon

½ cup diced strawberries, preferably organic

½ cup diced celery

⅓ cup plain nonfat yogurt

3 tablespoons apple cider vinegar

2 tablespoons chopped walnuts

Bring 2 cups of water to a boil, and add the Cabernet Medley rice packet. Bring the water to a second boil, reduce the heat, cover, and simmer for 25 minutes. Remove from heat and let cool for 5 to 10 minutes more. Toss the diced apples with lemon juice to prevent browning. In a separate bowl, mix the strawberries, celery, yogurt, and apple cider vinegar until blended well. Toast the walnuts if desired. Combine all the ingredients and mix well. Chill before serving.

Yield: 4 servings

Each serving contains approximately: Calories 150, Fat calories 23, Fat 2g, Saturated fat 0.3g, Cholesterol 0.3mg, Protein 3g, Carbohydrate 30g, Dietary fiber 2g, Sodium 21mg, Omega-3 fatty acids 0.35g

Allowances: ½ fat + 1 starch + ¾ fruit

We chose Indian Harvest Cabernet Medley because it contains the interesting and flavorful combination of white and red rice, whole-grain rye, and barley. When experimenting with this recipe, try substituting other rice combinations for the Cabernet Medley. Our favorite rice blends are brown basmati, jasmine, and Black Pearl Medley.

FRUIT SALAD BY LIZ

FRUIT

This mix was given to us by our dear friend and fellow Ricer Liz. She was inspired to remake this creation when she was at a café, enjoying a fresh fruit salad on her rice and fruit day. "Here's a new way to enjoy fruit salad with a refreshing twist of flavors."

½ cup diced mango
½ cup diced strawberries
2 teaspoons chopped fresh mint leaves
Juice of ½ lemon

Mix all the ingredients in a large bowl. Transfer to a clear bowl or plate and garnish with a sprig of mint leaves. Try this dish by itself or use as a filling for a salt-free pita, toasted and sprinkled with cinnamon, and topped with *Yogurt Cheese* (see page 143).

Yield: 1 serving

Each serving contains approximately: Calories 87, Fat calories 4, Fat 0g, Saturated fat 0.1g, Cholesterol 0mg, Protein 1g, Carbohydrate 23g, Dietary fiber 3g, Sodium 3mg, Omega-3 fatty acids 0.1g

Allowances: 1½ fruits

BARLEY APPLE PUDDING

FRUIT

Pudding is not just for dessert anymore! Have it for breakfast or as a side of fruit to top off a meal. This pudding was inspired by a recipe from Tao Herb Farm. The barley's chewiness has great texture, but you can, of course, substitute other grains. Why not do yourself a favor and buy and experiment with barley soon?

½ cup cooked barley

2 cups apples, peeled and sliced

Juice of ½ lemon

⅓ cup orange juice

2 teaspoons canola oil

2 tablespoons maple syrup

½ teaspoon cinnamon

Boil the barley until the desired texture is achieved, following directions on the package (1½ hours for hulled barley, 50 minutes for pearled barley).

Preheat the oven to 350 degrees F. Arrange the apple slices to cover the bottom of a lightly greased baking dish. Drizzle lemon juice over the apples. Mix the remaining ingredients with the cooked barley and spoon over the apple slices. Bake for 30 minutes. Serve hot or cold.

Yield: 2 servings

Since barley has been shown to lower cholesterol and stabilize blood sugar (better than any food other than oats, oat bran, and dried beans), experiment with it often. Substitute it for pasta or any other grain—in soups, pilafs, and casseroles—its texture is to die for!

Each serving contains approximately: Calories 216, Fat calories 45, Fat 5g, Saturated fat 0.4g, Cholesterol 0mg, Protein 2g, Carbohydrate 44g, Dietary fiber 3g, Sodium 4mg, Omega-3 fatty acids 0.46g

Allowances: 1 fat + 1 starch + 1½ fruits

LIZ'S STRAWBERRY SALAD   FRUIT

Here's the spinach salad that we've all been waiting for! Thanks to Liz, our friend and fellow Ricer, we don't have to wait any longer. The berries are not overpoweringly sweet but make this garden-fresh mix absolutely mouthwatering.

1 cup baby spinach, washed and patted dry

⅓ cup strawberries, hulled and halved

⅓ cup blueberries

1 tablespoon *Wonderful Walnuts* (page 141)

1 tablespoon raspberry vinaigrette, preferably Consorzio Raspberry Balsamic
    Vinaigrette Dressing ○

Place the spinach in a large bowl. Top with the strawberries, blueberries, and walnuts, then add the dressing and toss.

Yield: 1 serving

Each serving contains approximately: Calories 104, Fat calories 47, Fat 5g, Saturated fat 0.5g, Cholesterol 0mg, Protein 2g, Carbohydrate 15g, Dietary fiber 4g, Sodium 40mg, Omega-3 fatty acids 0.7g

Allowances: 1 fat + ½ fruit + 1 vegetable

PINK LADIES FRUIT SALAD

Sometimes the best discoveries fall upon you when you least expect them! One night after work, the dietitians were sitting around chatting over a bowl of fruit. We had balsamic vinegar, strawberries, and watermelon, but never intended for this blend to catch us the way that it did!

2 cups strawberries, hulled and halved
1 tablespoon balsamic vinegar, preferably Villa Manodori Balsamic Vinegar ○
2 cups fresh watermelon, cut into chunks, chilled

Combine the strawberries and balsamic vinegar in an airtight container and refrigerate for 4 hours. Pour the strawberry mixture over the chilled watermelon and enjoy this delicious treat.

Yield: 4 servings

Each serving contains approximately: Calories 67, Fat calories 3, Fat 0g, Saturated fat 0.1g, Cholesterol 0mg, Protein 1g, Carbohydrate 17g, Dietary fiber 2g, Sodium 3mg, Omega 3-fatty acids 0.1g

Allowances: 1 fruit

We recommend Villa Manodori balsamic vinegar because of the intensely sweet flavor of this aged balsamic. So if you're using a grocery store brand of balsamic vinegar, you may need to add a tablespoon of powdered sugar.

PLANTAINS WITH MOJO

FRUIT

This recipe was a little new for us southern folk in the Carolinas. If you are not used to having your fruit with a kick, I encourage you to keep an open mind! Skip over this one, and you'll be missing out!

2 unpeeled green plantains
2 garlic cloves, peeled and minced
½ red or yellow onion, diced
1 teaspoon extra-virgin olive oil
Juice of 1 lime or lemon
1 tablespoon chopped fresh cilantro

Rinse the plantains and cut into 1-inch slices, leaving the skin on. Place the plantains in a saucepan, cover with water or vegetable broth, and cook for about 30 minutes, or until soft. Peel the skin off the plantains, then quarter the slices. Set to the side. To make your mojo, sauté the garlic and onion in olive oil until translucent; do not let it brown. Add the lime or lemon juice and the cilantro, and remove from heat. Stir the mojo sauce into the plantains and serve.

Yield: 4 servings

Each serving contains approximately: Calories 132, Fat calories 14, Fat 2g, Saturated fat 0.3g, Cholesterol 0mg, Protein 2g, Carbohydrate 32g, Dietary fiber 3g, Sodium 5mg, Omega-3 fatty acids 0g

Allowances: ¼ fat + 1¼ starches + ½ vegetable

ENTRÉES

SOUPS

STARCHES

FISH AND SEAFOOD

CHICKEN

VEGETARIAN PROTEIN

SOUPS

COUSCOUS VEGGIE SOUP
STARCH

This is another Forum contribution that was a great find. You can add more couscous if you want it to be more stewlike. This is so good, and the chipotle and curry together are yum!! If Mrs. Dash chipotle seasoning is not available, chipotles (which are smoked jalapeños) would impart this great flavor; otherwise jalapeños would work.

1 cup red and yellow bell pepper, halved and sliced lengthwise into strips
½ cup onion, chopped
1 cup sliced mushrooms
1 teaspoon extra-virgin olive oil
3 cups vegetable broth, salt free, preferably using Rapunzel's Vegan, No Salt Added,
    Vegetable Bouillon ○
1 teaspoon garlic powder
2 teaspoons curry powder
½ teaspoon Mrs. Dash chipotle seasoning
½ cup couscous
¼ cup frozen peas

In a medium saucepan, sauté the peppers, onion, and mushrooms in olive oil. When softened, add in the vegetable broth and spices. Stir well and bring to a boil. Then add the couscous and peas, turn off the heat, cover, and wait 5 minutes. Stir and enjoy!

Yield: 3 servings

Each serving contains approximately: Calories 188, Fat calories 37, Fat 4g, Saturated fat 0.3g, Cholesterol 0mg, Protein 8g, Carbohydrate 31g, Dietary fiber 4g, Sodium 136mg, Omega-3 fatty acids 0.04g

Allowances: ¼ fat + 1¼ starches + 3 vegetables

The Forum is a free online bulletin board on the Rice Diet Web site (www.ricediet.com). On the Forum, fellow Ricers share ideas, problems, support, and successes—and obviously recipes!

DR. ROSATI'S BORLOTTI BEAN SOUP STARCH

My husband, Bob, makes this soup at home, and it is absolutely wonderful. You'll have your best chances at finding borlotti beans at an authentic Italian store. If you have trouble, canned aduki beans (no salt added, preferably Eden Organic brand) may be used as well.

Two 15-ounce cans borlotti beans or aduki beans, no salt added, preferably Eden
    Organic brand ○
1 medium potato, chopped
1 medium onion, chopped
1 celery stalk, chopped
6 carrots, chopped
1 large bunch of kale leaves, stemmed and shredded
8-ounce can diced tomatoes, no salt added
1 fresh or dried bay leaf
2 fresh sage leaves or ¼ teaspoon dried
1 fresh rosemary sprig
¼ cup chopped flat-leaf parsley
6 garlic cloves, minced
½ cup pearled barley
3 anchovies
1 teaspoon freshly ground black pepper

In a large stockpot, combine one can of beans, vegetables, herbs, and garlic with 2 quarts of water. Bring to a boil and then reduce to a simmer. To enrich the soup's flavor, purée the other can of beans and add to stockpot.

Meanwhile, rinse and add the barley, along with the anchovies and black pepper, to taste, to the bean soup and cook for 1 hour more, or until the barley is very tender.

Yield: 6 servings

Each serving contains approximately: Calories 166, Fat calories 11, Fat 1g, Saturated fat 0.2g, Cholesterol 6mg, Protein 9g, Carbohydrate 33g, Dietary fiber 8g, Sodium 69mg, Omega-3 fatty acids 0.2g

Allowances: 1½ starches + 2 vegetables

STARCHES

FREGOLE WITH ROASTED VEGETABLES   STARCH

Fregole was our best culinary discovery last year. Fregole is from Sardinia. It is extra-large couscous, or round wheat pasta, that has been toasted. It can be cooked like pasta (in boiling water and then drained) or like risotto (stirred as a flavorful broth is added). At this time, fregole can be found only in Italian specialty stores or the Rice Diet Store, but it's still well worth the effort to try it. Your food-snob friends will be amazed you're eating this without adding sodium! If you have a difficult time finding fregole, Israeli couscous is a larger pasta that is toasted, and has a taste similar to fregole's. Either way, you are in for a treat!

2 red onions, peeled and cut into eight wedges

4 teaspoons rosemary-infused olive oil, preferably Villa Manodori brand ○

4 large portobello mushroom caps

2 garlic cloves, thinly sliced

1 cube vegetable bouillon, no salt added, preferably Rapunzel Vegan, No Salt Added, Vegetable Bouillon ○

2 cups water

1 cup fregole

2 tablespoons minced fresh chives

Preheat the oven to 450 degrees F.

In a roasting pan, toss the onion wedges with rosemary-infused oil. In a separate roasting pan, toss the mushrooms with the rosemary-infused oil. Place both roasting pans in the oven for 15 minutes. Remove the mushrooms from the oven and set aside. Add the garlic to the onions and return to the oven for 5 minutes more.

Dissolve the broth cube in 2 cups of boiling water. Add 2 teaspoons of the rosemary-infused oil to the saucepan and heat. Add the fregole and toss it well in the oil. Add ½ cup of broth and continue to cook until the broth evaporates. Add the broth, a ladleful at a time, as required, as if making risotto, stirring all the time. Cook the fregole until it is soft but still has a slight bite, 8 to 10 minutes. Toss in the minced chives. Serve about ½ cup fregole with 1 portobello mushroom cap and some of the onions and garlic to each person.

Yield: 4 servings (½ cup fregole, 1 mushroom per serving)

Each serving contains approximately: Calories 171, Fat calories 54, Fat 6g, Saturated fat 0.8g, Cholesterol 0mg, Protein 6g, Carbohydrate 24g, Dietary fiber 3g, Sodium 53mg, Omega-3 fatty acids 0g

Allowances: 1 fat + ¾ starch + 2½ vegetables

When using an infused oil, be sure to consider the quality of the olive oil itself. At 45 calories per teaspoon, you will want to get the best taste for the calorie load.

GREEK PITA

STARCH

If you want to take this to work or school, this meal is easy to prep ahead of time. Just store the "filling" in a separate container and fill your pita whenever you're ready.

2 tablespoons *Yogurt Cheese* (page 143) or nonfat yogurt

I teaspoon garlic, minced

I cup shredded lettuce

½ cucumber, diced

½ cup diced tomatoes

¼ cup minced red onion

I tablespoon chopped fresh mint leaves

I serving *Eilene's Pita or Pocket Bread* (or other salt-free, whole wheat pita bread or wrap)

In the blender, mix the yogurt and garlic. Stuff the lettuce, cucumber, tomato, onion, and mint into a pita bread or wrap. Pour the yogurt sauce over the salad and enjoy! *Yummy!*

Yield: 1 serving

Each serving contains approximately: Calories 198, Fat calories 25, Fat 3g, Saturated fat 0.3g, Cholesterol 1mg, Protein 8g, Carbohydrate 38g, Dietary fiber 6g, Sodium 32mg, Omega 3-fatty acids 0.08g

Allowances: ½ fat + 1 starch + 2 vegetables + ¼ dairy

MOCK MACARONI AND CHEESE   STARCH

Susan and her husband, Jay, have created a Rice Diet variation on a common vegan dish. Because of the fat content, they suggest that you make only enough servings for one meal—it is way too easy to eat more than one portion. If you are feeding more than one person, this recipe multiplies with great success.

1 teaspoon almond butter, no salt added

¼ teaspoon sesame oil

½ teaspoon nutritional yeast

Juice of ½ lemon

¾ cup pasta, cooked

Preheat the oven to 350 degrees F.

Mix all the ingredients, except for the pasta, adding water and lemon juice to taste. Set aside. Cook and drain the pasta. Mix the pasta with the sauce, put into a baking dish, and bake for 15 minutes. You can substitute cauliflower for the pasta with great results.

Yield: 1 serving

Each serving contains approximately: Calories 217, Fat calories 47, Fat 5g, Saturated fat 0.7g, Cholesterol 0mg, Protein 7g, Carbohydrate 36g, Dietary fiber 2g, Sodium 2mg, Omega-3 fatty acids 0.05g

Allowances: 1 fat + 2 starches

Nutritional yeast is a wonderful way to enhance both flavor and nutritional value. It is an excellent source of protein, as well as rich in vitamins, especially B-complex and folic acid.

QUICK CAULIFLOWER AND GARBANZO CURRY STARCH

Susan was inspired by the wonderful meals with garbanzo beans, lentils, and cauliflower that she has found served in vegetarian Indian restaurants. She says that using the "shortcut" of adding Mr. Spice Indian Curry Sauce may not result in the same complexity as a recipe with twice the ingredients, but it has the advantage of less shopping and preparation time with very tasty results.

Half a 15-ounce can garbanzo beans, no salt added, preferably Eden's
    Organic brand ○
½ onion, diced
2 garlic cloves, minced
½ jalapeño pepper, seeded and minced
2 tablespoons Mr. Spice Indian Curry Sauce ○
Cauliflower florets, ½ head
¼ teaspoon freshly ground black pepper
1 tablespoon Ginger People Sweet Ginger Chili ○

Drain the beans and reserve the liquid. Heat 2 tablespoons of bean juice in a wok or skillet. Stir in the onion, garlic, and jalapeño and cook for 5 minutes. Add Mr. Spice Indian Curry Sauce and the cauliflower, cover, and cook for 10 minutes. Add the garbanzo beans and black pepper, stir well, cover, and cook for 10 minutes more. Add more bean juice or water if liquid is needed. Serve with Sweet Ginger Chili as a condiment.

Yield: 2 servings

Each serving contains approximately: Calories 172, Fat calories 8, Fat 1g, Saturated fat 0.03g, Cholesterol 0mg, Protein 8g, Carbohydrate 34g, Dietary fiber 7g, Sodium 54mg, Omega-3 fatty acids 0.05g

Allowances: 1½ starches + 2 vegetables

Any sweet and spicy sauce would be a good replacement for the Sweet Ginger Chili. Remember to read the label, though; surprisingly high sodium content is often found in sweet products.

RACHELLE'S FRIED RICE

STARCH

Rachelle, our former dietitian and very dear friend, created this recipe for cooking class. She writes, "Here is a healthy fried rice recipe that uses the smokiness of Spanish paprika to replace the bacon of yore. Also, the green onions, peas, and toasted sesame oil merge together beautifully for a quick and tasty dinner dish."

1 tablespoon canola oil

1 medium red onion, chopped

Hot Spanish paprika to taste, preferably Hot Pimentón de la Vera ○

3 cups long-grain white rice, cooked and cooled to room temperature

7 to 8 large shrimp, peeled, deveined, and cut into thirds

1 teaspoon low-sodium Worcestershire sauce, preferably Angostura ⊙

1 cup frozen peas, no salt added

Freshly ground black pepper, to taste

1 whole egg plus 1 egg white, lightly beaten

3 large green onions, sliced

1½ teaspoons toasted sesame oil

This recipe goes fast, so you need to have everything prepared before you start cooking. Prepare all the ingredients and set aside in individual bowls. Heat the canola oil in a small wok or skillet. Sauté the onions for a few minutes in the canola oil, then add the paprika. Add the rice and stir-fry it for a minute or two (be sure to mix well).

Add the shrimp and cook until they turn pink in color, 2 to 3 minutes. Drizzle in the Worcestershire sauce and stir a few times. Fold in the peas, season with black pepper to taste, and allow to heat through. Pour in about half of the beaten eggs and mix gently until the egg begins to cook through. Repeat with the remaining egg mixture. Fold in the green onions and just heat through. Remove the skillet from the heat and drizzle on up to 1½ teaspoons of toasted sesame oil.

Yield: 6 servings

Each serving contains approximately: Calories 282, Fat calories 63, Fat 7g, Saturated fat 1.1g, Cholesterol 72mg, Protein 10g, Carbohydrate 43g, Dietary fiber 3g, Sodium 95mg, Omega-3 fatty acids 0.41g

Allowances: ½ fat + 2 starches + ½ vegetable + ¾ protein

RACHELLE'S WILD MUSHROOM RISOTTO STARCH

We used this recipe in a cooking class and were able to concoct a creamy and satisfying version of risotto without the use of dairy products and with little added fat. This is a gorgeous meal, and totally within the Rice Diet guidelines.

1 tablespoon extra-virgin olive oil

2 shallots, minced

1 pound wild mushrooms

1 cup Arborio rice

5 cups vegetable stock, no salt added, preferably Rapunzel's Vegan,
   No Salt Added Vegetable Bouillon ⊙

1½ tablespoons nutritional yeast

1 to 2 tablespoons minced chives

Heat the oil in a large, heavy saucepan over medium heat. Sauté the shallots for about 1 minute. Add all the mushrooms and cook for about 5 minutes, without allowing the liquid to evaporate completely. Add the Arborio rice and cook for about 1 minute. Add 1 cup of the vegetable stock and simmer strongly, stirring frequently, until the liquid is absorbed. Continue to add broth, ½ to 1 cup at a time, stirring frequently along the way, until the liquid is absorbed. Repeat until the rice is swollen and tender and the mixture is creamy, about 20 minutes. Top with the nutritional yeast and chives.

Yield: 6 servings

Each serving contains approximately: Calories 186, Fat calories 42, Fat 5g, Saturated fat 0.4g, Cholesterol 0mg, Protein 8g, Carbohydrate 31g, Dietary fiber 2g, Sodium 112mg, Omega-3 fatty acids 0.02g

Allowances: ½ fat + 1½ starches + 1¾ vegetables

ELIZABETH'S BLACK AND BLUE TACOS   STARCH

A word from our friend and fellow Ricer Elizabeth: "After cooking just about every recipe from Kitty's first two books, I was more than happy to contribute a recipe to her latest endeavor. So many of those foods have become staples for me. In fact, I use her 'Boss' Black Beans in this favorite."

4 corn taco shells with no salt or hydrogenated fat added, preferably Garden of
  Eatin' Blue Corn Taco Shells

1 cup cooked rice, such as brown or Texmati

1 cup canned black beans, no salt added, preferably Eden Organic brand

1 cup leaf lettuce, shredded

½ cup chopped onion

½ cup *Yogurt Cheese* (strained nonfat plain yogurt) (see page 143)

½ cup salsa, no salt added, preferably Enrico's No Salt Added Salsa ○

Prepare the taco shells according to package directions.

Combine the rice and beans. For each shell add the following: ½ cup bean and rice mixture, 4 tablespoons lettuce, 2 tablespoons onion, 2 tablespoons yogurt cheese, and 2 tablespoons of salsa.

Yield: 4 servings (1 taco per serving)

Each serving contains approximately: Calories 204, Fat calories 36, Fat 4g, Saturated fat 0.3g, Cholesterol 0.6mg, Protein 7g, Carbohydrate 34g, Dietary fiber 5g, Sodium 56mg, Omega-3 fatty acids 0.01g

Allowances: ¾ fat + 2 starches + ¼ vegetable

• We love the crunchy Blue Corn Taco Shells; but if you can't find these no-salt-added shells, you may want to look for low-sodium flour tortillas.

• Enrico's is one of our favorite salsas. Be mindful when shopping, because the company makes the same salsa with added salt. Desert Pepper Peach Mango Salsa is another alternative.

MEXICAN LETTUCE WRAPS

STARCH

It's a taco without the taco! When we are portioning our starches (or we're out of salt-free tacos), this wrap-up is a good way to leave out the shell without leaving out the taco!

15-ounce can black beans, no salt added, preferably Eden Organic brand ○
¼ avocado, peeled and chopped
½ cup chopped tomatoes
¼ cup chopped cucumber
Juice of ½ lime
Chili powder, no salt added, to taste
1 bunch fresh cilantro, chopped
8 crisp lettuce leaves, washed and thoroughly dried
3 tablespoons salsa, no salt added, preferably Enrico's No Salt Added Salsa ○

Mix all ingredients (except for lettuce and salsa) in a large bowl. Ladle ¼ cup of mixture onto middle of lettuce leaf, top with some salsa, and roll.

Yield: 2 servings

Each serving contains approximately: Calories 240, Fat calories 35, Fat 4g, Saturated fat 0.6g, Cholesterol 0mg, Protein 14g, Carbohydrate 42g, Dietary fiber 14g, Sodium 113mg, Omega-3 fatty acids 0.17g

Allowances: 1 fat + 2¼ starches + 1 vegetable

Of course this recipe is ripe for all sorts of substitutions like *Kitty's Refried Beans* in place of black beans. If you have your own homemade salsa, that's even better!

REFRIED BEAN AND ROASTED PEPPER LETTUCE WRAP

STARCH

Are you in the mood for a little Mexican food? Susan's wrap will do the trick with the freshest ingredients this side of the border.

2 red bell peppers

15-ounce can refried beans, low fat, no salt added, preferably Bearitos brand ○

½ cup salsa, no salt added, preferably Enrico's Hot Chunky Salsa ○

Juice of 1 lime

2 tablespoons chopped fresh cilantro

1 jalapeño pepper, seeded and minced

8 crisp lettuce leaves, washed and thoroughly dried

2 green onions, chopped

Preheat oven to 400 degrees F.

Cut the peppers into quarters and remove the stem, seeds, and ribs. Place on a baking sheet and roast in the oven for 20 minutes. Flip the peppers to the opposite side and roast for an additional 15 minutes; the skin should be black in most places. Keep the peppers in a closed container for 15 minutes. Steaming the peppers in this way will allow you to peel away the skin easily.

In a medium bowl, mix the beans, salsa, lime juice, cilantro, and jalapeño to taste. Assemble the wraps by placing one-eighth of the bean mixture, a piece of pepper, and a sprinkle of green onion in a lettuce leaf. Wrap around filling and enjoy!

Yield: 2 servings

Each serving contains approximately: Calories 306, Fat calories 41, Fat 4g, Saturated fat 0.1g, Cholesterol 0mg, Protein 14g, Carbohydrate 57g, Dietary fiber 19g, Sodium 156mg, Omega-3 fatty acids 0.03g

Allowances: 3 starches + 3 vegetables

RICE HOUSE TACOS

STARCH

This is a big hit down at the Rice House, impressive in taste, as well as presentation. Just how do they do it? Here you go . . .

6 salt-free corn taco shells

MEAT SAUCE

½ onion, diced

I large tomato, diced

½ green bell pepper, diced

½ red bell pepper, diced

2 tablespoons garlic, minced

Freshly ground black pepper, to taste

I teaspoon ground cumin

I teaspoon chili powder, no salt added

I teaspoon extra-virgin olive oil

I cup water

I ounce tomato paste, salt free

¼ cup textured vegetable protein (TVP) ○

SPANISH RICE

½ onion, diced

½ green bell pepper, diced

I large tomato, diced

I teaspoon extra-virgin olive oil

2 tablespoons tomato purée, salt free

3 cups cooked rice

TACO SALAD

1 small head iceberg lettuce, shredded

1 large tomato, diced

½ onion, diced

½ red bell pepper, diced

½ green bell pepper, diced

¼ cup red wine vinaigrette

1 teaspoon minced garlic

Pinch of freshly ground black pepper

1 tablespoon chopped fresh cilantro

To make the sauce: Sauté the vegetables and spices in the olive oil until tender. Add the water and tomato paste and bring to a boil. Add the TVP, turn off the heat and let sit.

To make the Spanish rice: Sauté the vegetables in olive oil until tender. Add the tomato purée and rice. Mix well (feel free to add a little water if your rice seems too dry).

Place all the ingredients for the salad in a large bowl. Add the red wine vinaigrette, minced garlic, black pepper, and fresh cilantro. Set aside.

After the meat sauce, Spanish rice, and taco salad are made, fill the taco shells with ⅙ of the Spanish rice topped with meat sauce and the taco salad. *Kitty's Refried Beans* could easily replace the meat sauce for a taco variation.

Yield: 6 servings

Each serving contains approximately: Calories 266, Fat calories 50, Fat 6g, Saturated fat 0.1g, Cholesterol 0mg, Protein 8g, Carbohydrate 46g, Dietary fiber 6g, Sodium 23mg, Omega-3 fatty acids 0.14g

Allowances: 2¼ starches + 1½ vegetables + ½ protein + ½ fat

RICE HOUSE TWO-BEAN CHILI

STARCH

Who doesn't love a good hearty chili on a cool day? This recipe makes a lot, but it keeps well. Put it in an airtight container, and you can throw it in the refrigerator or freeze it.

7 to 10 cups water

18 ounces dried white navy beans

18 ounces dried black beans

1 small Vidalia onion, finely diced

½ cup frozen corn kernels

¼ cup diced red bell pepper

½ cup diced green bell pepper

¼ cup diced fresh tomatoes

1 teaspoon honey

1 teaspoon black pepper

1 teaspoon chili powder, no salt added

1 teaspoon ground cumin

Place the water and beans in a large pot and boil until tender (about 1½ to 2 hours). Add all the other ingredients and mix well. Let simmer 15 to 20 minutes over low heat.

Yield: 14 servings

Each serving contains approximately: Calories 220, Fat calories 6, Fat 1g, Saturated fat 0g, Cholesterol 0mg, Protein 14g, Carbohydrate 41g, Dietary fiber 13g, Sodium 30mg, Omega-3 fatty acids 0g

Allowances: 2½ starches + ¼ vegetable

RICE AND RYE

Here's another gem from Susan. She comments, "I made this dish for the first time for a group of seventy-five neighbors. I was concerned that it might be a little *too* healthy as a buffet offering. Wasn't I surprised when every grain was gone by the end of the meal? Here is the same recipe reduced to an appropriate quantity for home use. If you have any left over, it will keep well, stored in an airtight container. Bring to room temperature before serving."

4 large carrots, diced
1 tablespoon extra-virgin olive oil
½ cup brown rice
½ cup whole-grain rye (rye berries)
1 to 2 tablespoons caraway seeds, slightly crushed

Preheat the oven to 400 degrees F.

Toss the diced carrots with oil in a shallow baking pan and roast for 20 minutes, or until tender. Cook the rice and rye together in a rice cooker following the manufacturer's directions for rice-to-water ratio. Toss the cooked rice and rye with the roasted carrots and caraway seeds. Serve at room temperature.

Yield: 4 servings

Each serving contains approximately: Calories 220, Fat calories 45, Fat 5g, Saturated fat 0.6g, Cholesterol 0mg, Protein 6g, Carbohydrate 40g, Dietary fiber 6g, Sodium 44mg, Omega-3 fatty acids 0.03g

Allowances: 1 fat + 2 starches + 1 vegetable

YUMMY BROWN RICE SALAD   STARCH

This dish came to us from the Rice Diet Forum. The creator of this recipe has found that if it sits for over an hour, the flavors really meld together.

2⅔ cups cooked brown rice

½ cup chopped cooked chicken breast

½ large red bell pepper, finely diced

1 stalk celery, finely chopped

3 to 4 green onions, finely chopped

½ green apple, diced

2 tablespoons chopped walnuts

Juice of ½ lemon

¼ cup apple cider vinegar

1 tablespoon extra-virgin olive oil

Mix it all up and enjoy!

Yield: 4 servings

Each serving contains approximately: Calories 295, Fat calories 69, Fat 7g, Saturated fat 0.9g, Cholesterol 17mg, Protein 12g, Carbohydrate 46g, Dietary fiber 5g, Sodium 41mg, Omega-3 fatty acids 0.4g

Allowances: 1¼ fats + 2 starches + ½ vegetable + ¼ fruit + ½ protein

FISH AND SEAFOOD

BILLIE'S FLOUNDER IN LEMON REDUCTION

This recipe is an easy, quick, and delicious way to include fish in your week's menu. You can use flounder or any fresh white fish—all you need on hand is a few lemons and white wine!

3 lemons, halved and seeded
½ cup dry white wine
6 ounces flounder fillet, washed and patted dry

Preheat the oven to 425 degrees F.

    Squeeze the lemons into a shallow baking dish, and add the white wine. Then place the fish in the dish; the liquid should almost cover the fish. Cover the dish with aluminum foil and bake in the preheated oven for 12 to 15 minutes. The fish is done when it separates easily with the touch of a fork. Remove the dish from oven and place the fish on a serving plate. Pour the liquid into a shallow sauté pan and heat on the stove top, letting it reduce by half, then pour over the fish just before serving.

Yield: 1 serving

Each serving contains approximately: Calories 220, Fat calories 27, Fat 3g, Saturated fat 0.6g, Cholesterol 82mg, Protein 36g, Carbohydrate 35g, Dietary fiber 16g, Sodium 147mg, Omega-3 fatty acids 0.6g

Allowances: 4 proteins

DEBBIE'S BAKED OR GRILLED TILAPIA

PROTEIN

Debbie, part of the Rice Diet extended family, donates this recipe as her family's favorite beach meal! You don't have to use this method for just tilapia—grouper or orange roughy can be used with it as well.

2 6-ounce tilapia fillets

1 teaspoon freshly ground black pepper

1 tablespoon grated lemon zest, preferably organic

1 lemon, sliced into rounds

Place the fish on a sheet of nonstick aluminum foil. If baking in the oven, preheat the oven to 350 degrees F and place foil on a broiler pan. If grilling, preheat the grill and place the aluminum foil directly on grill.

Puncture slits in the foil to match the slits on the grill or broiler pan. Sprinkle the fish with the pepper and lemon zest, then place lemon slices on top. You could add a sprig of fresh dill under the lemon or, for a different twist, use lime and cilantro. Grill or bake for 30 minutes, or until the fish flakes easily.

Serve with your favorite rice dish and *Ryan's Grilled Veggie Skewers* (see page 200) for a quick-and-easy meal.

Yield: 2 servings

Each serving contains approximately: Calories 180, Fat calories 28, Fat 4g, Saturated fat 1g, Cholesterol 86mg, Protein 36g, Carbohydrate 8g, Dietary fiber 4g, Sodium 90mg, Omega-3 fatty acids 0.22g

Allowance: 3½ proteins

GRILLED MONKFISH WITH
ORANGE-ROSEMARY RELISH

PROTEIN

This marinade is composed of the freshest ingredients, thus creating one of the best finfish recipes we've found.

3 oranges, peeled and cut into segments (all membranes removed)

Juice of 1 lemon, preferably organic

1 teaspoon chopped fresh rosemary

1½ pounds monkfish

1 tablespoon extra-virgin olive oil

Freshly ground black pepper, to taste

1 tablespoon grated lemon zest, preferably organic

Preheat the grill to medium heat.

To make the orange relish, combine the orange sections in a mixing bowl with the lemon juice and rosemary and set aside. (This can be made in advance and stored in the refrigerator for up to a day or two. The relish should be served at room temperature.)

Brush the monkfish with oil and season with the black pepper and lemon zest. Place the fish on the grill and cook 10 to 12 minutes, turning once, then cooking until the fish flakes easily when tested with a fork. Top with the orange relish and serve immediately.

Yield: 4 servings

Each serving contains approximately: Calories 240, Fat calories 58, Fat 6g, Saturated fat 1.2g, Cholesterol 42mg, Protein 26g, Carbohydrate 20g, Dietary fiber 5g, Sodium 33mg, Omega-3 fatty acids 0.04g

Allowances: ¾ fat + 3½ proteins + ½ fruit

PAN-SEARED SEA SCALLOPS PROTEIN

It's true, finfish are a better choice than shellfish, in part, because of the higher cholesterol and sodium content in shellfish. But scallops are very low in saturated fat, and most people really enjoy them. If you want to spice up your seafood repertoire, this is a great one to throw into the mix!

5 jumbo "dry" sea scallops
Freshly ground black pepper, to taste
1 teaspoon extra-virgin olive oil
Juice of ½ lemon
1 tablespoon pesto, no salt added, preferably Racconto Traditional Basil Pesto ○
2 whole, fresh sage leaves
Lemon wedges for serving

Heat a nonstick pan until smoking. Season the scallops with pepper. When the pan is smoking, place the scallops in the dry pan; do not turn them! You want to sear the scallops well. After about 5 minutes, remove the pan from the heat and turn the scallops. Pour in the olive oil, lemon juice, pesto, and sage leaves, which will fry in the hot oil. Place the scallops onto your plate, top with lemon and herb juices, and serve with lemon wedges.

Yield: 1 serving

Each serving contains approximately: Calories 190, Fat calories 52, Fat 6g, Saturated fat 0.7g, Cholesterol 37mg, Protein 21g, Carbohydrate 13g, Dietary fiber 2g, Sodium 193mg, Omega-3 fatty acids 0.26g

Allowances: 1½ fats + 2 proteins

RYAN'S CRISPY FISH STICKS

PROTEIN

Many people struggle to find recipes that can be enjoyed by everyone in the family. This family favorite is "Ricer friendly" and loved by kids and grown-ups alike! Eat these by themselves, or take Susan's advice and stuff them in a fish taco full of fresh veggies and salsa (no salt added, of course).

2 cups shredded wheat, salt free

1 tablespoon paprika, preferably Sweet Pimentón de la Vera ○,

    or 1 teaspoon chili powder, no salt added

1 tablespoon garlic powder

¼ teaspoon freshly ground black pepper

8 ounces tilapia fillet, cut into strips

3 tablespoons honey mustard dressing, no salt added, preferably Honeycup

    Mustard Dressing ○

Preheat oven to 400 degrees F.

Crush the shredded wheat with a rolling pin to yield 1 cup. Place in a large mixing bowl, then add the spices. Coat the fish strips in the mustard dressing, then roll in the cereal mixture to coat evenly. Place on a shallow nonstick baking sheet and bake for 12 to 15 minutes, or until the strips are opaque.

Yield: 2 servings

Each serving contains approximately: Calories 239, Fat calories 20, Fat 3g, Saturated fat 0.7g, Cholesterol 57mg, Protein 26g, Carbohydrate 31g, Dietary fiber 3g, Sodium 62mg, Omega-3 fatty acids 0.14g

Allowances: 1 starch + 3 proteins

THREE-PEPPER SNAPPER   PROTEIN

One way to develop a recipe is to think of things that you have liked from other dishes, and experiment! This method of baking fish came together much that way. As long as you have a cabinet stocked with staple items that you use frequently (peppers, onions, olive oil, veggie stock, and wine), you can just play with variations of a dish and create your own. We'll lend you this one for a springboard!

3 medium sweet onions, sliced crosswise into rings

1 pound red snapper fillets

2 medium red bell peppers, sliced crosswise into rings

2 medium green bell peppers, sliced crosswise into rings

1 tablespoon extra-virgin olive oil

⅛ teaspoon freshly ground black pepper, to taste

¾ cup vegetable stock, salt free, preferably using Rapunzel's Vegan, No Salt Added
    Vegetable Bouillon ○

½ cup dry white wine

1 to 2 garlic cloves, minced

Fresh parsley sprigs, to garnish

Preheat the oven to 350 degrees F.

Place the sliced onions in bottom of a 13 × 9 × 2-inch baking dish; arrange the red snapper fillets over the onions. Then arrange the bell pepper rings over the fillets. Combine the olive oil, pepper, bouillon, white wine, and garlic and pour over the fish. Bake for 25 to 30 minutes. Garnish with fresh parsley sprigs; toasted slivered almonds could be another topping variation.

Yield: 4 servings

Each serving contains approximately: Calories 202, Fat calories 49, Fat 5g, Saturated fat 0.8g, Cholesterol 31mg, Protein 20g, Carbohydrate 18g, Dietary fiber 4g, Sodium 86mg, Omega-3 fatty acids 0.35g

Allowances: ¾ fat + 3 proteins + ½ vegetable

ANGELA'S GRILLED SALMON WITH CILANTRO-TOMATO SAUCE

PROTEIN

We have been blessed to have Angela, our dear friend and Ricer, pass down her wisdom from the kitchen. It seems that every dish to come out of her house receives an overwhelming stamp of approval!

1 tablespoon extra-virgin olive oil

1 large onion, chopped

4 garlic cloves, minced

28-ounce can whole tomatoes, no salt added, drained and chopped

1 pound mushrooms, thinly sliced

1 jalapeño pepper, seeded and minced

2 tablespoons red wine vinegar, preferably Badia a Coltibuono ○

½ bunch fresh cilantro, chopped

Juice of 1 lemon

16 ounces wild Atlantic salmon

Preheat your grill.

Heat the oil in a large skillet and sauté the onion and garlic. Next, add the chopped tomatoes and simmer for about 20 minutes. Add the mushrooms, jalapeño, vinegar, and cilantro and simmer for an additional 10 minutes until tender, adding the lemon juice as the last step. Grill the salmon to your liking and top with sauce.

Yield: 4 servings

Each serving contains approximately: Calories 301, Fat calories 103, Fat 11g, Saturated fat 1.6g, Cholesterol 62mg, Protein 23g, Carbohydrate 23g, Dietary fiber 7g, Sodium 95mg, Omega-3 fatty acids 2g

Allowances: ¾ fat + 3 proteins + 4 vegetables

SALMON WITH SUMMER SALSA   PROTEIN

We have another blue-ribbon winner from our recipe tasting—the dietitians and interns were fighting over this one tooth and nail! This is such a refreshing and versatile meal! You can make the salsa ahead of time, keep it in the fridge, and take it with you to a BBQ or picnic to add as soon as your salmon is hot off the grill. You can also use it for a snack with salt-free corn tortilla chips.

2 ripe mangoes, pitted, peeled, and diced (if unavailable fresh, jarred is next best)
2 cups halved red seedless grapes
¼ cup finely chopped red onion
1 bunch fresh cilantro, chopped
Juice of ½ lime
1 jalapeño pepper, seeded and minced
1 pound fresh salmon fillets, skin on
Freshly ground black pepper, to taste

To make the salsa, combine all the ingredients, except the salmon and pepper, in a large bowl and mix well. Cover with plastic wrap and refrigerate until ready to serve.

Place the salmon, skin side down, on the grill or in a skillet and cook until half of the fish begins to whiten on the sides. Sprinkle the black pepper over top as the fish is cooking. Flip the fish over to the flesh side, and gently peel back the salmon skin; it will come off very easily. Now lightly pepper this side of your fish and finish the cooking. Top the cooked salmon with the fruit salsa and serve with a starch and vegetable of your choice.

Yield: 4 servings

Each serving contains approximately: Calories 291, Fat calories 69, Fat 8g, Saturated fat 1.2g, Cholesterol 62mg, Protein 24g, Carbohydrate 34g, Dietary fiber 3g, Sodium 54mg, Omega-3 fatty acids 2.01g

Allowances: 3 proteins + 2 fruits + ¼ vegetable

SUCCULENT SALMON PROTEIN

Our friends at the Rice Diet Program Forum (www.ricediet.com) have shared another treat with us, and we can't get enough fresh finfish recipes to add to our collection. Both your eyes and your stomach will be impressed.

½ cup Dijon mustard, salt free, preferably Téméraire Dijon Mustard ○

1 to 2 teaspoons chopped fresh tarragon

1 pound fresh salmon steaks (4 steaks spproximately 4 ounces each)

Freshly ground black pepper, to taste

1 cup dry white wine

¼ cup freshly squeezed lime juice

4 slices red onion

4 sprigs fresh tarragon

In a small bowl, mix together the mustard and chopped tarragon; set aside for the salmon garnish. Season the salmon with pepper and place in a skillet. Add the wine, lime juice, and just enough water to cover the salmon. This will allow you to know how much water it takes to cover the salmon for the poaching process. Then remove the salmon and bring the liquid to a boil. Return the salmon to the skillet, and top each steak with an onion slice and tarragon sprig. Reduce the heat to a simmer, cover the pan with a lid or foil, and poach the salmon for 6 to 10 minutes. Serve each steak topped with a tablespoon of the mustard-tarragon mixture.

Yield: 4 servings

Each serving contains approximately: Calories 229, Fat calories 93, Fat 10g, Saturated fat 1g, Cholesterol 62g, Protein 25g, Carbohydrate 5g, Dietary fiber 0.3g, Sodium 94mg, Omega-3 fatty acids 1.96g

Allowances: 3 proteins + ½ vegetable + ¾ fruit

SUPEREASY SALMON PROTEIN

This recipe was inspired by Susan's friends John and Emily. We have modified it to create a low-sodium version. A low-sodium version of homemade pesto would be hard to beat in this recipe, but if you don't have the time or the fresh basil, Racconto pesto is good and superconvenient.

2 thin slices of lemon, preferably organic

I carrot, peeled and thinly sliced

2 thin slices of Vidalia onion

2 teaspoon Racconto Traditional Basil Pesto ○ (or mince your own basil, garlic, and 2 walnuts)

One 8-ounce salmon fillet, cut into two portions

Preheat the oven to 450 degrees.

Tear off two 12-inch sheets of aluminum foil (making 2 12-inch squares). In the center of each foil square, place 1 slice of lemon, half of the sliced carrots, and 1 slice of Vidalia onion. Spread a teaspoon of pesto on each piece of salmon (the side without skin). Place the salmon on top of the vegetables, pesto side down. Now seal the foil packets and bake for about 20 minutes, or until the vegetables are tender. Open carefully, remove from the foil, and serve.

Yield: 2 servings

Each serving contains approximately: Calories 226, Fat calories 98, Fat 11g, Saturated fat 1.5g, Cholesterol 62mg, Protein 23g, Carbohydrate 8g, Dietary fiber 2g, Sodium 73mg, Omega-3 fatty acids 2g

Allowances: ¾ fat + 3 proteins + 1 vegetable

RICE DIET-READY TUNA SALAD PROTEIN

This is a quick and delicious meal that you can serve with a big salad and crackers or stuff in pita bread. If you pack the tuna mixture in an airtight container, it may taste even better the next day for lunch on crackers or pita.

6-ounce can white tuna, packed in water, no salt added

¼ cup chopped celery

¼ cup fresh dill sprigs

2 tablespoons chopped flat-leaf parsley

2 tablespoons chopped green onion

⅛ teaspoon freshly ground black pepper

¼ cup plain nonfat yogurt

1½ teaspoons Dijon mustard, salt free, preferably Téméraire Dijon Mustard ○

Drain the tuna, reserving 1 to 2 tablespoons of the liquid from the can. In a bowl, mash the tuna with the reserved liquid. Add the remaining ingredients and mix well.

Yield: 2 servings

Each serving contains approximately: Calories 134, Fat calories 27, Fat 3g, Saturated fat 0.7g, Cholesterol 36mg, Protein 22g, Carbohydrate 4g, Dietary fiber 1g, Sodium 82mg, Omega-3 fatty acids 0.79g

Allowances: 2 proteins + ¼ dairy

SUSAN'S TUNA SALAD PROTEIN

Love tuna salad? Try Susan's recipe that skips the mayonnaise and uses mustard for more flavor without the fat!

6-ounce can tuna, packed in water, no salt added

1 tablespoon champagne mustard, preferably Cherchie's Champagne Mustard ○,
    or any mustard you prefer

1 tablespoon Cherchie's Pretty Hot Peppers ○ or blend of hot roasted peppers, like
    jalapeño and poblaños, or mince ½ of a chipotle pepper

Drain and flake the tuna. Mix all the ingredients, and serve over a large lettuce salad.

Yield: 2 servings

Each serving contains approximately: Calories 137, Fat calories 23, Fat 2.5g, Saturated fat 0.7g, Cholesterol 44mg, Protein 20g, Carbohydrate 6g, Dietary fiber 0g, Sodium 48mg, Omega-3 fatty acids 0.8g

Allowances: ¼ starch + 2 proteins

GRILLED SOFT-SHELL CRABS (AND ALL SEAFOOD)

PROTEIN

God is so good! In North Carolina, a popular belief is that God must be very thoughtful to have arranged for soft-shell crabs to be in season when oysters are not! Typically oysters are in season in months that contain the letter "R" and soft-shell crabs in the summer.

8 soft-shell crabs, cleaned
Kym's Seafood Marinade (see page 270)

Preheat your grill.

Rinse the soft-shell crabs and pat dry with paper towels. Place the crabs in a casserole pan and cover with half of the marinade, then turn over after 15 minutes for another 15-minute marination time. Then simply grill the crab for 5 to 7 minutes per side.

These are incredibly delicious. Crab is naturally quite high in sodium, so it will taste salty even to guests who are not accustomed to eating low-sodium food. And, note that they are less than one-third of the calories of sautéed crabs.

Yield: 4 servings (2 crabs per serving)

Each serving contains approximately: Calories 50, Fat calories 5, Fat 0.5g, Saturated fat 0.1g, Cholesterol 33mg, Protein 8g, Carbohydrate 4g, Dietary fiber 0g, Sodium 125mg, Omega-3 fatty acids 0.14g

Allowances: 1 protein

SAUTÉED SOFT-SHELL CRAB (AND OTHER SEAFOOD)

PROTEIN

Although I love almost all seafood, usually I choose finfish for health reasons. But when you've eaten the following recipe for soft-shell crabs, you'll understand how easy these are to justify!

4 small soft-shell crabs, cleaned

1 cup skim milk

2 tablespoons extra-virgin olive oil

¾ cup all-purpose flour

¼ teaspoon garlic powder

1 teaspoon lemon pepper, salt free

2 tablespoons chopped flat-leaf parsley

Juice of 1 squeezed lemon

Place the crabs in a shallow pan in a single layer, cover with milk, and let sit for 1 hour. Drain and discard the milk. Heat the olive oil in a wide sauté pan. Combine the flour, garlic powder, lemon pepper, and parsley in a ziplock bag. Dredge or shake the crabs, one at a time, in the flour mixture, and place in the heated oil. Sauté until brown, then turn and brown the other side. Pour lemon juice over the crabs, remove

Soft-shell crabs are great in season, from approximately May until August, but almost as good if you freeze them properly. Just buy in excess (more than you want to eat that day), rinse, and place 4 to 6 small crabs in small freezer bags filled with water; then put in freezer. Only a coastal cohort would know if they're fresh or frozen!

from pan, and serve with rice and a vegetable. You could easily make the *Easy Summer Slaw* (page 180) while your crabs saute!

Yield: 2 servings

Each serving contains approximately: Calories 243, Fat calories 130, Fat 14g, Saturated fat 2g, Cholesterol 33mg, Protein 10g, Carbohydrate 17g, Dietary fiber 0.5g, Sodium 189mg, Omega-3 fatty acids 0.23g

Allowances: 2½ fats + 1 starch + 1 protein

ANGELA'S SHRIMP WITH CRYSTALLIZED GINGER

PROTEIN

This recipe was the "hands down" favorite when testing these recipes. Everyone here was fighting over who got to take the leftovers home—it's simply amazing.

1 teaspoon extra-virgin olive oil

3 large red bell peppers, sliced into ⅛" strips, then halved

3 large garlic cloves, minced

1 large onion, chopped

2 tablespoons grated fresh ginger

5 to 6 tablespoons crystallized ginger, finely chopped

1 pound shrimp, cleaned

1 lemon, sliced, with rind (I prefer an organic lemon, quartered and then
   thinly sliced)

Heat the olive oil in sauté pan, add the red pepper, garlic, and onion and cook until soft. Add the fresh and crystallized ginger and sauté for another 5 minutes. Add the cleaned shrimp, sautéing another 3 minutes, or until tender. Approximately 30 seconds before serving, add the lemon slices (rinds and all!) and stir briefly.

Yield: 4 servings

Each serving contains approximately: Calories 195, Fat calories 35, Fat 4g, Saturated fat 0.5g, Cholesterol 172mg, Protein 25g, Carbohydrate 19g, Dietary fiber 4g, Sodium 173mg, Omega-3 fatty acids 0.5g

Allowances: ¼ fat + 1 vegetable + 3 proteins

If purchasing uncleaned, raw shrimp, add the shrimp to boiling water and cook until pink, approximately 1 minute. Then drain and cool in the refrigerator, or by putting ice cubes on top. (This step facilitates easy peeling of the shrimp, without disfiguring them.) When shrimp are cool, peel and devein.

RYAN'S SHRIMP SCAMPI

PROTEIN

This dish is a staple for Ryan and her fiancé to cook up for a "quality" meal together without any muss or fuss. It can be completed in about 15 minutes from start to finish, and the base "sauce" can also be used for other seafood dishes as well.

¾ cup orzo pasta, uncooked
2 teaspoons extra-virgin olive oil
3 garlic cloves, minced
⅓ cup dry white wine
¼ cup freshly squeezed lemon juice
3 tablespoons chopped, fresh basil
3 tablespoons chopped, flat-leaf parsley
Freshly ground black pepper, to taste
6 ounces raw shrimp, cleaned

Start by cooking the orzo in six cups of boiling water. Cook the pasta as directed on the package; this typically takes 6 minutes.

Heat the olive oil in a sauté pan placed over medium-low heat, then add the minced garlic (medium-low heat is best so that you won't burn your garlic). Add the wine and lemon juice, followed by the basil, parsley, and black pepper to taste. Add the shrimp and cook for about 3 minutes, then turn them over and cook on the other side for 1 minute, or until they have turned a light pink color. Toss with the drained pasta, and serve.

Yield: 2 servings

Each serving contains approximately: Calories 347, Fat calories 66, Fat 7g, Saturated fat 1.2g, Cholesterol 129mg, Protein 24g, Carbohydrate 38g, Dietary fiber 2g, Sodium 139mg, Omega-3 fatty acids 0.5g

Allowances: 1 fat + 2 starches + 2 proteins + 1 vegetable

SHRIMP CREOLE   PROTEIN

There's nothing like some soulful Shrimp Creole to slow down the pace of your week. Sit back, relax, and enjoy!

1 tablespoon extra-virgin olive oil

2 cups fresh or frozen chopped okra

2 cups chopped green bell pepper

2 cups sliced mushrooms

1 cup chopped onion

1 cup chopped celery

2 garlic cloves, minced

¼ cup tomato paste, no salt added

1 teaspoon ground oregano

¼ teaspoon Tabasco sauce

½ teaspoon sugar

¼ teaspoon paprika

28-ounce can whole tomatoes, no salt added

2 bay leaves

1½ pounds raw shrimp, cleaned

Heat the oil in a skillet over medium heat. Add the okra, peppers, mushrooms, onion, celery, and garlic and sauté for 10 minutes. Add the tomato paste, oregano, Tabasco, sugar, paprika, tomatoes, and bay leaves. Bring the mixture to a boil, stirring frequently. Cover, reduce the heat, and simmer for 10 minutes. Stir in shrimp and simmer for 3 to 4 minutes, or until shrimp turn a bright pink. Test a shrimp before removing the creole from the heat. When shrimp is done, spoon over rice.

Yield: 6 servings

Each serving contains approximately: Calories 236, Fat calories 42, Fat 5g, Saturated fat 0.8g, Cholesterol 172mg, Protein 27g, Carbohydrate 23g, Dietary fiber 7g, Sodium 253mg, Omega-3 fatty acids 0.6g

Allowances: ½ fat + 3 proteins + 2 vegetables

CHICKEN

CHICKEN AND SPINACH SALAD

PROTEIN

Susan created this dish after being inspired by a scallop recipe on the Chef Pascal Web site. The Orange, Ginger, and Coconut Sauce is used to flavor the chicken, and the Lemon Ginger Balsamique is used to flavor the spinach. However, combining those two ingredients makes an easy, elegant, and very tasty dressing for any salad or vegetable dish.

6 ounces boneless, skinless chicken breast, diced, preferably organic

3 tablespoons Chef Pascal Orange, Ginger, and Coconut Sauce Ⓞ

1 tablespoon Terres Rouges Lemon Ginger Balsamique Ⓞ

1 teaspoon Dijon mustard, no salt added, preferably Téméraire Dijon Mustard Ⓞ

4 cups spinach, washed and patted dry

4-ounce can clementines, drained, or mandarin oranges

Cut the chicken into at least twelve pieces and sauté in a hot skillet in 1 to 2 tablespoons water. When the chicken is fully cooked, 2 to 3 minutes, add the Chef Pascal sauce, toss lightly, and remove from heat. Mix the vinegar and mustard, then toss with

We love this sauce from Chef Pascal, and we keep finding new ways to use it. If you want to replace it with another sauce, just choose your favorite flavors and look for a brand that goes easy on the sodium. The balsamic vinegar that we use is tart and spicy. Experiment with the Two-to-Three-Ingredient Salad Dressings (page 276) for some interesting dressings; they don't have to be fruity to complement this salad.

spinach and clementines. Divide the salad and arrange on two plates. Top with equal amounts of chicken, and serve!

Yield: 2 servings

Each serving contains approximately: Calories 203, Fat calories 33, Fat 4g, Saturated fat 0.3g, Cholesterol 16mg, Protein 21g, Carbohydrate 16g, Dietary fiber 3g, Sodium 180mg, Omega-3 fatty acids 0.03g

Allowances: 3 proteins + ½ fruit + ¾ vegetable

MARINATED GRILLED CHICKEN WITH FRESH CORN SALSA
PROTEIN

If you are tired of old, boring chicken dishes, this one will perk you up with a south-of-the-border flair!

MARINATED GRILLED CHICKEN

1 cup nonfat plain yogurt

Zest and juice of 1 lemon, preferably organic

2 garlic cloves, minced

2 tablespoons molasses

¼ cup minced red onion

1 bunch fresh cilantro, chopped

Four 4-ounce boneless, skinless chicken breasts, preferably organic

CORN SALSA

2 teaspoons extra-virgin olive oil

1 cup fresh corn kernels (about 2 ears), cut from the cob

¼ teaspoon brown sugar

Freshly ground black pepper, to taste

14-ounce can stewed tomatoes, no salt added

¼ cup finely chopped red onion

¼ cup chopped cilantro leaves

Juice of 1 lime

2 tablespoons jalapeño pepper, seeded and finely chopped

Mix all the ingredients for the marinade in a large bowl, add the chicken, and toss to coat evenly. Cover the bowl and refrigerate for at least 4 hours, or overnight.

Preheat the grill.

Remove the chicken from the marinade and discard the marinade. Grill the chicken until the juices run clear, usually 6 to 8 minutes per side. To prepare the salsa: Heat the oil in a skillet over medium heat, add the corn, and cook for 2 minutes. Add the sugar, season to taste with pepper, and cook for another minute, then transfer the corn into a small bowl and cool slightly. Stir in the rest of your ingredients, and spoon over the grilled chicken.

Yield: 4 servings

Each serving contains approximately: Calories 252, Fat calories 35, Fat 4g, Saturated fat 0.7g, Cholesterol 51mg, Protein 25g, Carbohydrate 32g, Dietary fiber 4g, Sodium 127mg, Omega-3 fatty acids 0.05g

Allowances: ½ fat + 3 proteins + ½ starch + ¼ vegetable + ¼ dairy

STUFFED CHICKEN BREASTS PROTEIN

It's as easy as one, two, three! Try this easy method to make stuffed chicken breasts with just about anything you like. We have listed three of our favorite combinations for you to try, but then you can create your own!

Four 4-ounce boneless, skinless chicken breasts, preferably organic

1½ tablespoons extra-virgin olive oil

¼ cup balsamic vinegar

¾ cup vegetable stock, salt free, preferably using Rapunzel's Vegan, No Salt Added, Vegetable Bouillon ○

Cut a deep horizontal pocket in the side of each chicken breast, and spoon ¼ cup of "your stuffing" in the pocket of each chicken breast. Secure this with toothpicks and kitchen string along the side to close.

Heat the oil in a heavy skillet, and cook each side of the chicken until golden brown. Add the vinegar and vegetable bouillon and bring to a boil, then lower the heat and gently simmer the chicken for 2 or 3 minutes per side until cooked through. Remove the chicken breasts from the skillet and serve.

Yield: 4 servings

Each serving contains approximately: Calories 166, Fat calories 47, Fat 5g, Saturated fat 0.8g, Cholesterol 66mg, Protein 27g, Carbohydrate 2g, Dietary fiber 0g, Sodium 103mg, Omega-3 fatty acids 0.06g

Allowances: 1 fat + 3 proteins

VARIATION: *Stuffed Three-Pepper Chicken*

Four 4-ounce boneless, skinless chicken breasts, preferably organic

2 teaspoons extra-virgin olive oil

1 small red, green, and yellow bell pepper, seeded and sliced into thin strips

1 shallot, diced

Heat the oil in a skillet over medium heat, add the peppers and shallot and sauté for 4 to 5 minutes. Spoon "stuffing" into your chicken breasts, but continue to cook the remaining vegetables until reduced to a syrupy sauce. In another skillet cook the stuffed chicken breasts as initially described. Spoon the sauce over each chicken breast, and serve.

Yield: 4 servings

Each serving contains approximately: Calories 234, Fat calories 75, Fat 8g, Saturated fat 1.3g, Cholesterol 66mg, Protein 28g, Carbohydrate 11g, Dietary fiber 2g, Sodium 135mg, Omega-3 fatty acids 0.11g

Allowances: 1 fat + 3 proteins + 1 vegetable

VARIATION: *Stuffed Apple Chicken*

Four 4-ounce boneless, skinless chicken breasts, preferably organic

1 teaspoon extra-virgin olive oil

1 small Granny Smith apple, peeled and diced

4 tablespoons chopped fresh tarragon

Heat the olive oil in a skillet over medium heat. Cook the diced apple in the oil until tender, about 3 to 4 minutes, and set aside to cool. In a small bowl, gently toss the cooked apple with the tarragon. Spoon the "stuffing" into the chicken breasts, then cook as previously described. Continue to cook the remaining fruit until reduced to a thick syrup. Spoon the fruit sauce over each chicken breast, and serve.

Yield: 4 servings

Each serving contains approximately: Calories 195, Fat calories 59, Fat 7g, Saturated fat 1.3g, Cholesterol 66mg, Protein 27g, Carbohydrate 7g, Dietary fiber 1g, Sodium 104mg, Omega-3 fatty acids 0.07g

Allowances: 1¼ fats + 3 proteins + ¼ fruit

VARIATION: *Stuffed Chicken with Tomato and Basil*

8 sun-dried tomatoes, drained and chopped

½ bunch fresh basil, chopped

Four 4-ounce boneless, skinless chicken breasts, preferably organic

Prepare and combine the tomatoes and basil. Stuff the tomato mixture into the pocket in the chicken and continue to cook as previously described.

Yield: 4 servings

Each serving contains approximately: Calories 185, Fat calories 50, Fat 6g, Saturated fat 0.9g, Cholesterol 66mg, Protein 28g, Carbohydrate 6g, Dietary fiber 1g, Sodium 123mg, Omega-3 fatty acids 0.08g

Allowances: 1 fat + 3 proteins + ¾ vegetable

VEGETARIAN PROTEIN

BAKED TOFU

This is Susan's version of a vegetarian classic. "If you like tofu that is chewy and crumbly (as opposed to smooth and bouncy), this method of freezing and marinating works well for many stir-fried or baked variations."

1 package firm or extra-firm tofu; buy one with the highest calcium content
1 cup vegetable stock, salt free, preferably using Rapunzel's Vegan, No Salt Added, Vegetable Bouillon ☼
½ teaspoon extra-virgin olive oil
2 tablespoons nutritional yeast

To make crumbly tofu: Open the tofu package and drain. Press the tofu in a colander by weighing down with a plate. Let sit at room temperature, draining, for about 30 minutes. Wrap in plastic wrap, then place in a freezer bag and freeze overnight or up to 6 months. Thaw overnight in refrigerator.

Slice the tofu into 5 portions and marinate in vegetable stock or other no-salt-added marinade for about 2 hours. Preheat the oven to 450 degrees F, and coat a baking sheet with a little olive oil. Place the nutritional yeast on a plate and gently pat the yeast onto all sides of the tofu slices. Place the tofu in a single layer on the baking sheet, and bake for 10 minutes. Gently flip the slices over and bake for an additional 10 minutes.

Yield: 1 serving

Each serving contains approximately: Calories 74, Fat calories 40, Fat 4g, Saturated fat 0.8g, Cholesterol 0mg, Protein 9g, Carbohydrate 1g, Dietary fiber 1g, Sodium 26mg, Omega-3 fatty acids 0g

Allowances: ½ fat + 1 protein

APRICOT-HORSERADISH BAKED TOFU

VEGETARIAN PROTEIN

Susan uses this recipe when making *Baked Tofu*, a method she uses to create a firm and chewy texture (as opposed to smooth and bouncy). The fruit caramelizes in the oven, which only enhances the flavor and texture of this dish.

1 serving *Baked Tofu*

2 tablespoons apricot fruit spread, "fruit only" kind, no added sugar, preferably Bionaturae ◌

2 tablespoons full-strength, prepared horseradish, no salt added, typically found in chain grocery stores' refrigerator sections

Remove the tofu from the oven, and switch the oven to broil. Mix the fruit spread and horseradish and coat one side of the tofu. Now broil the tofu until the edges are crispy.

Yield: 1 serving

Each serving contains approximately: Calories 132, Fat calories 41, Fat 4.5g, Saturated fat 0.9g, Cholesterol 0mg, Protein 10g, Carbohydrate 15g, Dietary fiber 1g, Sodium 29mg, Omega-3 fatty acids 0g

Allowances: ¼ starch + 1¼ proteins + ¾ fruit

GRILLED TEMPEH

VEGETARIAN PROTEIN

For those of you who have not yet discovered tempeh, you are in for a treat! Who needs burgers and hot dogs loaded with sodium, saturated fat, and calories when you can enjoy a delicious source of protein with the health advantages of soy!

2 squares of tempeh

2 tablespoons sweet ginger chili sauce, preferably The Ginger People brand ○

Preheat the grill to medium-high. Brush the tempeh with the ginger chili sauce, and place on the grill for 7 to 10 minutes, turning once. Serve this up with *Ryan's Grilled Veggie Skewers* (page 200), and you've got a delicious meal, hot off the grill.

Yield: 6 servings

Each serving contains approximately: Calories 160, Fat calories 54, Fat 6g, Saturated fat 1g, Cholesterol 0mg, Protein 16g, Carbohydrate 13g, Dietary fiber 6g, Sodium 0mg, Omega-3 fatty acids 0g

Allowance: 3 proteins

Tempeh is a cultured soy product, made by cooking cracked soybeans, draining them, then inoculating them with a culture called *Rhizopus oligosporus*. Although this molded cake of pressed soybeans does look a little weird at first glance, it is no weirder than eating spoiled milk as cheese, yogurt, sour cream, or buttermilk! In Indonesia people enjoy tempeh as frequently as Americans do meat. And yes, they don't die nearly as frequently as we do of chronic diseases! So expand your limited vision and simply try this recipe or *BBQed Tempeh on Quinoa* in *Heal Your Heart;* they truly are fantastic!

RACHELLE'S SPICY THAI VEGETABLES WITH TOFU

VEGETARIAN PROTEIN

Hearty, healthy, and flavorful, this dish is a wake-up call for the senses! Using a low-sodium sauce, such as the Chef Pascal sauce, to create the flavorful foundation for your dish can be a great shortcut to a delicious meal.

2 teaspoons canola oil

1 medium red onion, chopped

2 to 3 cloves garlic, minced

1 cup broccoli florets, chopped

1 medium red bell pepper, chopped

1 to 2 jalapeño peppers, seeded and minced

2 teaspoons minced or grated fresh ginger

2 teaspoons low-sodium Worcestershire sauce, preferably Angostura ○

2 tablespoons Chef Pascal's Orange, Ginger, and Coconut Sauce ○

⅗ block firm, low-fat tofu, cubed

¼ cup chopped fresh cilantro

2¼ cups cooked long-grain white rice

Orange wedges for garnish

Prepare all the ingredients before you begin cooking.

Heat the oil in a small wok or skillet. Sauté the onion for a few minutes, then add the garlic and broccoli and sauté for another minute or two. Add the bell pepper to the mix and continue cooking for another minute. Add the jalapeños, ginger, Worcestershire sauce, and Chef Pascal sauce and stir in gently. Gently fold in the tofu so as not to pummel the tofu cubes. Add the cilantro at the end of the cooking and remove from the heat. Serve over the rice, and garnish the dish with orange wedges for a colorful and flavorful meal.

Yield: 4 servings

Each serving contains approximately: Calories 294, Fat calories 111, Fat 12g, Saturated fat 1.6 g, Cholesterol 0mg, Protein 14g, Carbohydrate 34g, Dietary fiber 3g, Sodium 9mg, Omega-3 fatty acids 0.71g

Allowances: ½ fat + 1½ starches + 1½ proteins + 1 vegetable

DRESSINGS AND TOPPINGS

FRUIT TOPPINGS

VEGGIE TOPPINGS AND SAUCES

DRESSINGS

FRUIT TOPPINGS

RICHTER GIRLS JAM
FRUIT

Our Rice Diet's Canadian ambassador, De-Anne, won the recipe contest on our Web site with this entry. This is tasty proof of how delicious simple food combinations can be. Congratulations, De-Anne!

3 to 4 cups frozen strawberries, no sugar added
4 dried pineapple rings

Place all the ingredients in a blender and leave out overnight. In the morning blend the ingredients until creamy and smooth. Serve as jam or sauce over cereal or toast.

Yield: 1 serving (2 tablespoons per serving)

Each serving contains approximately: Calories 25, Fat calories 0, Fat 0g, Saturated fat 0.0g, Cholesterol 0mg, Protein 0g, Carbohydrate 6g, Dietary fiber 1g, Sodium 2mg, Omega-3 fatty acids 0g

Allowances: ½ fruit

This dish is quick, health-promoting, and lasts all week (if you can pace yourself!). This method of creating jam also reduces pollution by not having to waste the energy used by factories making it, reduces the rise of landfills with useless containers and lids, and the list goes on. Why not enjoy locally grown, antioxidant-packed, organic fruits rather than commercially processed preserves with artificial food colorings and sweeteners?

EILENE'S DATE "HONEY" SPREAD

FRUIT

Eilene Bisgrove, my dear friend and son's godmother, is also part of the Rice Diet community. She teaches Old Testament Health and Food Politics at the program. She also enjoys cooking and sharing foods typical in biblical times. This spread would be great on her *Eilene's Pita or Pocket Bread* (page 125), or anywhere you would use fruit preserves.

8 ounces dried dates
½ cup water

Put the dates in a blender (dried date pieces [e.g., Sunkist] are best but whole pitted dates can be used, too). Add the water, and blend on medium speed until fully mixed. Add less water for a thicker spread, more for a thinner one.

Yield: 12 servings

Each 2-tablespoon serving contains approximately: Calories 54, Fat calories 2, Fat 6g, Saturated fat 0g, Cholesterol 0mg, Protein 1g, Carbohydrate 14g, Dietary fiber 0g, Sodium 2mg, Omega-3 fatty acids 0g

Allowance: 1 fruit

VEGGIE TOPPINGS AND SAUCES

JAY'S TOMATO-FENNEL RED SAUCE   VEGETABLE

Jay, Susan's husband, has donated this sauce from his collection, and we just love it over pasta or polenta. It's a sauce that's packed with flavor, as well as antioxidants, and goes with just about anything.

1 medium onion, finely chopped

3 cloves garlic, minced

1 teaspoon cracked black pepper

¼ cup chopped fresh basil

2 tablespoons chopped fresh oregano

2 tablespoons chopped fresh rosemary

1 tablespoon fennel seeds

14.5-ounce can diced tomatoes, no salt added

15-ounce can tomato sauce, no salt added

6 sun-dried tomatoes, quartered, preferably Sonoma brand ○

Sauté the onion and garlic in 2 tablespoons of water over medium heat until translucent, about 5 minutes. Add the spices, herbs, fennel seeds, and stir well to infuse flavor. Add the tomatoes and tomato sauce, reduce the heat, and simmer for 30 minutes. Add the sun-dried tomatoes and simmer for an additional 15 to 30 minutes. Serve with polenta or your favorite pasta!

Yield: 6 servings

Each serving contains approximately: Calories 63, Fat calories 4, Fat 0.5g, Saturated fat 0.1g, Cholesterol 0mg, Protein 2g, Carbohydrate 12g, Dietary fiber 3g, Sodium 37mg, Omega-3 fatty acids 0g

Allowances: 2½ vegetables

LIZ'S GARDEN FRESH "NO COOK" TOMATO SAUCE
VEGETABLE

This recipe has been given to us by our dear friend and fellow Ricer Liz. The sauce is super easy to put together, and a great alternative to a tomato sauce higher in sodium. It's so refreshing and tastes like you are eating straight from the garden.

8 plum tomatoes

4 garlic cloves

10 large fresh basil leaves

2 tablespoons extra-virgin olive oil

Freshly ground black pepper, to taste

2 tablespoons fennel seeds

4 sprigs flat-leaf parsley

Add all of the above ingredients to a blender and pulse until the mixture turns pink and frothy. Use this as a topping for a serving of whole wheat pasta, rice, or a salt-free pita.

Yield: 4 servings

Each serving contains approximately: Calories 101, Fat calories 70, Fat 8g, Saturated fat 1g, Cholesterol 0mg, Protein 2g, Carbohydrate 8g, Dietary fiber 3g, Sodium 10mg, Omega-3 fatty acids 0g

Allowances: 1½ fats + 1½ vegetables

KYM'S SEAFOOD MARINADE STARCH

I love recipes with history! Our dear friend and former intern Kym kindly shared this part of her life with us, and we thought that you would enjoy it too! Kym shares, "I gave this recipe to the chef at the country club to serve with shrimp/scallop kabobs for my wedding reception. He now uses it on a regular basis for similar dishes."

¼ cup rice vinegar

¼ cup orange juice or lemon juice concentrate

¼ Vidalia onion, diced

I tablespoon grated fresh ginger

½ teaspoon red pepper flakes

Combine all the ingredients and store in a ziplock bag or an airtight container. Use this to marinate seafood and finfish. It's also great for basting during grilling.

Yield: ¾ cup, 1 serving

Each serving contains approximately: Calories 66, Fat calories 4, Fat 0.5g, Saturated fat 0.1g, Cholesterol 0mg, Protein 1g, Carbohydrate 17g, Dietary fiber 1g, Sodium 6mg, Omega-3 fatty acids 0.03g

Allowances: ½ starch + ¼ vegetable + ½ fruit

RED PEPPER SAUCE VEGETABLE

This is such a versatile sauce. Use your imagination and stretch it any way you like! We received this recipe from our Rice Diet Forum, where one member has used this to top pasta, rice, and even potatoes. You can also use this as a dressing over veggies and salad.

6-ounce can tomato paste, no salt added

1 red bell pepper, chopped

1 garlic clove, chopped

1 small onion, chopped

Freshly ground black pepper, to taste

1 cup water

Blend all ingredients in a blender until smooth.

Yield: 4 servings

Each serving contains approximately: Calories 55, Fat calories 3, Fat 0g, Saturated fat 0g, Cholesterol 0mg, Protein 2g, Carbohydrate 13g, Dietary fiber 3g, Sodium 43mg, Omega-3 fatty acids 0g

Allowances: 2 vegetables

SUN-DRIED TOMATO PESTO   VEGETABLE

Susan created this combination and uses it as an easy recipe for pizza sauce, vegetable dip, or pasta topping, or as a base for salad dressing.

3-ounce bag sun-dried tomatoes, no salt added, preferably Sonoma brand ○

1 cup water

10 garlic cloves

1 teaspoon dried oregano

1 teaspoon dried thyme

Place the ingredients in a covered glass dish and microwave for 10 minutes. Let stand to cool and absorb the water. Purée in a food processor.

Yield: 4 servings

Each serving contains approximately: Calories 70, Fat calories 0, Fat 0g, Saturated fat 0g, Cholesterol 0mg, Protein 4g, Carbohydrate 4g, Dietary fiber 4g, Sodium 20mg, Omega-3 fatty acids 0g

Allowance: 3 vegetables

AL'S PRESTO CAULIFLOWER PESTO   FAT

Here's a great homemade recipe for pesto without the fat, donated by our fellow Ricer Al. Al's a great cook and put together this mix from fresh ingredients right out of his home garden.

1 cup fresh basil leaves
2 large garlic cloves
½ cup chopped fresh cauliflower
1 tablespoon pine nuts
Freshly ground black pepper, to taste
⅔ cup extra-virgin olive oil

Add all the ingredients, except the oil, to a blender or food processor, and blend until well processed. Add the olive oil, a little at a time, blending constantly until the pesto reaches a creamy consistency. If not using immediately, store in an airtight container or freeze.

Yield: 8 servings

Each serving contains approximately: Calories 95, Fat calories 85, Fat 9g, Saturated fat 1g, Cholesterol 0mg, Protein 1g, Carbohydrate 2g, Dietary fiber 1g, Sodium 3mg, Omega 3-fatty acids 0.16g

Allowances: 2 fats + ¼ vegetable

HOT AND SPICY VEGGIE TOPPERS

It's great to have a kicker like this ready to top baked potatoes, spaghetti squash, or frankly anything needing a flavor kick! Realize that the creator of this recipe likes it very hot; most people would prefer a variety of peppers that aren't as sizzling, such as poblanos, Anaheim, or banana peppers.

2 teaspoons extra-virgin olive oil
1 large onion, sliced in half and then thinly sliced lengthwise
16 medium jalapeño peppers, sliced in half, seeded, and thinly sliced lengthwise

Heat the olive oil in the skillet, add in the onion and peppers, and sauté until tender.

Yield: 2 servings

Each serving contains approximately: Calories 60, Fat calories 34, Fat 4g, Saturated fat 0.5g, Cholesterol 0mg, Protein 1g, Carbohydrate 6g, Dietary fiber 2g, Sodium 1mg, Omega-3 fatty acids 0g

Allowances: 1 fat + 1 vegetable

There are dozens of flavorful peppers available in most regions. Be sure that when handling hot peppers, and especially their seeds, that you don't touch your eyes before carefully washing your hands and scrubbing your nails with warm soapy water. Does this sound like it is written by someone who has made this mistake?!

DRESSINGS

JR'S CREAMY TOMATO-BASIL DRESSING   FAT

This Rice House dressing is always a favorite. Add this to top off your rice or grains with a little flavor, or use it as a salad dressing for your favorite veggies and greens.

1 cup cherry tomatoes

1 cup white wine vinegar

3 garlic cloves

2 teaspoons dried oregano

6 fresh basil leaves

Put all of the ingredients, except for the basil, in a blender or food processor and blend at medium speed for about 30 seconds. Add the basil leaves and blend for 30 seconds more, or until fairly smooth. Chill for 1 hour and enjoy!

Yield: 3 servings (½ cup per serving)

Each serving contains approximately: Calories 14, Fat calories 0, Fat 0g, Saturated fat 0g, Cholesterol 0mg, Protein 1g, Carbohydrate 3g, Dietary fiber 1g, Sodium 3mg, Omega-3 fatty acids 0.01g

Allowance: ½ vegetable

MANGO WASABI DRESSING   FRUIT

This dressing was created during a cooking class here at the Rice Diet. It's a great twist to dress up "slaw" with less fat and sodium. You can also use this to top a spinach salad.

1 mango

1½ teaspoons wasabi powder

1½ teaspoons water

2 tablespoons sushi ginger

1 tablespoon toasted sesame oil

2 tablespoons plain rice vinegar

Peel and chop the mango, then set aside. Mix the wasabi powder and water, and let sit for 10 minutes. Meanwhile, mince the sushi ginger. Place all these ingredients in a small food processor or blender and process until smooth. Add the oil and vinegar, toss with chopped cabbage, and serve.

Yield: 8 servings

Each serving contains approximately: Calories 31, Fat calories 9, Fat 1g, Saturated fat 0.1g, Cholesterol 0mg, Protein 1g, Carbohydrate 4g, Fiber 2g, Sodium 17mg, Omega-3 fatty acids 0.2g

Allowance: ½ fruit

SUN-DRIED TOMATO SALAD DRESSING   FAT

When Susan has leftover *Sun-Dried Tomato Pesto*, from the recipe on page 271, she likes to add it to her salads as well. To make this sauce a little more versatile, just add the following ingredients.

¼ cup *Sun-Dried Tomato Pesto*

2 tablespoons vegetable stock, preferably Rapunzel Vegan, No Salt Added
 Vegetable Bouillon ○

1 teaspoon red wine or balsamic vinegar, preferably Badia a Coltibuono ○
 or Villa Manodori ○

1 tablespoon extra-virgin olive oil

Mix well and enjoy!

2 tablespoons per serving

Each serving contains approximately: Calories 25, Fat calories 18, Fat 2g, Saturated fat 0.3 g, Cholesterol 0mg, Protein 1g, Carbohydrate 2g, Dietary fiber 1g, Sodium 60mg, Omega-3 fatty acids 0.01g

Allowances: ¼ fat + ½ vegetable

TWO-TO-THREE-INGREDIENT
SALAD DRESSINGS

FRUIT

These easy, throw-together dressings don't have any fat, yet are incredibly tasty. They give you the convenience of dressings from a bottle with the taste of homemade! Just mix a tablespoon of each for one serving.

• Chef Pascal's Orange, Ginger, and Coconut Sauce ○ and Terres Rouges Lemon Ginger Balsamique ○
• Cherchie's Cranberry Mustard ○ and plain rice vinegar
• Ginger People Sweet Ginger Chili ○ and plain rice vinegar
• Cherchie's Champagne Mustard ○ and raspberry vinegar
• L'Olivier Walnut Oil ○ and raspberry vinegar
• Honeycup Mustard ○ and balsamic vinegar
• White balsamic vinegar with freshly grated citrus peel
• Mr. Spice Ginger Stir-Fry ○ and Angostura low-sodium Worcestershire Sauce ○
• Badia a Coltibuono Red Wine Vinegar ○ with coarse mustard and fresh basil

- Orange juice, Badia a Coltibuono Red Wine Vinegar ○, and fresh tarragon
- Tomato juice (no salt added) and Badia a Coltibuono Red Wine Vinegar ○ (add garlic and cumin if desired)
- Apple cider vinegar with freshly grated nutmeg or ground cinnamon and juice of a clementine
- Rapunzel Vegan, No-Salt-Added, Vegetable Bouillon ○ with freshly grated ginger

DESSERTS

STARCHES

FRUITS

STARCHES

FIVE-MINUTE GRANOLA PIECRUST

The quickest and easiest piecrust I know is also the healthiest; it has no trans or partially hydrogenated fats! You can use packaged or homemade, but this crust works best with granola that doesn't contain dried fruit, like *Kitty's Gorgeous Granola* (page 109). I now prefer this crust to those that need to be baked; in addition to being fast and healthy, it also has a wonderful flavor and texture that becomes puddinglike as it absorbs the liquid from the filling.

¼ teaspoon canola oil

2 cups *Kitty's Gorgeous Granola,* or other processed type without dried fruit

5 to 6 tablespoons water

Lightly coat a 9-inch pie plate with oil.

Place the granola in a food processor, and using on and off pulses, break up any large lumps in the granola to create a fairly coarse meal. Empty the ground granola onto the pie plate, stir in enough water to moisten the granola, and press it evenly over the bottom. You can use this quick-and-easy piecrust for any pie recipe; just ignore any instructions for prebaking.

Yield: 6 servings

Each serving contains approximately: Calories 77, Fat calories 34, Fat 4g, Saturated fat 0.4 g, Cholesterol 0mg, Protein 2g, Carbohydrate 10g, Dietary fiber 2g, Sodium 29mg, Omega-3 fatty acids 0.01g

Allowances: ¾ fat + ½ starch

RICE DIET RICE PUDDING

STARCH

One Rice Diet Forum member has given us a way to make rice pudding the "Ricer-friendly" way. We are thrilled that the Forum has become such a wonderful resource for great recipes, as well as a support to help others make the Rice Diet transition a little easier and their success long-term.

¾ cup rolled oats, no salt added

½ cup raisins

¾ cup long-grain rice

6 cups skim milk

1 tablespoon vanilla

1–2 teaspoons ground cinnamon, to taste

2 tablespoon sugar or maple syrup

Add the first four ingredients to a saucepan and bring to a boil, then cover and reduce heat to low for 30 minutes. After 30 minutes, stir in the vanilla, cinnamon, and maple syrup. Enjoy immediately hot, or refrigerate for 4 hours or overnight.

Yield: 6 servings

Each serving contains approximately: Calories 238, Fat calories 11, Fat 1g, Saturated fat 0.3g, Cholesterol 3mg, Protein 9g, Carbohydrate 48g, Dietary fiber 2g, Sodium 89mg, Omega-3 fatty acids 0.01g

Allowances: 1½ starches + ½ fruit + 1 dairy

RISOTTO PUDDING

STARCH

This warm, creamy dish is just as sweet as any dessert but can be enjoyed as a breakfast treat as well. Please feel free to substitute any other dried fruit that you wish for the dates, giving the dish your own creative twist.

¾ cup rice, preferably short-grain Arborio rice
2½–3 cups soymilk, preferably WestSoy Plus
½ cup mashed bananas
¾ teaspoon finely grated orange zest, preferably organic
2 plump vanilla beans, split lengthwise, seeds scraped out (use both seeds and pod)
Large pinch of saffron threads, preferably Safinter's Saffron ✺
½ cup chopped dates

In a heavy-bottomed, 2-quart saucepan, combine all the ingredients except for the dates. Place the pot over medium-low heat and stir until bubbles break the surface. Reduce the heat to keep the mixture at a gentle simmer, and cook for 30 to 40 minutes. Stir frequently with a wooden spoon until the pudding is thick and creamy and the rice is tender and soft. Add the dates during the final 5 minutes of cooking, and serve the pudding immediately in warmed shallow bowls.

Yield: 3 servings

Each serving contains approximately: Calories 202, Fat calories 30, Fat 3g, Saturated fat 2.0g, Cholesterol 15mg, Protein 4g, Carbohydrate 40g, Dietary fiber 3g, Sodium 52mg, Omega-3 fatty acids 0g

Allowances: 1¼ starches + ½ fruit + ¾ dairy

FRUITS

BAKED PRUNE COMPOTE

FRUIT

Prunes, like many simple foods, are infinitely better if they are complemented by another flavor or two. The citrus and cinnamon intensify this dish with such synergy.

1½-ounce package pitted prunes

1 cup orange juice

⅔ cup water

Rind and juice of 1 lemon, preferably organic

Rind and juice of 1 orange, preferably organic

3-inch stick cinnamon

Preheat the oven to 325 degrees F.

I prefer the majority of my citrus rinds sliced and then quartered, then a smaller fraction grated. Combine all the ingredients and bake for 1 hour. You can serve the compote hot if you prefer, or cover and chill for at least 2 hours. Enjoy for breakfast or as a dessert.

Yield: 6 servings

Each serving contains approximately: Calories 58, Fat calories 3, Fat 0g, Saturated fat 0g, Cholesterol 0mg, Protein 1g, Carbohydrate 15g, Dietary fiber 3g, Sodium 3 mg, Omega-3 fatty acids 0.01 g

Allowance: 1 fruit

BANANA POPS

Frozen desserts don't have to be loaded with chemicals and refined sugar empty of nutrition; they can be a delicious, nutritious treat! Ryan made these with her dad when she was a kid. It's an easy dish that can be used as a side at breakfast or even for dessert.

1 ripe banana

¼ cup skim milk or soymilk, preferably WestSoy Plus

1 teaspoon vanilla extract

½ teaspoon ground cinnamon

2 paper cups

2 Popsicle sticks

2 sheets wax paper

Mash the banana, and put all the ingredients into a mixing bowl or blender. Mix well. Fill plastic popsicle-making forms with the mixture, or improvise, using two paper cups. Push a popsicle stick through the center of the wax paper and then insert into each cup. Place cups in freezer for 2 hours. Once you've frozen the banana pops, pop them out of the paper cups and enjoy your new tasty treat.

Yield: 2 servings

Each serving contains approximately: Calories 71, Fat calories 3, Fat 0g, Saturated fat 0.1g, Cholesterol 1mg, Protein 2g, Carbohydrate 16g, Dietary fiber 2g, Sodium 17mg, Omega-3 fatty acids 0g

Allowances: ¾ fruit + ¼ dairy

CHOCOLATE–BANANA CREAM CUSTARD

FRUIT

Chocolate lovers can always justify this treat since it is so rich in antioxidants, right? This is so incredibly delicious, and also the most nutritious chocolate dessert you've probably ever eaten. Of course, for "choc-o-holics," this may be your favorite potluck contribution; you can leave any leftovers with the hostess, rather than return with it home alone!

5 bananas, peeled and cut in half

10.5-ounce pack soft silken tofu

¾ cup unsweetened cocoa powder (also called cacao)

2½ teaspoons vanilla or almond extract

2 tablespoons Kahlúa, optional

16 fresh mint leaves

8 strawberries, sliced

⅓ cup granola or *Kitty's Gorgeous Granola* (page 109)

In a blender or food processor container, add the bananas and process for 2 minutes, or until very smooth and creamy. Add the tofu, cocoa, vanilla, and Kahlúa, and process for another couple of minutes, until the tofu is totally blended. When fully blended, place the custard in martini glasses and serve. Or for later use, transfer into a large bowl, cover, and chill in the refrigerator for 2 or more hours. Serve garnished with fresh mint leaves, fresh strawberry slices, and 1½ teaspoons of granola. What a scrumptious finale!

Yield: 6 servings

Each serving contains approximately: Calories 281, Fat calories 62, Fat 7g, Saturated fat 0.7g, Cholesterol 0mg, Protein 10g, Carbohydrate 46g, Dietary fiber 7g, Sodium 54mg, Omega-3 fatty acids 0.06g

Allowances: 1½ starches + 1½ fruits

DIANA'S SHREDDED CARROT HALVA
FAT

This recipe was inspired by Diana, a close friend of the Rice Diet family. The rich colors and sweet flavors of the nutmeg and spices make this dish especially popular in the fall.

1½ pounds (about 9 medium) carrots, washed, peeled, shredded, and pressed dry

3 to 4 cups of soymilk, preferably WestSoy Plus

8 whole black peppercorns

½ teaspoon cardamom seeds, coarsely ground

1 tablespoon extra-virgin olive oil

¼ cup sliced or slivered raw almonds

¼ cup dried cherries

¼ cup raisins or currants

¼ cup chopped walnuts

¼ teaspoon ground cloves

¼ teaspoon freshly grated nutmeg

¼ teaspoon ground cinnamon

2 tablespoons maple syrup or light honey

Combine the carrots, soymilk, and peppercorns in a heavy 5-to-6-quart nonstick saucepan and, stirring constantly, bring to a full boil over high heat. Reduce the heat to medium-high, continue stirring frequently, and cook for 25 to 35 minutes. Toward the end of the cooking time, reduce the heat to medium-low, and cook until the soymilk has reduced to a pasty fudge.

Add half of the cardamom and, stirring steadily to prevent scorching, cook for 10 minutes, or until the mixture is nearly dry. Remove the pan from the heat and set aside.

Heat the olive oil in a small pan over medium-low heat, add the almonds, and fry until golden. Remove with a slotted spoon and set aside. Add the hot oil to the carrot mixture along with the dried cherries, raisins or currants, walnuts, ground spices, and reserved almonds, and place the pan over the medium-low heat. Cook until the mixture begins to pull away from the sides of the pan. Remove the pan from the heat, discard the peppercorns, and stir in the maple syrup or honey. Transfer the halva to a decorative serving bowl or tray and garnish with the remaining cardamom.

Yield: 8 servings

Each serving contains approximately: Calories 234, Fat calories 64, Fat 7g, Saturated fat 0.7g, Cholesterol 0mg, Protein 5g, Carbohydrate 39g, Dietary fiber 4g, Sodium 145mg, Omega-3 fatty acids 0.3g

Allowances: 2 fats + 1 vegetable + 1 fruit + ½ dairy

GRANNY'S BAKED APPLES   FRUIT

Skip the processed piecrusts and go straight to the good stuff! This recipe is a wonderful way to enjoy the flavors of homemade apple pie, and it's still considered "Ricer friendly." Enjoy this dish as a side of fruit to top off any meal of the day.

2 Granny Smith apples
⅓ cup apple juice
2 slices fresh ginger
1 cinnamon stick
3 orange slices

Peel the top third of the apples. Place the apples in a baking or microwave dish. Add the apple juice, ginger, cinnamon, and orange slices. Bake in an oven, preheated to 350 degrees, for 10 minutes, or microwave for 4 minutes.

Yield: 2 servings

Each serving contains approximately: Calories 99, Fat calories 1, Fat 0g, Saturated fat 0g, Cholesterol 0mg, Protein 1g, Carbohydrate 27g, Dietary fiber 4g, Sodium 4mg, Omega-3 fatty acids 0g

Allowance: 1¾ fruits

GRILLED PEARS

FRUIT

Fruit can give your grilling a whole new meaning! You can use pineapple, mango, or papaya as well—simply place on the grill.

3 pears
2 tablespoons orange juice
1 teaspoon ground cinnamon, plus cinnamon for sprinkling
¼ teaspoon freshly grated nutmeg

Preheat a grill.

Cut the pears in half lengthwise, and remove the seeds and core. Mix the orange juice, cinnamon, and nutmeg together, and brush the pears with the mixture on the cut side. Place on the grill cut side down until lightly caramelized, about 5 minutes. Lightly sprinkle additional cinnamon over the top, and serve.

Yield: 3 servings

Each serving contains approximately: Calories 106, Fat calories 3, Fat 0g, Saturated fat 0g, Cholesterol 0mg, Protein 1g, Carbohydrate 28g, Dietary fiber 0g, Sodium 2mg, Omega-3 fatty acids 0g

Allowance: 1¾ fruits

NO-BAKE FRUIT PIE

FRUIT

How beautiful, clean, and delicious can a dessert be?! I feel so righteous and re-warded while eating this; the flavor is superb while offering antioxidants galore! Somehow the seaweed source of agar-agar appeals to me more than the alternative, gelatin, which comes from cow hooves and horns.

Five-Minute Granola Piecrust (page 279)

1 cup apple juice

1½ tablespoons agar-agar flakes

3 tablespoons freshly squeezed lemon juice

1 teaspoon vanilla extract

2 to 3 large ripe peaches, peeled, cut into ¼-inch slices

1 to 2 ripe kiwis, peeled, cut into ¼-inch rounds

6 to 8 medium strawberries, halved

1 cup blueberries

Prepare the piecrust and set aside.

To make the glaze: Heat the apple juice in a small saucepan, stir in the agar-agar flakes, and simmer until most of them are dissolved, 1 to 2 minutes. Transfer to a liquid measuring cup and stir in the lemon juice and vanilla. Place in the refrigerator to cool.

Arrange a circle of peach slices around the outer rim of the pie plate so that about one-third of the slice covers the rim of the pie plate and the remaining two-thirds of the slice tilts down into the pie. Cover the remainder of the crust with a layer of sliced peaches. Arrange the kiwi slices on top of some of the peaches, partially overlapping each other, in a concentric circle. Arrange the strawberry halves in a circle inside of the kiwis. Mound the blueberries in the center and dot them here and there between the kiwis and the peaches.

Once the glaze is at room temperature or cooler, pour it evenly over the fruit. The glaze should be thin enough to seep between the fruit. If the glaze is too thick to pour, return it to the pan and heat it slowly, while stirring.

Allow the glaze to set at room temperature for about 1 hour. Chill the pie if it is not needed within the next few hours, but for optimum taste, serve it at room temperature.

Yield: 6 servings

Each serving contains approximately: Calories 156, Fat calories 38, Fat 4g, Saturated fat 0.3g, Cholesterol 0mg, Protein 3g, Carbohydrate 28g, Dietary fiber 4g, Sodium 7mg, Omega-3 fatty acids 0.05 g

Allowances: ¾ fat + 1½ fruits + ½ starch

PINEAPPLE PIE FOR TWO

FRUIT

This little slice of heaven was donated to us by our friends on the Rice Diet Forum. Keep them coming, guys! We have been delighted with the little treasures that we have been able to find!

5 pieces whole wheat melba toast, salt free, preferably Old London Whole
    Grain brand ✹
1½ cups fresh pineapple, chopped
1 teaspoon ground cinnamon
1 teaspoon sugar, optional
1 tablespoon skim milk or soymilk

Preheat the oven to 350 degrees F.

Crush 5 pieces of whole wheat melba toast into coarse crumbs and divide between two tart dishes. Combine the pineapple, cinnamon, sugar (if desired), and soymilk in a mixing bowl, and divide equally between the two tart dishes. Bake in the preheated oven for 20 minutes. You can double this recipe and use an 8-×-8-inch baking dish.

Yield: 2 servings (1 tart per serving)

Each serving contains approximately: Calories 135, Fat calories 7, Fat 1g, Saturated fat 0.1g, Cholesterol 0mg, Protein 3g, Carbohydrate 31g, Dietary fiber 3g, Sodium 7mg, Omega-3 fatty acids 0.1g

Allowances: 1 starch + 1 fruit

RHUBARB–DRIED CHERRY CRUMBLE   FRUIT

Since I was raised in North Carolina, I had never seen or eaten rhubarb until I moved to Michigan in my 20s. We don't often see it fresh down South. If it's also hard for you to find, you may have luck in the frozen section of your health or gourmet grocery stores. I purposely make a big batch because it is great served right out of the oven, and for days as leftovers. Refrigerating this overnight creates a puddinglike texture, and freezing it for much later enjoyment is also tasty—and often saves me from overeating!

½ teaspoon olive oil

3 pounds rhubarb (approximately 9 cups), washed, trimmed (discard all leaves, they are poisonous) cut into 1-inch slices

½ cup strawberry preserves, fruit only, no sugar added

½ cup dried cherries, preferably organic

2 tablespoons flaxseed, freshly ground in a coffee mill or with a mortar and pestle

1 tablespoon finely grated or minced orange peel, preferably from an organic orange

¼ cup orange juice

1 teaspoon ground cinnamon

2 cups multigrain granola (try Ezekiel 4:9 Sprouted Grain Cereal)
Maple syrup, if desired

Coat a 13 × 8 × 2-inch heatproof pan with olive oil. Combine all remaining ingredients in the oiled pan. Don't be concerned if the mixture seems too dry, because the rhubarb releases significant liquid during the cooking process. Place the pan in a cold oven, set the oven to 375 degrees F, and bake uncovered for 15 minutes. Stir, and then continue baking until the rhubarb is tender yet firm, 10 to 15 minutes more. Add maple syrup only if more sweetness is desired.

Yield: 10 servings

Each serving contains approximately: Calories 169, Fat calories 19, Fat 2g, Saturated fat 0.1g, Cholesterol 0mg, Protein 5g, Carbohydrate 36g, Dietary fiber 5g, Sodium 82mg, Omega-3 fatty acids 0g

Allowances: ½ fat + 1 starch + ¾ fruit + 1 vegetable

SAMBA'S GINGERED PEAR CAKE   FRUIT

Occasionally, you'll find jewels like this on the Rice Diet's Web site Forum. Thanks for sharing and inspiring others to help themselves to health! You can make multiple servings of this at one time in a baking dish, then slice into individual portions and freeze. This would be a great dish for your rice and fruit day!

1½ canned pears in their own juice, drained
½ ripe banana, mashed
⅓ cup dry oats, no salt
¼ teaspoon ground cinnamon
¼ teaspoon freshly grated nutmeg
¼ teaspoon ground ginger

Preheat the oven to 350 degrees F.

Mix all of the ingredients together and put them in an individual baking dish. Bake for 30 to 45 minutes until browned.

Yield: 1 serving

Each serving contains approximately: Calories 228, Fat calories 20, Fat 2g, Saturated fat 0.5g, Cholesterol 0mg, Protein 5g, Carbohydrate 50g, Dietary fiber 8g, Sodium 6mg, Omega-3 fatty acids 0.1g

Allowances: 1¼ starches + 2 fruits

TOASTED GINGER PAPAYA   FRUIT

Here at the Rice House, we just love baked fruit! The natural sugars come out and caramelize, satisfying any sweet tooth!

1 tablespoon honey
1 tablespoon grated fresh ginger
2 medium papayas, quartered and seeded, skin on
1 teaspoon canola oil

Preheat the oven to 350 degrees F.

In a small bowl, combine the honey and ginger until well blended. Coat the cut sides of the papaya (but not the skin) with the honey mixture. Grease a nonstick baking sheet with the canola oil, and place the papayas on the sheet, skin side down. Bake for 15 minutes, or until golden brown.

Yield: 4 servings

Each serving contains approximately: Calories 103, Fat calories 12, Fat 1g, Saturated fat 0g, Cholesterol 0mg, Protein 1g, Carbohydrate 23g, Dietary fiber 3g, Sodium 5mg, Omega-3 fatty acids 0.02g

Allowances: ¼ fat + 1½ fruits

END NOTE

A WAKE-UP CALL
FROM MIMI

The recipes contained herein are community-inspired and truly reflect the loving, welcoming, supportive, and growing Rice Diet community. I hope that they inspire you not only to enjoy the many tasty flavors and nutritious meals but also to become more aware of how foods both nourish and nurture us. But as I've said throughout these pages and throughout the pages of *The Rice Diet Solution* and *Heal Your Heart*, the Rice Diet is much more than a diet plan that enables weight loss. It asks you to make a choice to live life in a different way.

Indeed, during twenty-five years of working with participants of cardiac rehabilitation and the Rice Diet Program, I have observed that in order for a diet to succeed long-term, you must do two things: remain steadfastly open to life's great possibilities (and your own wondrous potential), and be conscious and aware of who you are, what you want, and what is going on around you. If you are both—open and conscious—then this diet can lead you to create the health and life you desire.

The Rice Diet *dieta* is a lifelong commitment we Ricers have chosen to intentionally co-create the health and life we desire. It is an ongoing process to be open, to learn to listen to our bodies and mind and spirit, so that we are truly in this present moment and in the next present moment—without reacting habitually in a way that limits our potential for growth and peace and love. I happened to relearn the power of this truth very recently, as I wrote this book.

Last summer, as I vacationed in Italy with my family, Mimi, my closest friend of the last decade, died. When I awoke at 4:00 A.M., I was beating myself up for having indulged in a midnight decaf iced coffee and chocolate ice cream at Giolitti. After trying unsuccessfully to go back to sleep, all I could think about was the sleep I believed I needed before packing, renting a car, navigating out of Rome, and schlepping to Orvieto.

So I began to practice a body-scan technique for half an hour or more to let go of the belief that my dark chocolate and decaffeinated iced coffee would prevent my returning to sleep. Body scanning is a mindfulness meditation that includes breathing and scanning your body to notice sensations, thoughts, and feelings you are experiencing, so that you can recognize and release any tensions you may be holding.

In my mind, I revisited the prior day, which I had spent in long lines at the Vatican. I noticed and released my annoyance with all the ugly Americans and other tourists who were photographing the Sistine Chapel, despite incessant reminders from the loudspeaker not to photograph . . . and to offer the *silenzio* and respect the spiritually and artistically inspired place and visiting pilgrims deserved.

Like my ten-year-old son, I questioned why so many people seemed so disrespectful and disruptive of the holy ground beneath us. But eventually we found a few moments and created opportunities to get on our knees in St. Peter's Basilica. Despite the fact you can't physically get near Michelangelo's *Pietà* now and that even in one of the holiest places on Earth, it's a challenge to find a quiet and reflective space, I was excited to see my son's need and tenacity to do just that. He didn't say why, or for whom, he wanted to pray, but I sensed it was for our dear friend Mimi and her family.

I was soon flooded with gratitude for all the blessings and gifts I have received from God, revealed to me, of course, through his messenger Mimi. Rather than be frustrated for hours of restlessness or take a sleeping pill and miss the joy that followed, I realized that I had remained open and aware enough to benefit from a 4:00 A.M. spiritual wake-up call!

Mimi had been like a sister to me for the past decade. And despite the fact that she had been struggling for her life and health (and likely also because of it), we had shared a depth of love and friendship that is indescribable. As I lay there after my body scan, prayers, and meditation, I was flooded with the unconditional love of God, as well as my love for my dear friend Mimi. Instantly, I had the sense that Mimi had just left her body. It was then I knew why I was awake at 4:00 A.M.—Mimi was pointing me to yet another wake-up call. I could see her more clearly than if I'd been there, six time zones earlier, where she and her family had huddled for her last days—finally released from her suffering caused by her metastasized breast cancer. I also instantaneously released the fear I had of not being near her when she died, while I surrendered to the ecstasy of being closer to her in that moment than I ever could be physically.

Each day I realize in every cell in my body that I can choose to reside in love or fear . . . and I choose love. Mimi and I had modified my mother's loving game, which included the dare "I love you more; I love you to the moon and back." My last visit with her before I left for Italy ended with her addition "I love you to Jupiter and back." Then I said "I love you to infinity!" . . . and she extended it to "and beyond!"

There is an abundance of love for us all; it's there if we ask and seek, if we stay open and aware. I know that whenever a door closes, another is soon to open, and often this happens sooner rather than later, if we are receptive to and observant of the many opportunities available. And Mimi would want me to "pay it forward" (the title of a Helen Hunt movie that is a must-see!).

I share this very personal epiphany with you to illustrate the truth that the Rice Diet *dieta* is way beyond a food plan that offers weight loss and that this book includes far more than the recipes and menus. The success of maintaining an optimal diet and exercise regimen depends largely on staying conscious and aware of what you want, pursuing your heart's desire, and continuing to seek discernment on whether your will is in alignment with your Creator's and, thus, with your true purpose in life. When you stay open and aware, and seek out a loving and supportive community to inspire and nurture your life and health dreams, you will find an expansive and abundant life, filled with depth and joy.

Peace be with you as you co-create the life and health you desire.

APPENDICES

APPENDIX A

FOOD GROUPS DEFINED

Foods are divided into these categories because of similar caloric and nutritional content: Starches, Vegetables, Fruits, Protein, Dairy Products, and Fats, as well as Condiments.

STARCHES

The foods in the starch group contain an average of 80 calories or 15 grams of carbohydrate, 3 grams of protein, 1 gram of fat, only trace amounts of saturated fat, no cholesterol, and 5 milligrams of sodium per allowance, or small serving size. This group includes whole grains; slightly processed cereals, breads, and crackers; dried beans and peas; and starchy vegetables, such as potatoes, corn, peas, and winter squash.

As mentioned earlier, choose a minimum of 6 from this group per day, with the majority coming from the higher-fiber items. All whole grains—such as brown rice, oat groats (or steel-cut oats and oatmeal), barley (preferably the hull-less type), buckwheat groats, quinoa, millet, whole wheat berries (or cracked wheat), and rye kernels—are the ultimate base for your nutrition plan. Whole grains have more fiber and nutrients than do their processed counterparts, despite efforts to enrich these processed foods. Although all whole grains are good for you, rice is especially beneficial, offering some of the highest-quality protein of any grain. If these whole grains constitute the majority of your grain intake, then you can occasionally eat slightly processed grains, such as whole-grain crackers, breads, fat-free cookies, and pasta. Generally speaking, you would be getting plenty of fiber and nutrients as long as three-quarters of your grain intake is whole grain.

Dried beans and peas can be counted as a starch *or* as a protein allowance. These are the highest-protein members of the starch group and contain the richest amount of cholesterol-lowering soluble fiber. Other nutrient- and fiber-rich starches are the starchy vegetables, such as yams, sweet and white potatoes, corn, peas, and winter squash. To increase your fiber and nutrient intake, consume the skins of vegetables whenever possible, preferably organic.

Try to eat a variety of starches. Your body would prefer a cup of brown rice and ⅓ cup of black beans to 2 cups of potatoes. This is much more of a concern if you have unstable blood sugars, since refined, processed grains and potatoes become blood sugar faster than do these other carbohydrates. The high-soluble-fiber carbohydrates (oats, beans, and barley) should be on the daily menu of anyone with blood sugar irregularities, hypoglycemia (low blood sugar), and hyperglycemia (diabetes).

PORTION SIZE FOR 1 STARCH ALLOWANCE

The allowances, or serving sizes, for starches might be smaller than you would typically eat, but you usually will enjoy 2 to 3 per meal. An asterisk (*) indicates a high-fiber item.

BREADS

Bagels—½
Bread stick, 4 inches long by ½ inch in diameter—2
Bread (whole wheat*, rye*, oatmeal*)—1 slice

Croutons (homemade, without added fat and sodium)—1 cup

English muffin (whole wheat*, oatmeal*)—½

Hamburger or hot dog bun (whole wheat*)—½

Pita bread, 6 inches in diameter (whole wheat*)—½

Roll, plain (whole grain*)—1

Tortilla, corn* or flour, 6 inches in diameter (without lard)—1

GRAINS (COOKED, UNLESS SPECIFIED OTHERWISE)

Barley (hulled*)—½ cup

Buckwheat groats*—½ cup

Flake-type cereals (oat* and whole grain*)—¾ cup

Grits—½ cup

Oat bran*—3½ tablespoons raw

Oat groats, steel-cut oats, and oatmeal—½ cup

Polenta—½ cup

Quinoa—½ cup

Rice (brown*)—⅓ cup

Rye berries—½ cup

Wheat bran*—3⅗ tablespoons raw

Wheat berries*, cracked wheat (bulgur)—½ cup

Crackers, chips, and snacks:

Guiltless Gourmet no-fat/no-salt corn chips—⅘ ounce

Health Valley oat bran graham crackers—6½ crackers

Matzo crackers—¾ ounce

Old London Whole Grain Melba Toast, unsalted—4 crackers

Popcorn, popped with no fat—3 cups

Rice cakes—2 cakes

Ryvita sesame rye—2⅔ crackers

Unsalted sesame brown rice snacks—9 crackers

STARCHY VEGETABLES (COOKED)

Acorn squash* or butternut squash*—¾ cup

Corn*—½ cup

Corn on the cob*—1 ear, 6 inches long

Dried beans*, peas, or lentils*—⅓ cup

Green peas*—½ cup

Lima beans*—½ cup

Plantain or yam*—½ cup

Potato, baked with skin*—1 small (½ cup)

Sweet potato*—¼ cup

VEGETABLES

An allowance of vegetables has about 25 calories, 5 grams of carbohydrate, 2 grams of protein, trace amounts of fat, no saturated fat or cholesterol, and 10 milligrams of sodium. Note the large differences in calories and carbohydrates between the starchy vegetables (with 80 calories and 15 grams of carbohydrate) and these nonstarchy vegetables (with only 25 calories and 5 grams of carbohydrate). The sodium content of vegetables can vary widely, with an allowance of cooked celery and spinach offering 48 and 63 milligrams of sodium, respectively. But you don't need to worry about limiting your intake of naturally occurring sodium unless you have kidney or liver disease.

Choose a minimum of 4 servings per day, but choosing more will further assist with your weight loss. Again, it would be advantageous to enjoy plenty of the higher-fiber items. Since vegetables are the lowest-calorie food group and are packed with nutrition, it would be difficult to eat too many—if, of course, they contain no added fat or salt.

Eat as much of the following raw vegetables as you want without counting each as an allowance. They are considered "free" because raw, they have less than 20 calories per cup. Those high in fiber are marked with an asterisk (*).

Arugula	Escarole	Radishes
Broccoli sprouts	Green onion*	Romaine
Celery	Hot peppers	Spinach*
Chinese cabbage	Lettuce	Zucchini
Cucumbers	Mushrooms	
Endive	Radicchio	

One cup raw or ½ cup cooked of each of the following vegetables equals one allowance or serving. High-fiber items are marked with an asterisk (*).

Artichoke (½ medium)*	Cauliflower	Peppers
Asparagus	Eggplant*	Rutabaga
Beans (green, wax, Italian)*	Greens (collard, mustard,	Spinach
Bean sprouts	turnip)*	Tomato/vegetable juice, no salt
Beets*	Kohlrabi	added
Broccoli*	Leeks	Tomato (1 large)*
Brussels sprouts*	Okra*	Turnips*
Cabbage*	Onions	Water chestnuts
Carrots*	Pea pods	

FRUITS

One fruit allowance contains about 60 calories, 15 grams of carbohydrate, very little protein (usually less than 1 gram), trace amounts of fat, no saturated fat and cholesterol, and 1 milligram of sodium. As you might notice, the fruit group has the lowest content of fat, protein, and sodium per serving, which is part of the reason why fruit is great for people with many different chronic diseases. It is also one of the highest sources of cholesterol-lowering soluble fiber.

Choose a minimum of 3 servings per day, and frequently from the higher-fiber items. The darker the orange color in a fruit, the higher the beta-carotene content, so enjoy plenty of oranges, peaches, apricots, cantaloupes, and mangoes.

PORTION SIZE FOR 1 FRUIT ALLOWANCE

The allowances for many fruits are just what you would expect them to be—1 piece if it is raw, or ½ cup if it is cooked or juiced. Dried fruit might be the only surprise; ⅛ to ¼ cup of dried fruit is considered one serving because it is so calorically dense. Take care not to overeat dried fruit. Three or more allowances of fruits are recommended per day. Higher-fiber fruits are marked with an asterisk(*).

FRESH, FROZEN, OR CANNED FRUIT

Apple (raw, 2 inches in diameter)*—1

Applesauce (unsweetened)—½ cup

Apricots (canned)—½ cup or 4 halves

Apricots (medium, raw)—4

Banana (9" long)—½

Blackberries (raw)*—¾ cup

Blueberries (raw)*—¾ cup

Cantaloupe (5" across)—⅓

Cantaloupe (cubes)—1 cup

Cherries (canned)—½ cup

Cherries (large, raw)—12

Figs (raw, 2 inches in diameter)—2

Fruit cocktail (canned)—½ cup

Grapefruit (medium)—½

Grapefruit (segments)—¾ cup

Grapes (small)—15

Honeydew melon (medium)—⅛

Kiwi (large)—1

Mandarin oranges—¾ cup

Mango (small)*—½

Nectarine (2½ inches in diameter)*—1

Orange (2½ inches in diameter)*—1

Papaya—1 cup

Peach (2¾ inches in diameter)—1

Peaches (canned)—½ cup or 2 halves

Pear—½ large or 1 small

Pear (canned)—½ cup or 2 halves

Persimmon (medium, native)—2

Pineapple (canned)—⅓ cup

Pineapple (raw)—¾ cup

Plum (raw, 2 inches in diameter)—2

Pomegranate*—½

Raspberries (raw)*—1 cup

Strawberries (raw, whole)*—1½ cups

Tangerine (2½ inches in diameter)*—2

Watermelon (cubes)—1¼ cups

DRIED FRUIT

Apples*—4 rings

Apricots*—7 halves

Cherries—½ tablespoon

Dates*—2½ medium

Figs*—1½

Prunes—3 medium

Raisins—2 tablespoons

FRUIT JUICE

Apple juice/cider—½ cup

Cranberry juice cocktail—⅓ cup

Grapefruit juice—½ cup

Grape juice—⅓ cup

Orange juice—½ cup

Pineapple juice—½ cup

Prune juice—⅓ cup

PROTEIN

One low-fat protein allowance averages 55 calories, no carbohydrate, 7 grams of protein, 3 grams of fat, 25 milligrams of cholesterol (varies widely), and 51 milligrams of sodium. This group includes high-protein foods such as legumes, seafood, and, if you are preventing rather than reversing heart disease, poultry and lean meats. If you have heart disease or cholesterol over 150, it is important to remember that red meat (beef, pork, lamb, and veal) is highest in saturated fats; it is best to eliminate it from your diet entirely or consume it only on very special occasions. It is important to eat "grass-fed" organic meats. Depending on your need to lose weight and your motivation to reverse atherosclerosis (and its risk factors, such as high blood pressure and cholesterol), choose between 1 and 3 servings from this group every day.

We recommend that you eat animal products and dairy foods only if your health indicators suggest that they will benefit you. For instance, animal products except for fish would not be beneficial if you have heart disease or cholesterol that is greater than 150. You should limit animal products if your fasting blood sugar is more than 100, blood pressure is greater than 110/70, or weight is higher than ideal.

Legumes (beans and peas) are the optimal source of protein and can be counted in this group or the starch group. They are preferable to meats in that they offer similarly high protein and iron, without the accompanying sodium, saturated fat, and cholesterol, and with lots of cholesterol-lowering, blood-sugar-stabilizing soluble fiber, as well as B vitamins, calcium, and potassium.

PORTION SIZE FOR 1 PROTEIN ALLOWANCE

Protein is the only food group in which an allowance is much smaller than the average serving. All meats are cooked portions (4 ounces raw meat = 3 ounces cooked meat). Here are the amounts that equal one allowance of each of the following protein sources:

Beef—1 ounce (round is the leanest; use ground round instead of hamburger)

Dried beans, peas, lentils—⅓ cup cooked; tempeh and tofu—¼ cup; TVP, dry, unconstituted—3 tablespoons

Eggs—1 whole, 3 egg whites, or ¼ cup egg substitute

Fish—1 ounce, or ¼ cup flaked

Lamb—1 ounce

Meat, any type, lean, diced—¼ cup

Pork—1 ounce (tenderloin is the lowest in saturated fat)

Poultry—1 ounce (skinned white meat)

Roasted soybean, unsalted—1½ tablespoons

Veal—1 ounce

Wild game, except duck—1 ounce

DAIRY PRODUCTS

This group includes only those dairy products that are fat free with no salt added, and an average allowance contains 90 calories, 12 grams of carbohydrate, 8 grams of protein, no fat or saturated fat, trace amounts of cholesterol, and 150 milligrams of sodium. Select a maximum of 2 servings per day.

PORTION SIZE FOR 1 DAIRY ALLOWANCE

Most of the following dairy product allowances are similar to portions that you would typically consume, except for the frozen desserts. Here are the amounts of popular dairy choices that equal one allowance, or serving, which contains 90 calories:

Cottage cheese, ½ percent dry-curd type with less than 65 milligrams sodium—½ cup

Ricotta, fat-free type with less than 65 milligrams sodium—½ cup

Dry powdered nonfat milk—3½ tablespoons

Frozen dessert, no added fat or sodium—½ cup (limit to once a week if weight or triglycerides are a problem, as these can be high in sugar)

Grain milk and soymilk, nonfat—1 cup

Milk, skim—1 cup (1 percent milk still gets 22 percent of its calories from fat)

Parmesan cheese—2½ tablespoons, grated

Plain yogurt, nonfat—1 cup

Sour cream, nonfat—7 tablespoons

Sugar-free fruited yogurt, nonfat—1 cup

FATS AND OILS

An average allowance from this group contains 45 calories, no carbohydrate or protein, 4½ grams of fat, ¾ gram of saturated fat (although this varies widely), no cholesterol (if from a plant source), and no sodium. Depending on your need to lose weight and motivation to reverse atherosclerosis, choose from 0 to 4 servings per day from this group.

All fats and oils contain some saturated fat, so use all sparingly and choose those with the least saturated fat.

PORTION SIZE FOR 1 FAT ALLOWANCE

An allowance of fat is 1 teaspoon, though few people actually consume this little when they use it. Although you do not really need any added fat or oil to realize your optimal potential for health, it is included for your enjoyment and to enhance the odds that you can maintain this low saturated fat intake long-term. The amount of fat our bodies truly need is quite minimal. If you are overweight, the need drops even further. Fat is found naturally in many foods in a whole foods diet. Therefore, 0–4 added teaspoons of olive oil are usually quite adequate to meet one's needs. If you like nuts, it is suggested that you use them as condiments, not snacks, unless you remain very conscious of caloric quantity consumed. The following food portions are equal to one allowance of fat or oil:

OILS

Canola oil or rapeseed oil—1 teaspoon

Olive oil—1 teaspoon

Sesame seed oil—1 teaspoon

Soybean oil—1 teaspoon

Walnut oil—1 teaspoon

Nuts, seeds, and other high-fat foods:

Almonds—6 nuts

Almond butter—1½ teaspoons

Avocado—⅛ medium

Filberts (hazelnuts)—1 tablespoon

Flaxseeds—¾ tablespoon

Pumpkin seeds—1 tablespoon

Sesame seeds—1 tablespoon

Sunflower seeds—1 tablespoon

Tahini (sesame seed butter)—1½ teaspoons

Walnuts—1 tablespoon

CONDIMENTS

The following foods can be enjoyed as flavor enhancers or condiments, if you use their no-fat and no-salt-added forms. They contain fewer than 20 calories per portion and are great anywhere you previously would have used salt. You can use as much as you like of any except catsup.

Catsup, no-salt-added type—1 tablespoon

Herbs and spices

Horseradish, fresh root or full-strength prepared, with no salt added

Lemon

Lime

Mustard, no-fat/no-salt type

Salad dressing, no-fat/no-salt type

Vinegar, no-salt-added type

Wasabi powder

Wine, except for "cooking wines" or others with salt

APPENDIX B

GUIDE TO FAT, SODIUM, FIBER, AND RECIPE MODIFICATIONS

GUIDE TO FAT

To assess the calories and fat in processed foods that have a nutritional analysis, it is important to remember the typical amounts naturally occurring in the various food groups. Although the *Food Groups Defined* (in Appendix A) included this information, it bears repeating. If you remember the calories and fat inherent in each food allowance, you will be more astute at assessing how much fat is added to a processed food.

On average, the following foods (cooked) contain these amounts of calories and fat:

Starch (½ cup) and Bread (1 slice) 80, 1

Vegetable (½ cup) 25, 0

Fruit (1 piece) 60, 0

Dairy (1 cup skim) 86, 0.4

Fat (1 teaspoon) 45, 4.5

Protein (1 ounce lean) 55, 3

Sugar (1 teaspoon) 16, 0

This information also facilitates the "guesstimation" of exchanges within a mixed food product. For instance, if you read that two "no-added-fat" cookies contain only grains and fruits and have 140 calories, it is a safe guess that the two cookies could be calculated as a starch and a fruit.

The largest study assessing Internet data collected from successful dieters, who have lost 30 pounds and maintained the loss for two years, reported that the majority do so on a low-fat and high-complex-carbohydrate diet. A good goal is for your fat intake to be no more than 20 percent of total calories (AHA recommends 30 percent, while the Rice Diet recommends a 10 to 20 percent fat intake). Many think our very low (saturated) fat recommendations sound radical until they learn that the majority of research subjects consuming a 30 percent fat AHA diet experience a progression or worsening of atherosclerosis, whereas the majority experience a regression or improvement of atherosclerosis when they consume less than 20 percent fat. If you just follow the menu plans or daily add only 1 to 3 teaspoons of olive oil to a vegetarian plus seafood (or occasional lean meat) diet, you don't have to concern yourself with the details of figuring percent of calories coming from fat. For inquiring minds that want to know more detail, you can read *Heal Your Heart*.

To assess the amount of fat in a food, a good visual image to memorize is that 1 teaspoon of fat or oil = 1 pat of butter = 4.5 grams of fat = 45 calories. Fat is usually listed in grams (28 grams = 1 ounce), and 1 gram of fat equals 9 calories. All fats contain saturated, monounsaturated, and polyunsaturated fatty acids. Saturated fat intake is the most respected predictor of high cholesterol. The higher your saturated fat intake, the higher your blood cholesterol and risk of heart disease tends to be. Saturated fats have been shown to raise cholesterol about twice as much as mono- and polyunsaturated fats, which lower it. So to lower our cholesterol, we need to reduce our intake of saturated fat–rich butterfat (butter, cheese, whole milk, cream sauces/soups), beef, pork, coconut, palm or palm kernel oil, and hydrogenated fats. Hydrogenated fats are oils that have had hydrogen atoms added to them, which create smoother, creamier products with a longer shelf life. Unfortunately, it also creates a more saturated fat. The most commonly eaten hydrogenated fats include shortening, margarine, most processed grain products (such as cookies, crackers, cereals, and breads) and spreads, dressings, and sauces. I would avoid these as much as possible as no one fully understands what they do to us, but they do raise cholesterol. If your cholesterol is high, less than 5 percent of your calories should come from saturated fats. Your saturated fat intake will be this low if you follow this nutrition plan, which provides no more than 20 percent of calories from fat and dramatically limits meats, full-fat dairy products, and processed foods. It is a safe bet to assume that the lower your saturated fat intake, the faster and more significant your reversal of atherosclerosis.

Remember that all oils contain some saturated fat and thus can raise your cholesterol. The oils that are reported to be "good" oils are those that will lower cholesterol if substituted for more saturated fat–rich oil! Even so-called good oil can raise your cholesterol if consumed in large enough quantities. Since fat has more than twice the calories (per gram) that carbohydrate and protein do, we should obviously limit it if we have weight loss as a goal. Typically, the more we weigh, the higher our cholesterol will rise.

No one really needs more than 1 teaspoon, or 4.5 grams, of added oil per day. This includes those oils added to processed or packaged foods—so read the fine print! For your 1 to 3 teaspoons of added oil per day, I highly recommend olive oil and canola oil. Olive oil has been shown to lower cholesterol without lowering the "good" HDLs and is consumed in countries where relatively little heart disease is seen. Canola oil has less saturated fat than any other cooking oil we know. Other beneficial oils come from sesame seeds, almonds, and walnuts. Nuts and seeds are the ultimate source of fats if you mindfully eat a teaspoon or two rather than a compulsive cup.

Although limiting saturated fat is more important than limiting cholesterol intake (for most people), limiting your cholesterol intake to less than 100 milligrams per day is a healthy goal. If the food label does not reveal its cholesterol content, beware of foods that contain rich sources of cholesterol—like eggs, liver or other organ meats, dairy products that are not made from skim milk, and high-fat meats—in other words, any ingredient containing animal products. If it has a heartbeat, it has cholesterol! Seafood is the most justifiable animal product, but limit the cholesterol-rich shellfish.

SODIUM GUIDELINES

Note the milligrams (mg) of sodium listed in a product, as sodium inspires overeating. Many participants describe how sodium is even a more powerful trigger than is refined sugar. Becoming aware of hidden sodium in processed foods is key since this is where we typically ingest the greatest amount—without even knowing it! If you eat processed foods, becoming educated in assessing sodium content is of utmost importance. Who would guess that a product can advertise "no salt added," yet still contain other sodium-rich ingredients? Salt is actually sodium chloride, so it is necessary to avoid any products containing salt and anything with sodium in it—monosodium glutamate (a flavor enhancer), sodium benzoate (a preservative), soy sauce, etc.

The USDA guideline for sodium, in general, is to consume less than 2,300 milligrams per day. This is a far higher sodium allowance than is needed to inspire healthy blood pressure for most hypersensitives. Often patients are told they must not be sodium sensitive if their blood pressure did not lower on a 1,000-to-2,000-milligram sodium-restricted diet when the reality is that it often takes a much lower sodium intake to see beneficial results not only for hypersensitives but also for those suffering from kidney disease, edema, arthritis, and diabetes. Your body does not need more than 300 milligrams of sodium per day, which you can easily obtain naturally from foods—without adding any salt to your food. In fact, Rice Diet patients have flourished for years on less than 300 milligrams per day, but it is essential to be followed by an experienced doctor if less than 500 milligrams of sodium per day is consumed.

FIBER GUIDELINES

It is recommended that you get at least 25 to 50 grams of fiber per day. Some labels break this down into soluble and insoluble fiber. Research has shown that eating soluble fiber–rich oats, beans, and barley a couple of times per day can lower your cholesterol about as well as cholesterol-lowering medication without the side effects, which often aggravate other risk factors of heart disease. These soluble fiber–rich foods also do wonders for stabilizing blood sugars, which is dramatically beneficial for diabetics, hypoglycemics, and those desiring to lose weight. Since soluble fiber–rich foods have a slow transit time (from the time you eat to the time you excrete), they make you feel fuller per calorie than any health-promoting food. Thus, rather than view them as high-calorie foods, I view them as the healthiest foods I know to lend that sense of satiety that I need if I won't be eating for 4 to 5 hours.

While soluble fiber–rich foods are beneficial to enjoy often, large amounts of oats have been shown to increase one's risk of constipation. Since insoluble fiber–rich foods will stimulate regular bowel movements, consumption of both types of fiber is ideal. If you do get constipated, most people find that increasing their wheat bran, vegetable, prune, and water intake will take care of the problem. People who consume significant intake of insoluble fiber–rich grains also enjoy healthier gastrointestinal tracts in general; populations with high-insoluble-fiber intake have not only less constipation but less bowel cancer, hemorrhoids, and diverticulitis—all common in people with low fiber intakes.

Whole grains have more fiber and nutrients than do their processed counterparts, despite companies' efforts to enrich these processed foods. Always check the ingredients list to assess just how processed the food is. For instance, bread has gotten an unnecessarily bad reputation in general, because most of the highly processed breads in industrialized countries are inferior with respect to fiber and nutrients and they "trigger," or inspire, many to eat far more than they would if the product were made from whole grains. Whole-grain bread is eaten throughout the world in countries that have fewer chronic diseases than we have, but in these countries they truly eat *whole-grain* bread! We have been led to believe, through deceptive nutritional information on the package, that bread is "whole wheat" when it has whole wheat listed as the last ingredient in a long list of refined ingredients and chemicals. Don't be duped: The majority of breads I eat are bought from a health food bakery and are at least three times the weight of typical supermarket breads that are called "whole wheat." The exception to this is Ezekiel 4:9 bread (low sodium), which is available in the freezer section of natural foods groceries. In addition to being really heavy, obviously packed with whole grains, it also contains even more nutrient-packed sprouted ingredients—including legumes! And to end on an empowering note: Rather than waste any more energy and time on the dangers of processed foods, take responsibility for the freedom and choice we have to buy only (or largely) whole-grain foods that have a nutty, delicious flavor. When we do that, we exercise the tried and true "supply and demand" reality that has catapulted organic foods into one of the most financially successful growth markets of this century. When enough people buy (and thus create demand for) whole-grain products, more companies will get creative at developing and marketing a growing variety of healthier whole-grain products. We create our reality far more than we realize. We created highly processed, nutritionally inferior foods, and we can now, after years of realizing the negative health consequences of doing so, demand whole foods to be more and more accessible by buying them.

RECIPE MODIFICATIONS FOR LOWERING FAT, SUGAR, AND SALT AND INCREASING FIBER

1 whole egg	2 egg whites or ¼ cup egg substitute
1 egg yolk	1 egg white
1 cup butter or shortening	¼ cup of olive or canola oil, and replace the remaining volume with nonfat yogurt (or fruit purée if you want to also reduce the product's sugar)
1 cup whole milk	1 cup skim milk
1 cup buttermilk	1 tablespoon lemon juice or vinegar and skim milk to make 1 cup
1 cup light cream	1 cup evaporated skim milk
1 cup sour cream	1 cup plain nonfat yogurt or 1 cup blenderized ½ percent dry curd cottage cheese with lemon juice
½ cup cottage cheese	½ cup ½ percent dry curd cottage cheese or ricotta cheese (with no fat and less than 65 milligrams of sodium)
1 ounce baking chocolate	3 tablespoons powdered cocoa plus 1 tablespoon nonfat yogurt
1 cup thin white sauce	1 tablespoon olive or canola oil plus 1 tablespoon flour and 1 cup skim milk; can add up to 4 tablespoons of flour for a thick white sauce
2 tablespoons flour (50 calories)	1 tablespoon cornstarch (35 calories)

Cream of celery soup	1 cup thin white sauce plus ¼ cup of celery
Cream of mushroom soup	1 cup thin white sauce plus 1 cup mushrooms
1 tablespoon salad dressing	1 tablespoon no-added-fat-or-salt salad dressing (Pritikin) plus a little no-salt mustard
Cream cheese	Yogurt "cheese" or "curd"; if you cook with it, add 1 tablespoon flour to 1 cup yogurt cheese to prevent it from separating
Mayonnaise	Nonfat yogurt

APPENDIX C

FDA RECOMMENDATIONS FOR FISH, LEVELS OF MERCURY, AND OMEGA-3 FATTY ACIDS

As we indicated earlier, we recommend eating fish from three to five times a week (in 3- to 4-ounce servings). Fish, which contains the highest source of omega-3 fatty acids, has been shown to improve overall cardiovascular health. The American Heart Association agrees with this recommendation. However, some types of fish may contain high levels of mercury (Hg), polychlorinated biphenyls (PCBs), dioxins, and other environmental contaminants that in high amounts can interfere with the brain and nervous system (National Resources Defense Council). Again, exposure to mercury can be particularly hazardous for pregnant women and small children. Even in low doses, mercury may affect a child's development, delaying walking and talking, shortening attention span, and causing learning disabilities (National Resources Defense Council; www.nrdc.org).

So although you want to eat fish regularly, as a healthy source of omega-3 fatty acids, keep in mind that some large, predatory fish—especially shark, swordfish, tilefish, and king mackerel—have high levels of mercury. Use the following two graphs as a guide to assess the mercury level versus omega 3 fatty acid content of these popular seafood choices.

(Source: American Heart Association, www.americanheart.org)

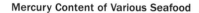

Mercury Content of Various Seafood

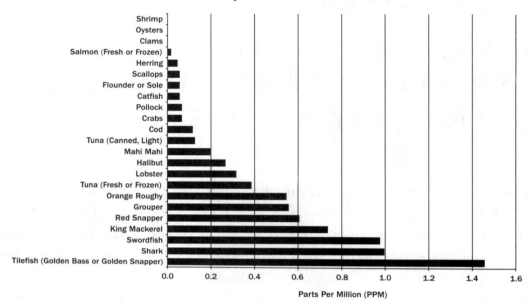

Omega-3 Fatty Acid Content of Various Seafood

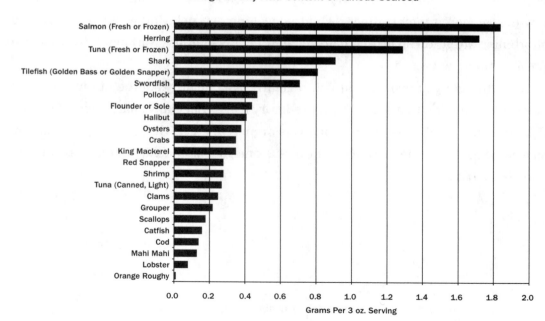

APPENDIX D

BASIC GUIDELINES FOR PREPARING GRAINS

Grain (1 cup)	Water (cups)	Cooking Time	Yield (cups)
Amaranth	2	20 minutes	2
Arborio rice	2	25 minutes	2½
Barley (hulled)	3	1½ hours + 10 minutes	3½
Barley (pearled)	3	50 minutes + 10 minutes standing	3½
Basmati rice	2½	20 minutes	3
Brown rice	2	45 minutes	3
Buckwheat groats*(kasha)	2	30 minutes	3
Bulgur wheat	2	20 minutes + 5 minutes standing	2¾
Couscous	2	1 minute + 5 minutes standing	3
Millet	2½	25 minutes + 5 minutes standing	3½
Oat groats	2¼	1 hour + 10 minutes standing	2½
Polenta	4	25 minutes, or 5-minute type	3
Quinoa (rinse well in cold water before cooking)	2	15 minutes + 5 minutes standing	3
Rye berries	3	1 hour	2½
Spelt	3	2 hours + 15 minutes standing	2¼
Triticale	3	1¾ hours + 10 minutes standing	2–2½
Wild rice	3	1 hour	3½
Whole-grain wheat berries	3	2 hours	2½

APPENDIX E

BASIC GUIDELINES FOR PREPARING BEANS AND PEAS

Legumes (1 cup dry)	Water (cups)	Cooking Time (hours), Soaked	Cooking Time (hours), Unsoaked	Yield (cups)
Adzuki	3	1–1½	2–3	2
Anasazi	3	1½–2	2–3	2¼
Black (turtle) beans	4	1½–2	2–3	2
Black-eyed (cow) peas	3	½	¾–1	2–2¼
Cannellini	3	1–1½	1½–2	2
Chickpeas (garbanzo)	4	1½–2	3	2½
Cranberry beans	3	1–1½	1½–2	2½
Fava	3	1½–2	2–3	2
Great Northern beans	3½	1–1½	2–3	2–2¼
Kidney beans	3	1	1½	2
Lentils	3	½	½–¾	2–2¼
Lima beans	2	¾–1	1½	2
Navy beans	3	1½–2	2	2
Pinto beans	3	1½–2	2–3	2–2¼
Red beans	3	1½–2	2–3	2
Split peas	3		¾	2–2¼

APPENDIX F

BODY MASS INDEX (BMI) AND WEIGHT GOAL EQUATION

In order to establish your weight loss goals, you need to figure out your Body Mass Index. The simplest and best common measure of weight for height is the Body Mass Index (BMI). BMI is calculated by dividing a person's weight (in kilograms) by the square of his height (in meters). Since Americans still use the English system, the formula for calculating BMI is as follows:

703 times your weight in pounds divided by your height in inches squared.

Most authorities consider a BMI less than 25 to be healthy; above that the person is considered overweight, and above 30, obese. Optimally your BMI should be less than 23.

The easiest way to figure your BMI is to use the table below. Find the appropriate height in the left-hand column, move across the row to the given weight, and the number at the top of the column is the BMI for that height and weight.

BMI (kg/m²)	19	20	21	22	23	24	25	26	27	28	29	30	35	40
Height (in.)	Weight (lb.)													
58	91	96	100	105	110	115	119	124	129	134	138	143	167	191
59	94	99	104	109	114	119	124	128	133	138	143	148	173	198
60	97	102	107	112	118	123	128	133	138	143	148	153	179	204
61	100	106	111	116	122	127	132	137	143	148	153	158	185	211
62	104	109	115	120	126	131	136	142	147	153	158	164	191	218
63	107	113	118	124	130	135	141	146	152	158	163	169	197	225
64	110	116	122	128	134	140	145	151	157	163	169	174	204	232
65	114	120	126	132	138	144	150	156	162	168	174	180	210	240
66	118	124	130	136	142	148	155	161	167	173	179	186	216	247
67	121	127	134	140	146	153	159	166	172	178	185	191	223	255
68	125	131	138	144	151	158	164	171	177	184	190	197	230	262
69	128	135	142	149	155	162	169	176	182	189	196	203	236	270
70	132	139	146	153	160	167	174	181	188	195	202	207	243	278
71	136	143	150	157	165	172	179	186	193	200	208	215	250	286
72	140	147	154	162	169	177	184	191	199	206	213	221	258	294
73	144	151	159	166	174	182	189	197	204	212	219	227	265	302
74	148	155	163	171	179	186	194	202	210	218	225	233	272	311
75	152	160	168	176	184	192	200	208	216	224	232	240	279	319
76	156	164	172	180	189	197	205	213	221	230	238	246	287	328

Body weight in pounds according to height and Body Mass Index.

APPENDIX G
YOUR JOURNAL

At the Rice Diet Program, our mission is to inspire you to choose a healthy diet, and to develop your life vision or dream. This dream when articulated by you and revisited by you will propel you into a fulfilling future. Jeff Georgi, our addiction specialist, and I are both quite excited about how articulating and contemplating your dream can inspire deep healing.

Create or imagine your dream by:

1. Being alive. Live each day to its fullest.

2. Being aware—of your life, your longings, your desires, your fears—be aware of all that you are.

3. Making an intention that furnishes content to your dreams. Periodically throughout the day, pause and focus on what you are doing, even seemingly mundane tasks. If we face all of life with awareness and intention, we will find greater focus and meaning.

4. Committing to love yourself. This may sound easy, or obvious. But the root cause of many people's overweight and disease is shame, or an inability to love oneself fully. So use your journal as a place to identify moments or feelings of shame; then replace these negative self thoughts with those that are positive and affirming.

As you go through your day, pay attention to these four ways to articulate *your* new life—be alive, be aware, be intentional, and be self-loving—record your thoughts, feelings and reflections in your journal. This record of your inner experiences will not only shore up your dreams and goals but will also reinforce each daily success on your Rice Diet *dieta*.

Take a look at the Sample Food Journal on the following page to give you a sense of how to begin this inspiring process. Below the sample, I've included a blank Journal page for you to use. And remember, you can always contact us and order your own *Journal for Health,* which includes space and inspiration for one month of journalizing commitment.

Your Diet Plan <u>1200 Calorie Phase III</u>   Date <u>1/9/07</u>

Today's Weight <u>243 pounds</u>   Blood Pressure/Other <u>160/98</u>

SAMPLE FOOD JOURNAL

Serving Size	Food		Cals / Fat / Sodium		
Breakfast	1 c. oatmeal		145	2	0
	3 prunes		60	0	0
	1 c. skim milk		90	0	120
	1 banana		<u>110</u>	<u>1</u>	<u>1</u>
		TOTAL	405	3	121

S= <u>II</u>   V= _____   FR= <u>III</u>   P= _____   D= <u>I</u>   F= _____

Lunch	1 c. brown rice		23	2	0
	1 c. steamed broccoli		46	1	41
	1 1/3 c. strawberries		<u>66</u>	<u>1</u>	<u>3</u>
		TOTAL	344	4	44

S= <u>III</u>   V= <u>II</u>   FR= <u>I</u>   P= _____   D= _____   F= _____

Dinner	3 oz. cooked snapper		109	2	48
	1 1/2 c. potato		240	0	13
	2 c. tossed salad		40	0	71
	1/2 c. stewed tomatoes		35	0	31
	1 c. fruit sorbet		<u>240</u>	<u>0</u>	<u>22</u>
		TOTAL	664	2	185

S= <u>III</u>   V= <u>III</u>   FR= <u>IIII</u>   P= <u>III</u>   D= _____   F= _____

Daily Total for Calories/Fat/Sodium: <u>1413</u>   <u>9</u>   <u>350</u>

TOTALS:

Starch = <u>8</u>   **V**egetables = <u>5</u>   **FR**uit = <u>8</u>

Protein = <u>3</u>   **D**airy = <u>1</u>   **F**at = <u>0</u>

Meal Plan Goals	Actual Intake	Differences (+/−) between Goals & Intake	
S= 8	8	_____	
V= 5	5	_____	
FR= 3	8	+5	
		(from fruit sorbet's 240 cals)	
P= 3	3	_____	
D= 1	1	_____	
F= 0	0	_____	

Daily Activity	Goal	Actual
Cardiovascular	60 mins. daily	60
Strength Training	30 mins. 2 x weekly	20
Flexibility (stretching)	Daily	60
Mind/Body Relaxation	30 mins. daily	60

Personal Notes:

Today I attended the journalizing class at the Rice Diet Program. I frankly wasn't expecting much from the experience but was amazed at what came up for me. When I asked myself where the last 50 pounds came from . . . I didn't know that I had the answer until I started writing about the safety my excess weight was providing me increasingly, since my assault. I was shocked that there was any connection between the two! My New Year's resolution is to journalize daily!!

P.S. That fruit sorbet was no fat but those 240 calories were sure not as nutritious, satisfying or filling as 4 cups of cold watermelon would have been.

If you can imagine it, you can achieve it.
If you can dream it, you can become it.
—*William Arthur Ward*

Your Diet Plan _____   Date _____

Today's Weight _____   Blood Pressure/Other _____

FOOD JOURNAL

Serving Size	Food	Cals / Fat / Sodium

Breakfast

TOTAL   ___   ___   ___

S= _____   V= _____   FR= _____   P= _____   D= _____   F= _____

Lunch

TOTAL   ___   ___   ___

S= _____   V= _____   FR= _____   P= _____   D= _____   F= _____

Dinner

TOTAL   ___   ___   ___

S= _____   V= _____   FR= _____   P= _____   D= _____   F= _____

Daily Total for Calories/Fat/Sodium: ___   ___   ___

TOTALS:

Starch = ____   **V**egetables = ____   **FR**uit = ____

Protein = ____   **D**airy = ____   **F**at = ____

Meal Plan Goals	Actual Intake	Differences (+/−) between Goals & Intake
S= _____	_____	_____
V= _____	_____	_____
FR= _____	_____	_____
P= _____	_____	_____
D= _____	_____	_____
F= _____	_____	_____

Daily Activity	Goal	Actual
Cardiovascular	60 mins. daily	_____
Strength Training	30 mins. 2 x weekly	_____
Flexibility (stretching)	Daily	_____
Mind/Body Relaxation	30 mins. daily	_____

Personal Notes:

_____
_____
_____
_____
_____
_____
_____
_____
_____
_____

We will not know how unless we begin.
—Howard Zinn

APPENDIX H

MAIL-ORDER SOURCES FOR HEALTH FOODS AND OTHER PRODUCTS

Listed below are several mail-order and online sources for foods that you may find challenging to obtain in your area. The following store information will assist you in finding very-low-sodium and low-saturated-fat ingredients, many of which are organic, that are mentioned in the recipes.

The Rice Diet Store
1644 Cole Mill Road
Durham, NC 27705
(919) 383-7276, ext. 2
www.ricedietstore.com

The Rice Diet Store carries pantry staples, including a large and interesting variety of whole grains, beans, cereals, dressings, and canned fish. From these basics to the finest imported olive oils and vinegars, the foods have been carefully selected by our nutrition staff to facilitate Ricers in living their *dieta* at home. The Rice Diet Store also sells a wide selection of support tools to assist you with your long-term success. *Your Journal for Health, T-Factor Fat Gram Counter*, teleclass and meditation CDs, yoga DVDs, and pedometers can renew and inspire your commitment to health for years to come.

Baking Products or Baked Goods

Toufayan Bakeries, Inc.   or   Toufayan Bakeries, Inc.
175 Railroad Avenue   3826 Bryn Mawr Street
Ridgefield, NJ 07657   Orlando, FL 32808
(800) 328-7482   (800) 233-7482
www.toufayan.com

Toufayan makes 8-ounce salt-free white and whole wheat pitas. Their pita-bread products, called Pitettes, measure 3½ by 4 inches in diameter and freeze beautifully. The website includes a complete product list, recipes, and contact information. If Toufayan products are not available in your area, they will gladly ship via UPS.

Food For Life Baking Company
P.O. Box 1434
Corona, CA 92878
www.foodforlife.com

Food For Life Baking Company, makers of the fabulous Ezekiel 4:9 breads, is a family-owned and -operated specialty bakery with a passionate commitment to natural foods. Among the products specifically developed to meet particular dietary requirements are two organic sprouted grain low-sodium breads. Access their Web site to find the retail store nearest you.

The Bean Bag
818 Jefferson Street
Oakland, CA 94607
(800) 845-BEAN (2326)
www.beanbag.net/organic.html

This is a great company for ordering dried beans, including many heirloom and organic beans and specialty grains.

Phipps Ranch
P.O. Box 349
Pescadero, CA 94060
(415) 879-0787
www.phippscountry.com/beanlist.htm

Another great legume source for the unusual varieties, including cannellini, cranberry, fava, flageolet, borlotti, wren's egg, pinquito, scarlet runner, and tongues of fire. They grow their products without using pesticides, but they are not a certified organic farm.

Boca Burger
1660 N.E. 12th Terrace
Fort Lauderdale, FL 33305
(305) 524-1977

This company specializes in textured soy protein products. Be aware that most of them have unnecessarily high amounts of sodium, but there are a few that are low-sodium enough to use as a quick, convenient meat substitute.

CapriFlavors
1012 Morrisville Parkway
Morrisville, NC 27560
(800)-861-5440
www.capriflavors.com

CapriFlavors is committed to bringing you the finest Italian imported food possible. They sell the pod system for making *My Orzo Eye Opener* (page 120).

APPENDIX I

HEAL YOURSELF AND YOUR WORLD RESOURCES

WEB SITES

Campaign to Label Genetically Engineered Foods—www.thecampaign.org

Chefs Collaborative—www.chefscollaborative.org

Chefs Collaborative is a national organization of the food community who promote sustainable cuisine by celebrating the joys of local, seasonal, and artisanal cooking.

Deirdre Imus's website, *The Deirdre Imus Environmental Center* for Pediatric Oncology—www.dienviro.com

To find farmers' markets in your area, go to www.ams.usda.gov/farmersmarkets/.

EarthSave—www.earthsave.org

EarthSave continues the educational work that *Diet for a New America* began and educates, inspires, and empowers people to shift toward a plant-based diet centered on fruits, vegetables, grains, and legumes—foods that are healthy for people and the planet.

Eat Well Guide—www.eatwellguide.org

The Eat Well Guide is a free online directory of sustainably raised meat, poultry, dairy, and eggs from farms, stores, restaurants, inns, and hotels, and online outlets in the U.S. and Canada.

Generation Green—www.generationgreen.org

Generation Green gives families a voice in public policy decisions. As consumers, we have the power to reject corporate policies that endanger us and our children.

Heritage Foods USA—www.heritagefoodsusa.com

Heritage Foods USA exists to promote genetic diversity, small family farms, and a fully traceable food supply.

LocalHarvest—www.localharvest.com

LocalHarvest maintains a definitive and reliable "living" public nationwide directory of small farms, farmers' markets, and other local food sources.

Niman Ranch—www.nimanranch.com

Niman Ranch is a network of more than three hundred farmers who raise their beef, pork, and lamb according to the company's strict standards against growth hormones, GMOs, and unnecessary antibiotics. Each piece of meat can be traced back to the farm and animal from which it was produced.

Nutrition Action—www.cspinet.org/nah/

Nutrition Action Healthletter is published by the Center for Science in the Public Interest, an advocacy organization whose twin missions are to conduct innovative research and advocacy programs in health and nutrition, and to provide consumers with current, useful information about their health and well-being. *Nutrition Action Healthletter* is the largest-circulation health newsletter in North America.

Organic Consumers Association—www.organicconsumers.org

The Organic Consumers Association (OCA) is an online and grassroots nonprofit public-interest organization campaigning for health, justice, and sustainability.

Seeds of Change—www.seedsofchange.com

Seeds of Change started in 1989 with a simple mission: to help preserve biodiversity and promote sustainable, organic agriculture by cultivating and disseminating an extensive range of open-pollinated, organically grown, heirloom, and traditional vegetable, flower, and herb seeds. Today you can buy certified organic seeds and plants online, or order by phone from their catalog.

Slow Food—www.slowfood.com

Slow Food, founded in 1986, is an international organization whose aim is to protect the pleasures of the table from the homogenization of modern fast food and modern life.

True Food Network—www.truefoodnow.org

The True Food Network offers a valuable resource called the True Food Shopping List. The Network is also the grassroots network of the Center for Food Safety.

USDA Agricultural Marketing Service—www.ams.usda.gov/farmersmarkets

The USDA Agricultural Marketing Service offers a state-by-state listing of local farmers' markets. It also lists the benefits of products sold at farmers' market for the consumer and the environment.

Vegetarian Society—www.vegsoc.org/

The Vegetarian Society is an organization that works to educate people about the merits of a vegetarian lifestyle and to protect vegetarianism by providing accurate information to the press—and by encouraging the food industry to improve its standards. It also offers nutritional advice and other information to individuals, companies, and organizations.

REFERENCES

INTRODUCTION AND CHAPTER ONE

CSPI. "Food Industry Accused of Salt Assault on America." Press Release, August 2005, Washington, D.C.

Dietary Guidelines for Americans, 2005. Washington, D.C.: USDA.

Tsang, Gloria. March 2006. UK Sets Salt Reduction Targets for Packaged Foods. www.healthcastle.com.

CHAPTER THREE

Brennan, P., et al. 2005. "Effect of Cruciferous Vegetables on Lung Cancer in Patients Stratified by Genetic Status." *Lancet* 366:1558–60.

Hasler, C.M. *Functional Foods: Their Role in Disease Prevention and Health Promotion.* A Publication of the Institute of Food Technologists Expert Panel on Food Safety and Nutrition.

Obisesan, Thomas O., Clemencia M. Vargas, and Richard F. Gillum. 2000. "Geographic Variation in Stroke Risk in the United States: Region, Urbanization, and Hypertension in the Third National Health and Nutrition Examination Survey." *Stroke* 31:19.

Shick, S.M., R.R. Wing, M.L. Klem, M.T. McGuire, J.O. Hill, and H. Seagle. 1998. "Persons Successful at Long-term Weight Loss and Maintenance Continue to Consume a Low Calorie, Low Fat Diet." *Journal of the American Dietetic Association* 98:408–413.

CHAPTER FOUR

Baker, B.P., et al. May 2002. "Pesticide Residues in Conventional, IPM-Grown and Organic foods: Insights from Three U.S. Data Sets." *Food Additives and Contaminants* 19(5).

Center for Children's Health and the Environment, "Regulating Pesticides in Food," Mount Sinai School of Medicine, www.childenvironment.org/factsheets/pesticides_in_food.htm.

CSPI. August 2005. Food Industry Accused of Salt Assault: on America. Press Release, Washington, D.C.

Curl, C.L., et.al. March 2003. "Organophosphorus Pesticide Exposure of Urban and Suburban Preschool Children with Organic and Conventional Diets," *Environmental Health Perspectives* 111(3).

Dietary Guidelines for Americans, 2005. Washington, D.C.: USDA.

Enos, W.F., J.C. Beyer, and R.H. Holmes. 1955. "Pathogenesis of Coronary Disease in American Soldiers Killed in Korea." *Journal of the American Medical Association* 158:912–14.

Fromartz, S. 2006. *Organics, Inc.: Natural Foods and How They Grew.* New York: Harcourt.

Heaton, Shane. 2001. "Organic Farming, Food Quality and Human Health: A Review of the Evidence." Soil Association.

Goodall, Jane. 2005. *Harvest for Hope.* New York: Warner Books.

Gouveia-Vigeant, Tami, and Joel Tickner. May 2003. "Toxic Chemicals and Childhood Cancer: A Review of the Evidence," in a publication of the Lowell Center for Sustainable Production at University of Massachusetts, Lowell.

Hasler, Claire, Ph.D. *Functional Foods: Their Role in Disease Prevention and Health Promotion.* A publication of the Institute of Food Technologists Expert Panel on Food Safety and Nutrition.

Hottinger, G. 2004. *The Best Natural Foods on the Market Today,* vol. 1, Boulder, CO: Huckleberry Mountain Press.

Lu, Chensheng, et al. March 2001. "Biological Monitoring Survey of Organophosphate Pesticide Exposure among Preschool Children in the Seattle Metropolitan Area." *Environmental Health Perspectives* 109(3).

———. "Organic Diets Significantly Lower Children's Dietary Exposure to Organophosphorus Pesticides." *Environmental Health Perspectives*, published online, September 1, 2005, http://ehp.niehs.nih.gov/members/2005/8418/8418.pdf.

Kempner, W. 1944. "Treatment of Kidney Disease and Hypertensive Vascular Disease with Rice Diet." *NC Med J* 5: 125–33.

———. *Treatment of Kidney Disease and Hypertensive Vascular Disease with Rice Diet*. Chicago: AMA.

———. 1944. "Treatment of Kidney Disease and Hypertensive Vascular Disease with Rice Diet II." *NC Med J* 5:273–74.

———. 1945. "Treatment of Kidney Disease and Hypertensive Vascular Disease with Rice Diet III." *NC Med J* 6: 61–87,117–61.

———. 1946. "Some Effects of the Rice Diet Treatment of Kidney Disease and Hypertension." *Bulletin of the New York Academy of Medicine* 22: 358–70.

———. 1947. "Treatment of Cardiac Failure with Rice Diet." *NC Med J* 8: 128–31.

———. 1948. "Treatment of Heart and Kidney Disease and of Hypertensive and Arteriosclerotic Vascular Disease with the Rice Diet." *Annals of Internal Medicine* 31: 687–88.

———. 1948. "Treatment of Hypertensive Vascular Disease with Rice Diet." *Am J Med* 4: 545–77.

Kempner, W., R.L. Peschel, and J.S. Skyler. 1975. "Treatment of Massive Obesity with Rice/Reduction Diet Program. An Analysis of 106 Patients with at least a 45-kg Weight Loss." *Archives of Internal Medicine* 135(12):1575–84.

Kempner, W., and C. Schlayer. 1958. "Effects of Rice Diet on Diabetes Mellitus Associated with Vascular Disease." *Postgrad Med* 24: 359–71.

National Academy of Sciences. 1993. *Pesticides in the Diets of Infants and Children*. Washington: National Academy Press.

Pollan, Michael. *The Omnivore's Dilemma: A Natural History of Four Meals* (New York: Penguin, 2006).

Ryan-Borchers ,T.A., J.S. Park, B.P. Chew, M.K. McGuire, L.R. Fournier, and K.A. Beerman. May 2006. "Soy Isoflavones Modulate Immune Function in Healthy Postmenopausal Women." *American Journal of Clinical Nutrition* 83(5): 1118–25.

Tsang, Gloria. March 2006. UK Sets Salt Reduction Targets for Packaged Foods. www.healthcastle.com.

GENERAL INDEX

RECIPE INDEX